CEYLON AND THE PORTUGUESE
1505-1658

CEYLON AND THE PORTUGUESE

1505-1658

P. E. PIERIS

ISBN : 978-93-5324-495-8 (HB)

First Published, Tellippalai, 1920

Published, 2020

Published by

Facsimile Publisher
12 Pragati Market
Ashok Vihar, Ph-2
Delhi-110052
E-mail: books@facsimilepublisher.com

Printed at: G. Print Process, Delhi.

Ceylon and The Portuguese
1505-1658

Author: P. E. Pieris

CEYLON AND THE PORTUGUESE

1505 - 1658

BY

P. E. PIERIS, LITT. D. (Cantab)

Ceylon Civil Service,

ASSISTED BY

R. B. NAISH, B. A. (Oxon.)

Ceylon Civil Service.

AMERICAN CEYLON MISSION PRESS.

TELLIPPALAI, CEYLON

1920

DEDICATION

Dear Lady Blake,

I have written this book in the hope that it will awaken in those of your fellow countrymen and fellow countrywomen whose hands it may chance to reach, an interest in Ceylon and a desire to understand her people. In that respect you and Sir Henry have set a shining example, and in grateful recognition I venture respectfully to dedicate this work to you.

Yours sincerely,

Kandy,
3rd June, 1920.

P. E. PIERIS.

"Son of man, stand upon thy feet."

Ezekiel.

PREFACE

The period of the history of Ceylon which is covered by the present work has been already dealt with by me in another book which, inasmuch as it was addressed primarily to the people of that country, assumed in the reader a degree of knowledge which no one who has not resided there for many years can have, and was burdened with a minuteness of detail which, however novel and interesting to the local student, cannot but weary, if not repel, the general reader. And yet the story of the Portuguese in Ceylon is of more than local interest, for it depicts for us a characteristic phase of the beginning of European expansion in the East. A hundred and fifty three years after the Portuguese first landed in Ceylon they were expelled from the country, leaving the gloomy word *Failure* writ large over all their actions. That however was not all, for they left the Sinhalese a broken race, with their ancient civilisation brought to the verge of ruin, and their scheme of life well-nigh destroyed.

In 1796 the British flag was unfurled over the country; and though perhaps the old romance of life has gone, never again to return, a material prosperity and a personal security such as have not been known before have grown up under its protection. It is difficult for the West to understand the East, and for that reason this book has been re-written for the English reader as some contribution to the increase of that knowledge. For the matter contained therein I am solely responsible; any credit which may be considered due for the manner in which that material is presented to the reader, should be ascribed to Mr. Naish, for whose incisive and illuminating criticism I cannot too deeply express my gratitude. A complete Bibliographical List will be found in the first Volume of 'Ceylon, the Portuguese Era.'

P. E. P.

CONTENTS OF CHAPTERS

CHAPTER I

CHAPTER II

CHAPTER III

CHAPTER IV

CHAPTER IX

CHAPTER X

CHAPTER XI

CHAPTER XII

draw. Dom Jorge de Almeida as General. Treaty of 1633. The condition of Portugal. Financial Chaos. Death of Senerat. Raja Sinha and the Hollanders. Diogo de Melo and the Court. Hostilities recommence. The Parangi Hatane. Battle of Gannoruwa. The King's thank-offering.

CHAPTER XIII

Capture of Batticaloa. Treaty of Batticaloa. The policy of the Hollanders. Quarrel between the King and Wijaya Pala. Capture of Negombo. Sinhalese medicine. The fort of Galle. The assault. Division of the spoil. The Portuguese in consternation. Coster at Court. The King's reply. Death of Coster. Desertion at Galle. The Portuguese dominion threatened. Joao de Ribeiro. Negumbo retaken. Revolt of Wijaya Pala. The Prince at Colombo. He leaves Ceylon. The obsequiousness of the Hollanders. Hostilities. The approach of peace. Negumbo occupied by the Hollanders. Declaration of peace.

CHAPTER XIV

Adrian van der Stel. Capture of Pannara. The Hollanders non plussed. Their policy. Raja Sinha in peace time. His fondness for animals. European music. His views on inter-marriage. The King as God. The Portuguese administration. Excesses of the Generals. Peculation. Oppression by minor officials. The law courts. The Military. The Religious Orders. The pledge at Malwana. Sinhalese Law. Caste among the Sinhalese. The Portuguese and caste. Palanquin bearers. Petty oppression of the tenants The arecanut boom. The Chalias. The Lascarins. The dignity of the Sinhalese. Hostilities renewed. The Portuguese disorganised. Gaspar de Figueira. Further fighting. The origin of the Esala Perahera. Its celebration. Arrival of Hulft. Fall of Kalutara.

CHAPTER XV

The fortification of Colombo. The siege begun. Raja Sinha and his dignity. Tennekon Appuhami. An Assault. The Hollanders repulsed. The King annoyed. The tactics of the besiegers. Mine and countermine. St. Thomas' image. Ferocity of Hollanders towards noncombatants. Underground fighting. Portuguese appeal to the King. Hulft appointed the King's Director General. Plague in the town. Hulft before the King. His death. The King's grief. The Portuguese defensive. The last assault. The resistance. Terms of surrender. The evacuation of the fort. Raja Sinha disillusioned. He breaks off with the Hollandars. Colombo re-fortified. The King withdraws. Fall of Manar. The siege of Jaffna. The surrender. Thanksgiving.

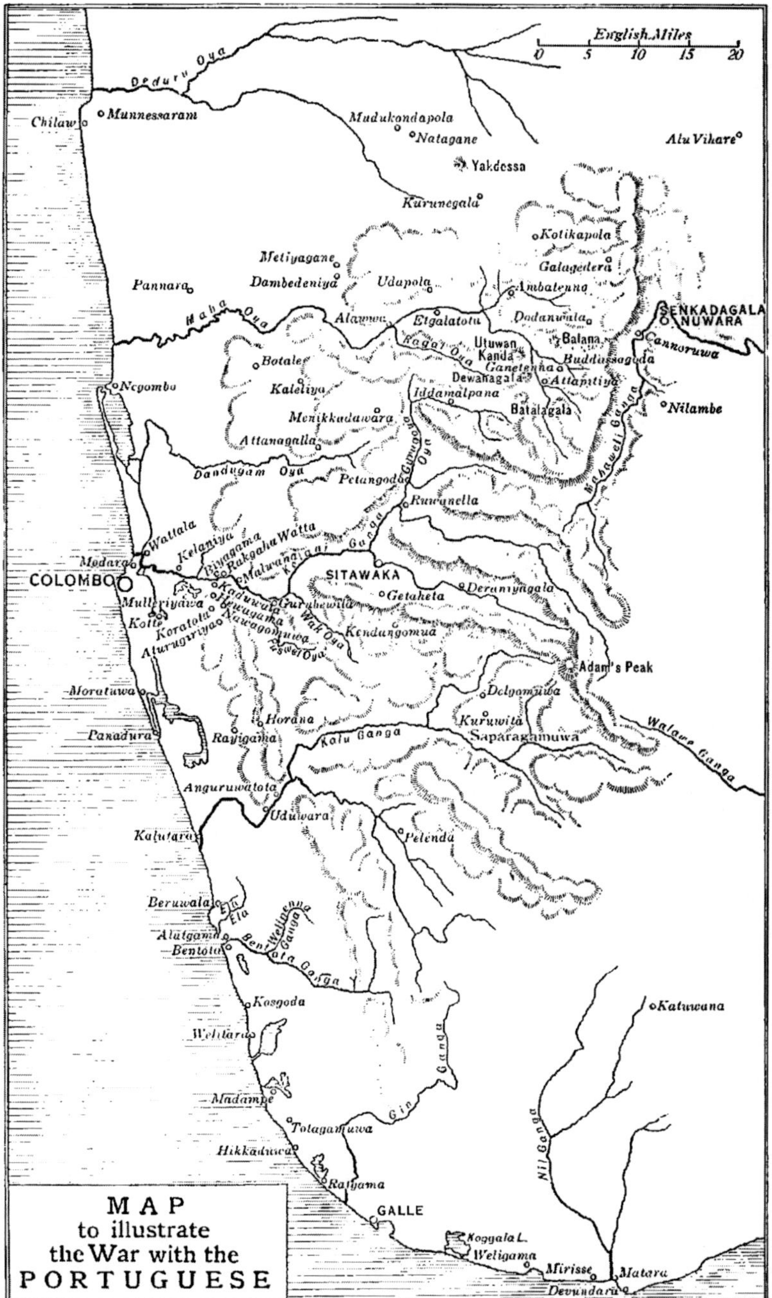

MAP
to illustrate
the War with the
PORTUGUESE

WAXTYPE

GEORGE PHILIP & SON, LTD.

CHAPTER I.

The great Indian Epic of the Ramayana, however much involved in legend and myth, has, there is no reason to doubt, preserved for us the record of events which did actually take place in the early dawn of the history of Ceylon. It tells how Ravana, the fierce Island King, had captured the beautiful Sita, the wife of Rama Chandra,[1] a North Indian Prince, and how, to avenge the insult, her husband led a mighty army across the water to the invasion of Ravana's mysterious land. He was met by the army of Ravana, which, after a fierce battle, was driven back in confusion. Rama Chandra thereupon advanced to Ravana's fabled fortress, and after a siege of ten years succeeded in killing the King and rescuing the Princess.

More certainty attaches to the story of the next invasion from India. It was the time of the full moon of the month of Wesak, 543 years before the birth of Christ, when over the loveliness of "the loveliest parcel of land the Creator has placed in this Earth,[2]" was thrown the warm embrace of the glowing Eastern Moon. Far away at Kusinara, Gautama Buddha, the Perfectly Enlightened one, had reached Eternal Peace, and to the protection of Sekraya the Great God he commended Wijayo, the Lion born, who, exiled from India, that day had reached Ceylon with his seven hundred followers. And by the command of the god the Lotus-hued Vishnu, now appointed Protector of the Kingdom and the Faith which were to be, hastened to bless the Prince and to sprinkle holy water on his men, in preparation for the new life which was opening before them. Wijayo's attempts at colonising were successful, a portion of the aboriginal Yakkas[1] joined themselves to him, and in a few years his position was so firmly established that he was able to obtain a suitable consort from the most prominent of the ruling families of South India.

The Kingdom of the Pandyans was known to the Greeks, and is mentioned by Ptolemy as the *Regnum Pandionis.* Its capital, Madura, from which more than one embassy visited the court of Augustus, was for many centuries the centre of Dravidian learning. Wijayo's marriage with the daughter of the Ruler of this country was a recognition of his position among the Princes of India, though this advantage was secured by sacrificing Kuweni, the aboriginal Princess whom he had married, and whose influence had been loyally exercised to consolidate his power.

Nature has scattered her gifts over this happy Island of Ceylon with an unstinting hand. Jutting out as it does like a mole from the Indian Peninsula, it is the meeting-ground of the two monsoons. Twice in the year, in May and in November, as the wind changes from the north-east to the south-west and back again, the moisture-laden clouds roll up from the ocean and pour their wealth in torrents on the thirsty land. The fierce tropical sun blazes forth, and in a short time the soil, however poor it may be, is covered with the rankest vegetation. The sun is always there, and if only this wealth of water can be secured from waste, the health and happiness of the people is in a large degree insured. For rice is the food of the tropics, and given water and sun, only a little scratching of the soil is required to provide an abundant harvest. Religious ceremonies mark every stage of its cultivation, and the proudest in the land would take his share in what is still esteemed the most honourable of all occupations.

From the earliest times the Sinhalese set themselves to solve the problem of the conservation of the water, and so successful were their efforts that for generations the surplus of the grain which they produced was sent to feed the neighbouring continent. Mighty dams were constructed across great valleys, and the water stored behind them was led by a skilful system of channels to irrigate wide tracts of country. Thus, within fifty years from the arrival of Wijayo, there was constructed the Abhaya Wewa, the first of that series of marvellous reservoirs which form the most amazing product of Sinhalese industry and science; and in two centuries the nation had reached a stage of prosperity the extent of which can be gauged from the fact that five hundred low-caste Chandalas had to be constantly employed in the task of scavenging its capital, Anuradhapura.

Then there came that tremendous religious movement which has covered the Island with those mighty buildings the remains of which still compel our wonder and amazement, and which has left to the Sinhalese that heritage of high ideals, gentleness and contentment of which neither the centuries of ruthless warfare, nor the more insidious attacks of modern commercialism, has succeeded in robbing them. This religious movement dates from the arrival in Ceylon of Mihindu, the son of the Emperor Asoka, in B. C. 307, as the first Missionary of Buddhism. He was soon joined by his sister Sanghamitta, who brought with her in a vase of gold a sprig, which was planted at Anuradhapura, of that Bo tree under the shadow of which Gautama had attained to Perfect Knowledge.

It is doubtful if any other single incident in the long story of their race has seized upon the imagination of the Sinhalese with such tenacity as this of the planting of the aged tree. Like its pliant roots, which find sustenance on the face of the bare rock and cleave their way through the stoutest fabric, the influence of what it represents has penetrated into the innermost being of the people, till the tree itself has become almost human. The loving care of some pious observer has left on record in sonorous Pali, and with minute detail, the incidents of the day when the soil of Ceylon first received it; and to-day the descendants of the princely escort who accompained it from India continue to be its guardians. The axe of the ruthless invaders who for so many centuries to come were destined to spread ruin throughout the country, was reverently withheld from its base. And even now, on the stillest night, its heart-shaped leaves on their slender stalks ceaselessly quiver and sigh, as they have quivered and sighed for twenty-three centuries. The Buddhist looks forward to no greater happiness than once in his lifetime to make the pilgrimage to this tree, and there after offering his bloodless sacrifice of oil and sweet-smelling flowers, to renew his vows not to take life' and not to drink strong drinks.

Three objects are essential for the sanctity of every Buddhist place of worship. There must be a Bo tree, usually planted on a mound of earth supported by an ornamental stone railing; an image of the Buddha, who is usually represented in one of three postures—erect, sedent or recumbent; and finally the *dagoba*[6], or reliquary.

As in every other age and country, relics have commanded the utmost reverence amongst the Sinhalese, and their zeal has been nowhere more prominently displayed than in the great structures which they erected for the protection of the relics of the Buddha. These dagobas were invariably bell-shaped, and rested on a solid platform of bricks. The tiny relic was enclosed in a leaf of gold, and formed the centre for an immense pile of bricks which was built round it in concentric circles of ever-widening diameter. A graceful solid spire, itself springing from a square base, crowned the structure and terminated in a finial of gold or bronze. The whole of the brickwork was coated with a strong cement prepared from lime, and whether in the bright sunlight, or when illuminated by thousands of tiny oil-lamps at night, it threw off a sheen of speckless white. Such was the Thuparama, the earliest and the most graceful of the dagobas of the Island, which was erected as a receptacle for the Buddha's Refection Bowl; and round it thousands of pilgrims bow in worship to-day.

Mihindu died in B. C. 258 when his body was cremated with extraordinary pomp, the whole Island joining in the celebration of the obsequies, which lasted several days.

The Island was at this period of its history divided into three Kingdoms or *Ratas*. The most northerly of these was named Pihiti Rata, and also Raja Rata, the Country of the Kings, as it contained the Royal Capital. Its southern boundary was mainly defined by two rivers. Of these the first was the Maha Weli Ganga, the Great Sandy River, which has its source in the mountain known to Europeans as Adam's Peak, and flows in a north-easterly direction till it reaches the sea near the great harbour of Trincomalee. The second was the Deduru Oya which runs west from the central mountain plateau as far as Chilaw. Southward from the Maha Weli Ganga and the plateau lay the Kingdom of Ruhuna, which included the flat country as far as the Kalu Ganga, which joins the sea twenty-five miles south of Colombo. The central mountainous district and the rich western low country between the Kalu Ganga and the Deduru Oya formed the third Kingdom of Maya Rata.

The peace and goodwill which followed the message of Mihindu could not last, and by 200 B. C.

an invader from the Choromandel Coast, Elara by name, had seized the throne of Anuradhapura. Usurper and stranger though he was, even the priestly Buddhist chroniclers bear witness to the eminent qualities of this King, who "ruled the kingdom for forty-four years, administering justice with impartiality to friends and to foes." But a greater than Elara had already been born in the person of Gamani, the son of Kawan Tissa, the King of the Ruhunu Rata, a district which was always noted for the turbulent independence of its people. Intense and fiery patriotism characterised Gamani from his earliest years. As a boy of twelve when his mother, who had found him sleeping curled up in bed, advised him to lie with limbs outstretched, he had bitterly retorted. "Confined by the Damilas beyond the river, and on the other side by the unyielding ocean, how can I lie down with outstretched limbs ? " and no sooner had he reached man's estate than he began to prepare the army with which he hoped to drive the invader out of the country.

But Kawan Tissa was cautious and withheld his consent, and the disappointed Prince in bitter jest sent his father a present of a female ornament, remarking : "Friends, my father if he were a man would not say so. Let him therefore wear this." The irate King gave orders for a golden chain to be prepared for the punishment of his impetuous son, and Gamani had to flee from the Court, thus earning the epithet of *Duttha*, or the Disobedient, which, in spite of his subsequent glorious career, has always been applied to him in history.

The King did not long survive this incident, and Gamani at length found himself in a position to put his cherished plans into execution. A great army of horse and foot, of elephants and chariots, forced its way northwards. The forts guarding the road to Anuradhapura were soon captured, and at length the Sinhalese army appeared before Elara's capital and entered upon the construction of elaborate siege works. Elara thereupon marched out of the city to attack the enemy, and redoubt after redoubt fell before him till he came to where the King himself was stationed. Here the fight raged hottest, but Dighajantu, Elara's brave commander, was killed at the very feet of Gamani, and his men turned back in confusion. The Sinhalese hurried in pursuit, and the two Kings met near the southern gate of the city. Elara fell before the javelin of his rival, the city was captured, and before long the whole of the island recognised the sovereignty of Gamani. The body of Elara was cremated with all honour and a mound erected over his ashes; while in acknowledgment of the goodness and chivalry of his foe, a decree was promulgated by the generous conqueror that royalty itself on passing that mound must dismount and silence its music—a decree which was loyally observed so long as a King reigned in the Island of Ceylon.

Gamani now had leisure to attend to the improvement of the country. Numerous tanks were constructed, and the nine-storied *Lowa Maha Paya* at Anuradhapura raised on its sixteen hundred columns of granite for the accommodation of the priesthood. Silver and gold and precious stones were lavished without stint on the adornment of this superb structure, which was roofed throughout with copper. An exquisite throne of ivory with the emblems of the Sun and the Moon embossed in silver and gold occupied the main hall, while above it the white *chatra* or parasol, the symbol of dominion, glittered on its silver staff. A stupendous dagoba, the Ruvanveli Seya, was next begun, the whole cost being met out of the Royal Treasury.

Gamani did not however live to see this task completed. As he lay on his deathbed he was carried out to where he could gaze on the unfinished structure, and there single-handed he fought his last fight with death, cheered by the assurance that for his meritorious acts his place was secure in heaven. His regenerate figure was seen to circle the great structure three times, and then to disappear into space in sight of the assembled multitudes ; and even today his memory is revered among the Sinhalese as that of one of the greatest of the rulers of Ceylon.

It was one of Gamani's successors, Walagamba, who erected the Abhayagiri Dagoba, the mightiest of its kind, which rising from its square platform of eight acres in extent, originally exceeded 400 feet in height. In his reign also, throughout the length and breadth of the country, every recess in the hard rock which could be converted into a human abode was prepared for the occupation of those devotees who desired to retire from the distractions of life and pass their time in contemplation.

But it is a different work which has secured for him fame more indestructible than the living rock out of which his caves were fashioned. For nearly five centuries the *Dharma*, the Doctrine of the Buddha, had been handed down by word of mouth alone amongst the priesthood, just as even today the ritual of each ancient shrine is preserved only in the memories of those whose inherited duty it is to carry it out. It was, however, recognised that the time had come to record the Dharma in a form which would obviate any risk of unauthorised alteration. About eighty years, therefore, before the beginning of the Christian Era, five hundred of the most learned priests in the country met at the King's summons, among the rugged crags of the Alu Vihare[8] ; there, with infinite patience, they inscribed on long strips of palm leaf in the Pali language the profound Metaphysics of the Buddha, his discourses on Morality, and his code of Discipline.[9]

A series of undistinguished rulers now occupied the throne in rapid succession. It was during this period that, as recorded by Pliny, four ambassadors from Ceylon made their way to Rome on a complimentary mission to a State the intercourse with which is still evidenced by large finds of Roman coins in the Island; but no event of special importance marked the history of the country till the accession to the throne of Gaja Bahu, who, early in the beginning of the second century of the Christian era, invaded Tanjor with a great army. The expedition was entirely successful. The King of Tanjor, intimidated by the overwhelming power which accompanied Gaja Bahu, was glad to make peace, surrendering to him not only the 12,000 Sinhalese prisoners and the Bowl Relic which had been captured during a previous invasion of Ceylon, but 12,000 more of his own subjects.

A hundred years later Voharaka Tissa, who humanised the administration of justice by the abolition of torture, was faced by the problem of a threatened religious schism. An attempt was made to introduce a new doctrine known as the Waitulya, which embraced a considerable amount of Brahminical teaching, as the genuine *Dharma* of the Buddha; but the King ordered the destruction of the work and the degradation of the priests of the Abhayagiri establishment who had adopted it.

The rigid adherence of the eccentric saint-king Siri Sanga Bo to the letter of the *Dharma*, reduced the country to a state of anarchy. The prohibition against taking life was regarded by him as forbidding the infliction of capital punishment on condemned criminals, who consequently were often secretly released from custody, while the bodies of those who had died from natural causes were exposed to view at the place of execution. Various miracles are stated to have been brought about by the power of his virtues; and when at last a rebellion broke out headed by his minister Gothabaya, rather than be the cause of bloodshed he abdicated the throne and fled from Anuradhapura. At Attanagalla he miraculously separated his head from his body and sent it to the rebellious minister in the hands of a poor peasant who had shared his meal with him, so that he might obtain the reward which had been promised for its production; and there are still shown there the plants, self-sown, which yearly spring up in the pond into which the saint threw a handful of the boiled rice which had formed the peasant's meal.

A great temple was erected by Gothabaya to mark the place of the King's death, and his vigorous repression of the Waitulyan heresy, which once again broke out at Abhayagiriya, won for him the support of the powerful priesthood. His own son Maha Sena, however, did not escape the taint, and under him the Lowa Maha Paya was razed to the ground, till a threatened rebellion compelled him to alter his views and once again to drive out the Waitulyans. The ponderous mass of the Jetawanarama, together with numerous temples and sixteen tanks, including the great Minneriya Wewa which once irrigated many thousand acres of fields, marked the closing years of his reign.

In A. D. 305, during the reign of his son Kit Siri Mewan, the right Eye Tooth of the Buddha, which for eight hundred years had been preserved at Dantapura, was brought to Ceylon by the Princess Ranmali, daughter of the King of Kalinga,[9] whose country had been invaded by enemies, and delivered to the Sinhalese King. Even today no relic on earth commands the veneration of a larger number of the human race than this, the *Danta Dhatu*. Among the Sinhalese it obtained the position which the Palladium held in Imperial Rome, for the sovereignty of the country could not be denied to the possessor of the relic. Wherever the violence of the invader forced the King to establish his Court, the *Maligawa*, which housed the sacred object, rose within the Royal precincts—smaller, but incomparably more beautiful in its workmanship, than the *Wasala* of the King. The wealth of the country was freely poured out to render it honour; its attendants formed an establishment which was kingly in its size and arrangement; entire villages were dedicated to it for the supply of the offerings of rice and flowers and oil; ivory and gold and gems concealed the massive frames of the narrow doors which guarded the approach to the shrine, where one King at least offered up all the ornaments of royalty which he wore upon his person.

The village of Kirawella was set apart for the maintenance of the Princess Ranmali and her Consort, and the royal rank of their descendants was recognised even by the Portuguese.

Jeta Tissa the artist, Bujas Raja the surgeon, and Upatissa who fed the squirrels in his park and built homes for incurables and maternity hospitals till the faithlessness of his wife led to his assassination, bring us to the times of Mahanama, when the eloquent Buddhist Brahmin Buddha Gosha, The Voice of Buddha, so famous as the missionary of Burmah, translated the Commentary of the *Pitakas* into Pali, and Fa Hian the Chinese traveller visited Ceylon, of which he has left us a valuable account.

An invasion from South India once more compelled the Royal Family to take shelter in the Ruhuna, till Dhatu Sena (458-476 A. D.) was able to re-establish himself at Anuradhapura. The Kala Wewa with its great dam six miles in length, which still feeds Anuradhapura by its fifty-four mile Canal, is the chief surviving monument of this able King, under whose directions the great historical chronicle of the *Mahawansa* was begun by his own uncle. The cruelty and avarice of Kasyapa, his son by one of the junior wives, led to the deposition of the King and his terrible death by being walled up alive. Moggalana the rightful heir fled to India, and the frightened parricide built for himself the amazing rock fortress of Sigiriya, whence he attempted to win the favour of his subjects. But the day of retribution was fast approaching. Moggalana landed with an army of mercenaries, and Kasyapa unwisely leaving his stronghold gave him battle in the open field. Kasyapa's army was defeated and fled in confusion, and the wretched man, rather than fall into the hands of the avenger, killed himself on the field of battle.

A thousand of the parricide's partisans were put to death, and numerous others were punished by having their ears and noses cut off and being banished from the country. Moggalana richly rewarded those who had shown kindness to his father when he had fallen from power. For the first time also in the history of the country a naval force was organised for the purpose of coast defence; and the King's happiness was completed by the arrival from India of a fresh relic, a Hair of the Buddha.

His son Kumaradas immolated himself on the funeral pyre of his friend the poet Kalidas who had been foully murdered by a courtesan, and for many years no king of outstanding ability occupied the throne. A dreary tale of murder, civil war and foreign invasion fills up the greater portion of this chapter in the history of the Island, interspersed however with strange flashes of romantic chivalry. Princes settle their claims to the throne by single combat in the presence of their armies, and the victor entreats the defeated rival not to kill himself in his despair, a prayer unheeded in the depth of shame. Poetasters who had attained to the regal power would send men round their dominions upon elephants, singing the songs composed by their royal masters. In other cases the work of government would be neglected while the King coaxed his children into attending to their studies. Learning, however, maintained a hold on the country, several poets of merit flourished at this time, and in various places important colleges were established.

In the eighth century Dapula II transferred the seat of Government to Polonnaruwa, fifty-five miles to the South East of Anuradhapura. This King it was who was the first to realise the importance of preserving authentic records of all legal proceedings, which he ordered to be deposited in the palace itself. A gentle and kind-hearted man, he established hospitals in various parts of the country and took a delight in entertaining children. Even the beasts of the field and the birds of the air were not forgotten by him, and the tact and delicacy of his sympathy is proved by what the ancient chronicler of his acts has recorded, that he used to send food to destitute ladies under cover of the night.

In spite of the political weakness of the country the Buddhist virtues were enthusiastically cultivated during the recurring intervals of peace. Kings divided among the poor their weight of treasure, and set an example to their people in dutiful affection to their mothers. More than one of them expounded the most complicated dogmas of the Dharma before congregations of priests, while others were authors of works of considerable learning. The establishment of free hospitals, the endowment of colleges, and the construction of tanks and places of worship, were tasks in which kings vied with each other, and their ministers and generals followed their example ; while Mahindo IV (964-980 A. D.) exempted all temple lands from the payment of the royal dues for ever.

But the dissensions within the country once again attracted the attention of the Indian marauders. Anuradhapura was occupied and sacked by the Pandyans in the middle of the ninth country, and a heavy indemnity alone secured their withdrawal to their own country. The Sinhalese, however, had not to wait long for their revenge; within a generation the sack of Madura more than compensated for the plunder of Anuradhapura. In the middle of the next century an invasion was attempted by the Choliyans, but they were brought to bay and were glad to return with what booty they could. A Sinhalese army followed them beyond the sea into their own country, and compelled them to make good the plunder which they had seized. The tide of invasion thus temporarily checked returned with overwhelming force; the North of the Island was wrested foot by foot by Dravidian tribes from the Sinhalese Kings; and by the beginning of the eleventh century the power of the latter was confined to the Ruhuna district.

Once more the Choliyans swooped on the Island. By treachery they succeeded in capturing the King with his jewels and treasure. The temples and dagobas were plundered, "and like unto the demons who suck up the blood, they took to themselves all the substance"[10] that was in Ceylon. The exasperated Sinhalese led by two of their noblemen erected a stronghold from which they maintained so stubborn a resistance that the Choliyans had once more to withdraw to the North of the Island. Nevertheless the power had departed from the hands of the Sinhalese Princes, and for many years the country was little more than the hunting ground of the Indian warriors.

But the spirit of resistance was strong within the people, and a leader came forward in the person of Wijaya Bahu. In spite of internal dissensions which intensified the difficulty of his task, he patiently developed his plans till he found himself strong enough to place two armies on the field. Fortress after fortress fell before his generals, and at last he himself took the field, and appeared before Polonnaruwa. The Choliyans, who fought with more than their usual courage, were defeated, and had to shelter themselves behind the walls of the capital. For six weeks more the struggle was kept up with the utmost desperation ; then at last the Sinhalese succeeded in scaling the ramparts and carrying the place by storm. Every one of the hated Choliyans was put to the sword.

Once more the Sinhalese flag floated over the whole of Ceylon, and Wijaya Bahu set himself vigorously to create order out of the chaos that the Indians had left behind. Courts of Justice were organised, priests were obtained from Pegu[11] to restore the sacerdotal succession, the capital was strengthened and beautified, numerous tanks were constructed, and amidst all these labours the King found time to devote himself to literature. The latter part of his long reign of fifty-five years was tranquil and prosperous, and when he died in A. D. 1109 the terror of the Choliyan domination was a thing almost forgotten in the Island.

His death was once again the signal for internal discord, but a mighty figure had appeared on the stage. Great things had been prophesied at the birth of Parakrama Bahu, the son of the Princess Ratanavali, and the thoughtful quiet prince was given an education suitable to his future destiny. Not only was he carefully trained in those warlike accomplishments of riding, archery and swordsmanship which the necessities of the times rendered essential to every Prince, and in that knowledge of jurisprudence which is expected from the chief judge of a country, but also in the more refining arts of poetry, music and elegant writing ; and from his youth he took a share in the practical administration of the government. High thoughts welled within his breast. "If I who am born of a princely race should not do a deed worthy of the heroism of Kings, my life would be of none avail[12]." Taking only his arms with him he travelled in disguise through the country, and organised a system of spies by means of which he made himself conversant with the disposition of the people and also with the various strategic routes. His succession to the government of the Ruhuna brought the fulfilment of his long-cherished schemes within the range of possibility. Garrisons were formed on the frontier outposts, and on every side all land suitable for rice cultivation was irrigated and utilised, so as to render the country independent of foreign supplies in case of prolonged hostilities. The local bodies of troops were systematically drilled in manoeuvres, mercenaries were obtained from India in large numbers, the artificers were organised for the preparation of the necessary weapons, and the sons of the nobility trained in arms at his own palace.

Money, however, was lacking, and a special Minister was delegated to supervise the collection of the revenue. Gold and silver are not found in the Island, but the lack of these has been compensated for by the abundance of her gems. The country lying between the Kelani Ganga and Walawe Ganga on the South, and stretching inland within the mountain zone, has from the remotest times been renowned for the beauty and the lustre of the rubies, sapphires and the catseyes which are there met with in such abundance. Great mounds of earth still mark the diggings of Indian visitors who came in search of them probably before the arrival of the Sinhalese, and the markets of that country were always ready to absorb all that the Island could produce. Gems have from the earliest times been the property of the King, and the work of digging for them was now energetically taken in hand. Gem-mining is not an expensive undertaking, for the debris of the crystalline rocks in which the precious stones are found is reached at a depth of about twenty feet. This is washed in circular baskets of cane and the gems picked out by hand. The Sinhalese knew that inorganic crystals grew and multiplied and reproduced their kind, or, as they put it, that gems ripened under the action of the sun, and mining would not be carried on at the same spot more often than once in twelve years. The exploitation of this source of revenue soon brought the necessary treasure to the coffers of the King, and when everything was ready he openly declared war.

Polonnaruwa was soon taken by storm, but the riotous conduct of Parakrama's soldiers so exasperated the inhabitants, that they drove his generals away from the city. Parakrama Bahu was not long in raising a second army, and Polonnaruwa once again fell into his hands. A confused period of fierce struggle followed. Manabarana, who led the opposing faction, after a terrible battle which lasted seven days, fled from the field to die; and Parakrama Bahu was crowned King of the whole of Ceylon, amidst scenes of amazing pomp and splendour.

The consolidation of the Kingdom being successfully achieved, Parakrama Bahu next took in hand the reform of the Buddhist religion, which by the oppression of the foreigner and the negligence of its votaries was in a critical condition. By the exercise of his tact and authority the dissensions among the various fraternities were healed, and the priesthood itself purified. Polonnaruwa was strengthened by a chain of ramparts; a magnificent palace with a large theatre and parks added to the beauty of the city; a hospital which was regularly visited by the King, gave proof of his sympathy for suffering mankind; while the precious Bowl and Tooth relics were transferred to the capital.

The insulting attitude assumed by the King of Pegu towards the Sinhalese ambassadors accredited to his Court, and his seizure of a Sinhalese Princess on her way to Cambodia, led to the despatch of a punitive expedition which took his capital, put the King to death, and returned to Ceylon after imposing a tribute on the conquered. Another army was despatched to assist the Pandiyans against the Choliyan King Kulasekara. The campaign which followed was triumphantly successful, and coins struck in the country with the superscription of Parakrama Bahu were left behind in token of his suzerainty.

The thirty-three years of his reign were indeed among the most flourishing in the history of the Island. A Civil Service was carefully organised in its various departments; the ancient edifices at Anuradhapura were restored; numerous parks were laid out with fruit trees and flowers; over six thousand image houses and seventy-three great dagobas were erected; and thousands of tanks were repaired in addition to the one thousand four hundred and seventy-one reservoirs which were newly constructed; while hospitals and libraries were established in various parts of the country. So efficient was his administration that it was said "Even a woman might traverse the length of the Island with a precious jewel, and not be asked what it was.[12] The great King died in the year 1197; Ceylon never again produced his like.

Not a generation had elapsed after the death of Parakrama Bahu, when once again Ceylon was overrun by Indian hordes, starting this time from the Kingdom of Kalinga[13]. Twenty thousand merciless warriors swept through the country, plundering, ravishing, mutilating, and slaughtering. Even the yellow robe of the ascetic could not avail to save the person of the priest. The holiest shrines were violated and overthrown. Ruwanweli Seya, "which stood like the embodiment of the glory of all the pious Kings of old,"[12] was despoiled of its priceless relics. In sheer wantonness they loosed the cords which held together the rare palm-leaf books, and scattered the leaves to the winds. The King himself was taken prisoner and blinded, and then the marauders established themselves at Polonnaruwa, while another capital was erected by the Sinhalese at Dambadeniya. The vigorous action, however, of Pandita Parakrama Bahu (1235-1270 A. D.), a King distinguished as much for his success in the field as for the splendour of his intellectual attainments, compelled them to abandon Polonnaruwa and retreat towards the continent; but they were intercepted at Kala Wewa and put to the sword.

Repeated invasions from India followed the death of Pandita Parakrama Bahu, and the Tooth Relic was captured by the Pandiyans; it was, however, restored on the personal intercession of the King, who proceeded to India for the purpose. It was about this time that the *Sidat Sangarawa*, the most important work on Sinhalese Grammar, was written[14].

Meanwhile a Tamil settlement had been formed in Jaffnapatam, the sandy peninsula in which the Island terminates on the North, and its King Arya Chakrawarti was attempting to spread his dominion over the Sinhalese territory. The feeble Bhuwaneka Bahu maintained a nominal rule as King of the mountain region, while the country below was administered by the powerful Minister Alakeswara Mantri. The new fortress of Jayawardhana Kotte, six miles from the Colombo of today, which was erected by him, served as a rallying point for the Sinhalese, and the defeat of two Tamil armies was the auspicious prelude to the reign of Rukule Parakrama Bahu, which began in 1415 A. D. Kotte now became the Capital and thither the Tooth Relic was transferred. An invasion of the Canarese[15] was successfully repelled, and a naval expedition punished the piratical Malabar Prince of Vira Rama Pattanam for the seizure of a Sinhalese trading vessel.

The lofty plateau which formed the eastern portion of the Maya Rata was at this period a subordinate principality known by the descriptive name of Kanda Uda Rata,[16] the country above the Mountains. Its capital was the small town of Senkadagala, known today among Europeans as Kandy, and it was ruled by a Prince named Jaya Sinha. Being however suspected of treasonable designs, he was reduced to subjection by the younger son of the King; while his elder son occupied Jaffna, which became his principality till he succeeded his father at Kotte. His short reign of seven years was marked by a great rebellion in the South, suppressed by his brother, who subsequently ascended the throne as Wira Parakrama Bahu. He in turn was succeeded by his son Dharma Parakrama Bahu, during whose reign the Portuguese visited the Island for the first time.

NOTES TO CHAPTER I

1. Rama Chandra is worshipped as an Incarnation of Vishnu. The ruling Rajput families of Jeypur and Udaipur claim descent from him.

2. So says the Portuguese Captain Joao Ribeiro, who was in the Island from 1640 to 1658.

3. Wijayo claimed to be the grandson of a Lion, *sinha*; his followers are the Sinhalese, the Lion Race. The month of Wesak corresponds to May—June.

4. There can be little doubt from the narrative contained in the ancient Sinhalese chronicle, the *Mahawansa,* that the Yakkhas had attained to a considerable pitch of civilisation, and that the new settlers freely intermarried among them. No traces of their civilisation, however, can be recognised today.

5. The *Ficus Religiosa*; four Buddhas are said to have visited the world, and a different variety of the fig tree is sacred to each of them.

6. From *Datu,* relic; *Garbham,* receptacle. These are probably more familiar under the Indian name of *tope.*

7. The Eastern Coast of India, from Pt. Calimere to Orissa. Chola, Chera, and Pandya were the three ancient divisions of the Dravida country of South India.

8. A Vihare is a temple of the Buddhist religion.

9. Commonly known as the *Tri Pitakas,* the Three Baskets of the Buddhist Canon.

10 Mahawansa.

11. This is Chryse, the Golden, of the Periplus; the Swarna Bhumi, the Land of Gold, of ancient Oriental writers. At one time it took its place among the greatest Empires of the East, and its close connectton with Ceylon is well set out in the famous Kalyani inscription at Pegu, dated A. D. 1476.

12. Mahawansa.

13. Kalinga is the Northern Circars of today, extending from the Kistna to the Mahanudi.

14. The date of the Sidat Sangarawa is a matter of some doubt, but it is usually considered to have been written early in the 14th century.

15. On the West Coast of India, and to the North of Malabar.

16. The Portuguese formed the name Candia from the Sinhalese *Kanda,* mountain, and applied it both to the principality and also to the Capital, the full name of which in official Sinhalese is Senkanda Saila Sriwardhana Pura. The name Kandy is unknown to the Sinhalese.

CHAPTER II.

The early history of Portugal and of the great maritime enterprises upon which she engaged under the impulse of the movement created by Prince Henry the Navigator, grandson of John of Gaunt, has been frequently told. In 1498 when Dom Manuel was on the throne, the first Portuguese vessels under Vasco da Gama reached Calicut; and seven years later, on the 25th of March 1505, Dom Francisco de Almeida set out from the Tagus with the pompous title of Viceroy of India.

De Almeida was more than a pirate or conqueror, for he was also a statesman with a far-sighted and wise policy. The Eastern trade had filled the treasuries of Venice with almost limitless wealth, and his desire was to direct this stream of gold into his Royal Master's coffers. In the Indian waters the carrying trade was in the hands of the hated Mohammedan races. The Soldan at Cairo was the undisputed master of the Red Sea, while the Turk, from Bussorah, controlled the Persian Gulf; and it was over these two sheets of water that the Eastern merchandise found its way to the vessels which awaited it on the coasts of the Mediterranean. De Almeida's aim was to divert this traffic to Portugal by way of the newly discovered Cape route, but its fulfilment could only be brought about by first securing the undisputed control of the sea. It was not likely that the Mohammedans would surrender the supremacy which they had held so long without a fierce resistance, and both the Egyptian and the Turk had navies and artillery powerful enough to challenge the best that Europe was likely to send. De Almeida therefore devoted his energies to strengthening his navy and deprecated the erection of fortresses except where they were absolutely necessary for the protection of the trade factories. He advocated the maintenance of friendly relations with the Indian Rajas, and the making of alliances with them, under which they would look after the factories and supply the merchandise which was required, while the Portuguese in return would guarantee the protection of their coasts against all attack by sea.

Early in November 1505 the Viceroy's son Dom Lourenco was sent by his father with a fleet of nine vessels to attack the Moorish[1] spice ships which were reported to be making for the Red Sea by way of the Maldives, when adverse winds drove him to the coast of Ceylon in the neighbourhood of Galle. Two generations before Sri Rahula of Totagamuwa, the great hierarch[2] whose versatile genius has not been surpassed by that of any Sinhalese since his time, had sung the praises of Galle "where the shops were resplendent with gold and gems and pearls, as if the depths of every ocean had been searched to procure them." Its great bay afforded a welcome shelter to the Portuguese while they replenished their stock of water and fuel before setting sail for Kolon Tota, always spoken of by their writers as Colombo. The unbroken stretch of coconut palms which covered the shore with a garment of exquisite verdure, the soft scented breeze of the cool morning, the green hills crowned with their snowy white dagobas flashing like silver in the blazing sun, above all the fresh luxuriance of the vegetation, made a picture well calculated to fill with delight the hearts of men who had recently faced the buffettings of the stormy ocean. At length on the 15th of November the fleet anchored off Colombo.

Mud-walled houses with thatched roofs slanting low towards the sea as a protection against the fierce attack of the South-west Monsoon, formed the main street of the town. High above them arose the white walls of two mosques, standing out clear from the background of green. The light canoes of the hardy fishermen were drawn up on the stretch of sand, and near them a shouting crowd of men and boys dragged in the great net over which the seagulls hovered in their circling flight. West of the town lay the stretch of marshy ground which connected the lagoon with the sea, and beyond, sweeping to the North, rose a bleak headland which formed the extremity of the natural rampart known as the Galbokka. The harbour was crowded with shipping; some of the vessels were taking aboard the elephants[3] and cinnamon for which the island has been always famous throughout the East; others were being laden with copra and fresh coconuts; here logs of satinwood and ebony were being hauled to the shore for transport to the great mart of Ormuz in the Persian Gulf; while elsewhere vessels from the further Eastern waters were landing their goods for transhipment to the Red Sea. The trade of the port was in the hands of a colony of Moors, of Indian origin. Their ancestors had settled in the country some five hundred years before, and had been received with the liberality which ever characterised the conduct of the Sinhalese towards strangers who did not prove themselves unworthy of it.

The arrival of this flotilla of white strangers was immediately reported to the Court, whither the reputation of the Portuguese had preceded them; a Council of State was summoned, and it was decided to receive them amicably. A message was sent demanding of the strangers what they desired at the King's port. Dom Lourenco sent back a reply that he was a merchant, a servant of the King of Portugal, who had been driven out of his course to

Ceylon, and that he would be glad to open a friendly trade. The King directed that the Portuguese should send a representative to discuss matters with him, and an officer named Fernao Cotrim set out with a Sinhalese escort. For three days he travelled crossing hills, and fording numerous streams ; for the Sinhalese had no desire to let the foreigners learn that their Capital was but two hours' journey from the sea. "As the Parangi' went to Kotte" is the Sinhalese proverb which still preserves the memory of this ruse.

Cotrim was accorded an interview with the King's Ministers, to whom he explained the errand on which the Portuguese were come. He asserted that their only desire was for peaceful trade. If the King wished for this, he should send an yearly present as a token of friendship to the King of Portugal, who would send him presents in return. Moreover, the Portuguese would undertake to protect his coasts against all enemies.

The offer found acceptance with the King and his Council, and they consented to the terms proposed. Cotrim returned to the fleet and reported the success of his mission. De Almeida was highly gratified; in celebration of it he ordered a salvo of artillery to be fired, to the great terror of the peaceful inhabitants of the port, who regarded it as a hostile demonstration.

Another officer, Payo de Sousa, was now sent with full powers to conclude a treaty with the King. He was conveyed to the Capital, Jayawardhana Kotte, on elephant back with the same precautions as were observed in the case of his predecessor. This royal city was built on a triangular tract of elevated land, the apex of which lay to the North. On its two sides it was flanked by the waters of the Diyawanna Oya and its tributary streams, which approached each other so closely at the base that the narrow neck joining the fort to the *Pita Kotte* or town was a bare fifty paces across. Strong walls of dressed *cabook* or laterite taken from the quarries in the neighbourhood added to the security afforded by the water, which teemed with crocodiles. At the base was the *Periya Kotte* or Main Guard, where additional stone-works and a broad moat guarded the entrance to the citadel from the land side. Within lay the Palace, side by side, as was always the case, with the three-storied Dalada Maligawa, the Temple of the precious Tooth Relic. A few of the great dignitaries connected with the Court also had their residences within the walls. Half a mile to the South of the Periya Kotte a considerable moat crossed by a bridge protected the town.

Sri Rahula in his *Selalihini Sandesaya* has left us a charming description of the Capital as he saw it. To him it was a city of the gods, with stately mansions and tinkling bells, filled with the odours of sandal wood and champac-flowers, where every woman was lovely, and every heart was joyous; but it does not appear rash to assert that at the beginning of the sixteenth century there was not in the Island one town which surpassed in its extent and population a large English village of today. Towns are the creation of trade or of manufacture on a large scale, but the Sinhalese were never a commercial race, and their manufactures did not rise above the level of handicrafts. Seaports like Colombo, Beruwala, and Weligama, owed their importance to the presence of the foreign trading element, chiefly Mohammedan; the Sinhalese himself lived at a distance on the land which he cultivated. In this fortunate climate the social scheme was one which was eminently calculated to produce contentment in the majority; everyone had a sufficiency of land for the maintenance of himself and his family, and there was always an abundance of forest available for the occupation of the more enterprising. Of money there was but very little, and the luxuries which money could procure were few.

The house of a Sinhalese was little more than a temporary protection against the inclemency of the weather. The houses of the greatest contained no chair or table; the furniture at best would consist of a few stools. Till he entered the actual precincts of the palace, the town as it revealed itself to the eyes of de Sousa must have seemed very dingy. One or two of the houses of the great noblemen which he passed would have two storeys, with narrow balconies and painted walls. The strict sumptuary laws which prevailed there no less than in South India limited the rest of the small populace to thatched roofs and unplastered walls. All magnificence was centred round the King, and the religion of which he was the patron, and often the servant. The magnificence, however, was that of artistic beauty and not of size. Dwelling houses were always small, and individual rooms cramped and suffocating. The practice of eating and drinking in crowds as a means of social enjoyment was unknown, hence there was no need for stately halls where such crowds could meet, for temporary structures could always be erected with little trouble to house the gathering which assembled at a marriage.

The courteous but frankly inquisitive crowd which gathered to watch de Sousa's progress through the town would contain as many women as men, for the Mohammedan habit of seclusion was unknown in the country, except in the case of noble women who considered it a disgrace to be seen by any man but their husbands. Both sexes wore their hair long and tied in a knot behind, and the ear-lobes of both were bored and weighed down with heavy pieces of jewellery. A cloth wrapped round the waist, whether the coarse product of their own country or the fine muslin of the Indian looms, formed the main portion of the costume of the males. The women wore little more, though all of them were covered with jewellery which varied in quality according to the caste. The little children were, as now, innocent of clothing, save perhaps a silver chain. Most of the girls would have flowers entwined in their black hair, and their faces would be daubed with a paste made of the sweet-smelling sandalwood finely ground; all of them would be chewing the one stimulant of the Sinhalese, the betel leaf and slice of arecanut.

The golden gem-set spire which surmounted the Palace attracted the eye as the ambassador was led through the narrow gates of the Sumangala Prasada, the massive door-frames of which were of elaborately carved stone. From the palace eaves hung a row of flags of all colours, the tiny bells which were attached to them tinkling with every breeze. According to Sinhalese custom the audience took place by candle-light. De Sousa was ushered into a large hall hung with the fabrics of Persia, its sombre gloom relieved by lamps and torches on silver stands. The place of audience was filled with the crouching figures of numerous courtiers, and on either side were rows of warriors, their naked swords by their sides and shields on their arms.

At one end of the hall rose a massive canopy of stone shaped like the head of the fabulous *Makara,*[5] and surmounted by the figures of the deities who preside over the four quarters of the universe. Above it was raised the white *chatra* of dominion, which overshadowed the "Lion Throne" of the Race of the Lion. On this massive seat of ivory, which rose on six stages and was covered with cloth of gold, was seated Dharma Parakrama Bahu, Overlord of Ceylon. A white tunic covered the upper portion of his body, while his head dress, which was studded with gems and large pearls, fell in two points over his shoulders. Round his waist was wrapped a cloth picked] out with silver and reaching to his feet, which were protected by sandals studded with rubies. A profusion of rubies, diamonds and emeralds covered his fingers and weighed down his ears till they reached nearly to his shoulders.

Advancing between the rows of armed men, de Sousa halted at a respectful distance and made a profound obeisance. After a grandiloquent harangue on the greatness of the King of Portugal and of his people, he explained the object of his mission. In reply the King after consulting with his Ministers promised to allow the Portuguese four hundred *bahars*[6] of cinnamon a year, on condition of their protecting his coasts from all external attack. A *Sannas* to this effect written in Sinhalese on a sheet of gold was presented to the ambassador, who was then given permission to return to his vessel.

"It was on account of the cinnamon that the Romans and other nations came to Ceilao; I fear, Senhor, that those who have obtained the taste for it will come behind us on its scent." So wrote the veteran Portuguese warrior Miguel Ferreyra to the Viceroy at Goa as he left Ceylon in 1540. Nature laid a heavy curse on the Island when she decreed that this delicious spice was not to grow in any other country of the world. The shrub—for it can hardly be dignified by the name of tree—the inner bark of which supplies the coveted article, was not the object of cultivation, but grew wild in abundance in the forests. The trade in cinnamon was always a Royal monopoly, and the preparation and collection of the bark was a service which had to be rendered by the caste of Chalias, who were confined, under circumstances of great hardship, to some of the royal villages along the southern and western coasts. A definite amount had to be provided by the caste every year, and an elaborate system had been devised for the control of the men and the supervision of their work. The bark was dried in the form of long quills and tied in bundles of a fixed weight, which were then wrapped in mats and conveyed to the King's *Bangasalai* or Store at Colombo. This store was in charge of a high official under whose directions the article was sold by weight to the foreign merchants. It was from this trade that the King obtained the largest portion of his revenue. The cinnamon, stored in the holds of vessels along with loose pepper to preserve it from deterioration, was conveyed to Ormuz or the Red Sea on its way to Europe.

Next in importance from the point of view of the Royal Revenues was the trade in elephants. These animals had always been, as they are to-day, the property of the Crown, and roamed about in great herds over the less thickly populated districts of the Island. The Ceylon elephant surpassed all others in sagacity, and the Portuguese, speaking from what they witnessed in after years at the dockyard at Goa, used to declare that its superiority was acknowledged by the animals brought from other parts of the world, which would make obeisance to it. The Sinhalese themselves distinguished ten classes among their elephants, just as they recognise a royal caste among cattle and a low caste among the cobras.

The usual method of capturing elephants was by driving the herd within a great stockade: but individuals would sometimes be taken by means of trained decoys. The chief hunt was maintained where Ptolemy had indicated the existence of their feeding grounds, namely, towards the eastern extremity of the Ruhuna. Other hunts were held not far from the capital itself, while large numbers were obtained from the dry regions in the North and centre of the island; but these were considered inferior to the others both in intelligence and stamina. Several villages were attached to the hunt, and the services which their inhabitants had to render were entirely connected with the capture, taming, and maintenance of the beasts. Certain villages also in the North Central districts, where herds of deer abounded, furnished the stout ropes made of deer hides which were used for securing the newly captured animals. The traffic in elephants was carried on almost exclusively with India. In the seventeenth century at the Court of the Great Mogul, a tusker from Ceylon was a means of conveyance reserved for the Royal Princes. Whether it was for purposes of dignified ceremonial, as a means of transport, or for purposes of war, the elephant stood unmatched at this period of the history of the East, and the *Gajanayaka Nilame*—the Chief of the Elephants—who was at the head of the establishment, ranked among the highest Household Officers of the Sinhalese Court.

A short time after de Sousa's return the promised cinnamon arrived with two little elephants, and a great quantity of fruit and other provisions for the use of the fleet. It had been customary for the fleets which were sent from Portugal on voyages of discovery to take with them stone pillars called *padroes* to be set up in the newly discovered countries. These *padroes* were surmounted with a cross, below which the Royal Arms were sculptured. Dom Lourenco now asked for and received permission from the Sinhalese King to engrave such a cross and the Portuguese arms on a boulder overlooking the Bay; and this memorial of the first arrival of the Portuguese may still be seen, though bearing the inexplicable date 1501. In addition to this a small hut was erected on the hill behind the boulder, and dedicated as a chapel to Sao Lourenco, de Almeida's patron Saint, after whom also the promontory was named. This done the fleet sailed away, leaving a few Portuguese behind in charge of a temporary Factory where they could collect the produce of the Island for export to Europe.

So pleased was Dom Manuel with this new discovery, that he ordered a commemorative painting to be prepared, while at the Papal Court a solemn procession was conducted in honour of the event on St. Thomas's Day, 21st December 1507. It should be remembered that at this time the Portuguese did not possess a foot of territory in Asia, and that the Viceroy himself had to rely on the hospitality of the Raja of Cochin. Dom Manuel therefore suggested that Ceylon was, by virtue of its central position and excellent climate, the most suitable residence for his representative in Asia. The time, however, was unfavourable for the development of this scheme, as the Viceroy's energies were concentrated on repelling an Egyptian fleet which had defeated and killed his son Dom Lourenco. The Factory at Colombo was neglected, while the attempt of the Portuguese to monopolise the trade of the port only served to rouse the resentment of both the Sinhalese and the Moors. In a few years the men who had been left in charge were recalled, while the demand for cinnamon was met by trade or piracy.

But Dharma Parakrama Bahu's reign was not a peaceful one. There were dissensions among his own subjects, and the corsairs from the mainland from time to time harried his coasts, till they were attacked and defeated by the Prince Sakala Kala Wallabha. A rebellion in the Uda Rata, where a certain Wikrama Bahu was in power, occurred not long after, but after two short campaigns the district was reduced to submission by the Prince.

In the meantime Affonco de Alboquerque had succeded de Almeida, and his occupation of the three great ports of Goa, Malacca, and Ormuz marked the commencement of a new policy of territorial aggrandisement. The appetite of Portugal was whetted by a fuller realisation of the immensity of the wealth which could be obtained from the Eastern trade, and she was determined to secure this for herself. It was not, however, possible for her to hope for success by peaceful rivalry, for the Eastern Princes fully appreciated the fair dealing of their long-standing customers. The Mohammedan trade had therefore to be destroyed by force, and powerful forts established in order to sweep the Moors from the Eastern seas.

The inhuman barbarities which accompanied the execution of this policy, the utter callousness to human pain and suffering—a callousness which knew no distinction between man, woman and child—were discussed with horror from the Cape to Nagasaki. Alboquerque himself was fortunately too busy in India to turn his attention to Ceylon, but in 1518 his successor, the Governor Lopo Soarez de Albergaria, arrived at Colombo with a large fleet, and applied for permission to erect a fort; he urged on the King the advantages he would derive from the trade which was sure to follow, and the importance of driving the Moors out of the country, expressing at the same time his firm determination never to cease in his hostility towards them.

The Moors watched the new development with anxiety, and a deputation of their leading merchants waited on the King, and begged him earnestly not to be led astray by the flattery of the Governor; for their experience in India had warned them not to trust the Portuguese, whose sole object was to aggrandise themselves at the expense of the countries which they visited. The Sinhalese, they asserted, would find too late that the sovereign power had been wrested from them. They emphasized their own good services to the country of their adoption; they had never interfered with its political affairs, while their trade had brought wealth and prosperity in its train; they had not attempted to obtrude their religion on anyone, but they warned the King that the arrival of the Portuguese would be speedily followed by the downfall of the national religion. Their vehement expostulations stirred up the populace to a condition of frenzied excitement. A few cannon which the Moors had presented to the King were dragged to the shore, and an ill-directed fire was opened on the ships, whose reply however soon drove away the angry rabble. The next morning the Portuguese landed and erected a stockade guarded by a moat across the narrow isthmus. Protected by these they began the erection of a small fort.

The King, however, was averse to hostilities; and a conciliatory message from him led to the resumption of negotiations, which terminated in his issuing his *Sannas* promising the Portuguese 400 *bahars* of cinnamon and twenty rings set with rubies and ten elephants every year, on the same condition as formerly, namely, their undertaking the defence of his coasts. The fort, named Nossa Senhora das Virtudes, was soon completed, whereupon the fleet sailed away leaving a garrison behind under the command of Dom Joao de Silveira.

On the north-west coast of Ceylon, there are in the bed of the ocean a cluster of elevated patches on which the eyes of all Asia have from the earliest times been fixed with admiring envy. For these patches are the banks where, long before the days of Wijayo, the loveliest pearls in the world used to be found. The peculiar lustre of the pearls of Ceylon is popularly ascribed, as is that of her gems, to the effect of her sun; however that may be, the fact remains that the pearls which are obtained in such quantities from the same species of mollusc in the Persian Gulf, can invariably be detected by their inferior lustre.

The Pearl Banks have always been royal property; but the divers employed in the collection of the oysters were usually obtained from South India, and were not Sinhalese. The revenue yielded by the

Fishery was precarious in its nature, for the millions of oysters, whose growth was carefully watched till they attained maturity, might any day disappear into the depths of the surrounding ocean. The hundreds of boats which were engaged in the fishing were furnished not by the King but by private persons, and each day's catch was divided according to certain recognised rules between the King, the boat owners and the divers.

Before the fishery commenced incantations were performed in order to render the terrible sharks and other monsters of the deep harmless to the divers, and then the men plunged into the water. They employed a heavy stone to assist them in their descent from the ship's side. On reaching the bottom they threw themselves on their faces and collected what oysters they could into a net bag secured at their waists. When their ear-drums began to ring they gave a signal by a cord which was attached to their bodies, and were hauled up by their companions in the boat. The Fishery began in the middle of March and ceased with the setting in of the south-west Monsoon towards the end of April, a great Fair, which attracted merchants from all parts of Asia, being maintained on the barren shore so long as the Fishery lasted. The oysters of each group of owners were piled up within an enclosure of thorns on the beach, and there they remained till their fleshy contents had rotted away, when the shells were carefully examined for the pearls. These, when collected, were sorted by being sifted through a series of nine brass sieves. The finest would be immediately secured for the Indian Courts, and the inferior kinds as well as the seed pearls transported to Europe to be used in the *aljofar* work of the Moors, which bedecked the Court dresses of the Iberian beauties.

By order of the Governor a report was prepared of the possibilities of this Fishery and of the trade prospects of the country in general, for transmission to Lisbon. A careful examination of the coast was also begun. At the same time the indefatigable priests began the work of conversion among the Sinhalese ; for under the Papal Bull of Alexander VI. issued in 1494, one of the conditions of the sovereignty of new discoveries being vested in Portugal was the propagation of the Catholic Religion.

King Dharma Parakrama Bahu died not long after, and the vacant throne was offered to Sakala Kala Wallabha ; but with rare self-denial he rejected the proffered honour in favour of his half-brother Wijaya Bahu, who was accordingly proclaimed King. Early in 1520 Lopo de Brito reached Colombo with 400 men in succession to de Silveira. His arrival was not a day too soon, for the clay walls had already begun to crumble under the torrential rains of Ceylon. Pearl shells were fetched to provide the necessary lime, and the rebuilding of the walls and barracks taken in hand. But so unpopular had the Portuguese become, that the inhabitants first refused to furnish them with provisions, and finally began to cut off all soldiers found outside the walls. The garrison retaliated by making an attack on the town, and succeeded in setting fire to a portion of it, but was driven back with a loss of thirty men. The tension increased, for Wijaya Bahu's sympathies were with his subjects, and the alternate flattery and threats which de Brito employed towards him only served to delay for a short time the appearance of a Sinhalese army before the fort.

The two armies which were now face to face were in strange contrast to one another. Behind the protecting walls stood a highly efficient body of professional soldiers, who would have lost little by comparison with the finest troops in Europe. Their numbers were scanty, but they were all more or less veterans, wearing defensive armour, and a fair proportion of them supplied with firearms. To them the enemy must have seemed merely a tumultuous rabble, without discipline and only formidable by reason of the war-elephants which could be seen in their ranks.

Under the system of land tenure which prevailed in the Island from the earliest times, all occupied land was divided into *Pangu* or allotments, which varied in size and importance. To each allotment was assigned a portion of high land which could be planted with trees, a mud land capable of being sown with rice, and an extent of waste land which would be cleared in patches, according to the exigencies of the seasons, for less permanent cultivation. On the high land would be the cottage where the family of the tenant lived, and round it would be planted the coconut, jak and other trees which were so important an item in the domestic economy of the villager. Each allotment was liable to contribute towards the maintenance of the common wealth whether by personal service, called *Rajakariya,* on the part of the tenant, or by payment in money or in kind. Some *pangu* would have to supply soldiers with their weapons, consisting in the main of bows and arrows, pikes and other similar instruments of warfare. The professional soldier was unknown, unless it were among the members of the *Attapattu,* who formed the Royal Guard; or the trained Indian mercenaries who were maintained at Court.

When the summons to arms arrived, the cultivator would exchange his plough for the bow, provide himself with a scanty stock of rice and a few dried palm leaves which were to serve him as a tent, and join the rest of his fellows at the appointed rendezvous. Over each group of twenty or thirty men there would be an *Arachchi* armed with his lion-headed sword of native steel, short and small handled, as befitted a slightly built race. To act as Arachchi would be the service which his *Panguwa* carried with it. The superior officers were known as Mudaliyars.

Each caste among the soldiery would be grouped separately, and no one of a low caste could take command over a man of a higher caste. Other *pangu* would supply the wood-cutters, who formed an important element in an army whose fighting was mainly guerilla. They would bring their own axes. Others would attend to haul the trees they felled, and to convey the baggage and ammunition. The tom-tom beaters held always a prominent place, for their noisy drums not only inspirited the men on the march and in the attack, but also conveyed messages over great distances. The smiths sent their contingent to furnish and repair the necessary weapons; others again brought the charcoal which was required at their forges; while a few *pangu* would supply a man with a horn or the raucous conch-shell. In the nature of things those whose duties were connected with the care and manoeuvring of elephants had a better and more systematic training, but as a rule it was left to each man to render himself efficient in the line of service to which his allotment was liable.

This army was meant for purposes of defence. Each individual who went to make it up was liable to serve only for a certain number of days, and there were limitations to the distance which he was expected to travel from his home[7]. Carefully prepared registers existed of the various holdings, and the number of men who could be called up at any time was known. When a man died, a member of his family would step into his place and continue in the enjoyment of the *panguwa* on the same terms. The fact that there were several able-bodied members in a family made no difference, for it was the *panguwa* and not the individual which was liable, and so long as the service was rendered the tenancy could not be altered.

Anything in the nature of a uniform was unknown. In the tropics dress, except in its most meagre form, is not a necessity. Each man dressed himself as he liked, which made little practical difference, for the Sinhalese fought bare-bodied, with merely a strip of cloth tied round his waist and tucked up behind. Each district had its distinctive flag, round which the men of the district were grouped.

Probably there was not one amongst those who were gathered before the little fort who had previously attacked a walled position. Unused as they were to this kind of warfare, the Sinhalese progressed but slowly; nevertheless step by step they drew nearer. Earthworks were thrown up, and on these were mounted several hundered machines, some of them throwing wooden darts ten palms in length. From others fire-bombs were hurled on the thatched roofs within the fort, while two bastions constructed of the trunks of the coconut palms which grew in abundance in the neighbourhood, rendered the task of supplying the fort with water, which had to be fetched from outside the walls, one of great peril. An urgent demand for help was sent to the Governor at Cochin, but he was powerless to assist; he advised de Brito to pacify the enemy if he could do so without discredit to his sovereign, and to wait till sufficient forces should be available for an attempt to obtain vengeance. For the rest he promised that as soon as the weather changed, the first ship which left the harbour should sail to his assistance.

For six months more the little garrison held out, though famine was hovering over it and everything was doled out with the most rigid care. At last on the 4th of October a galley reached Colombo, to the great delight of the besieged, and a joint attack by sea and land drove the Sinhalese back into the town. They soon returned supported by twenty five of the war elephants, and made a determined attempt to carry the place by storm ; but the firearms of the Portuguese rendered the task a hopeless one, and at last Wijaya Bahu withdrew from the field, whereupon the Portuguese entered the town and set it on fire. Both sides however were anxious for the cessation of hostilities. Peace was accordingly concluded, and friendly relations re-established.

NOTES TO CHAPTER II

1. This term was applied indifferently by the Portuguese to all who professed the Mohammedan Faith.

2. He held the office of Sanga Raja, or King of the Priesthood, with the honorific name of Wijaya Bahu. His poem, the *Paravi Sandesaya,* from which this quotation is taken, was written about 1450 A. D.

3. In 1500 the Portuguese had found a ship of Cochin conveying seven elephants from Ceylon. This vessel was of 600 tons. The Sao Gabriel, in which Vasco da Gama reached India, did not exceed 120 tons.

4. *Parangi* is the Sinhalese form of *Feringhee.*

5. A fabulous sea-monster with the tail of a fish. The *chatra* is the parasol of dominion

6. The *Bahar* was approximately 176.25 kilo.

7. Cf. the Anglo-Saxon *fyrd,* or county militia.

CHAPTER III

In the meantime a family quarrel had broken out with regard to the succession to the throne. Marriage among the Sinhalese is purely a social contract, without any of that glamour of religion with which Christianity has after many centuries succeeded in surrounding it in some countries of Europe. The position of the Sinhalese wife in the early part of the sixteenth century was in some ways curiously in advance of the age. Marriage did not reduce her to the condition of her husband's chattel; she retained her right of private property, and enjoyed large privileges in regard to divorce. The circle of choice, however, was limited not only to the caste, but even to the special class of the caste to which either party to the marriage belonged. It was a near relative and not the priest who performed the actual marriage ceremony by tying together the little fingers of the man and woman with cotton and pouring over them the sacred water; and it was the father who followed this up by an admonition on the duties and responsibilities of matrimony.

The fact of marriage could operate in one of two ways. In the first case the husband was absorbed into the family of his wife. The position of such a husband has always been the object of a certain degree of ridicule among the Sinhalese; as their proverb puts it, he takes with him only his mat to sleep on and a torch to guide him on his way back when he is turned out by his wife. In the second case the wife separated herself from her family and divested herself of all right of inheritance of the ancestral property, being absorbed into the family of her husband.

Polygamy was not practised, though, where an important family was in danger of extinction, a husband was permitted to take a second wife with the consent of the first. A husband who detected his wife in the act of adultery was entitled to put her to death; but side by side with this severe regulation for the preservation of what was dearer to him than life, untainted blood, there obtained the peculiar custom of polyandry. This custom, which prevailed among the Spartans, and was common in Britain in the time of Julius Caesar, is still found in various parts of India, among races so diverse as the Rajputs and the Nairs. Under it a wife marrying into her husband's family, becomes the wife of all her husband's brothers in common, if they so desire. The practice probably originated in the exigencies of a system of land tenure under which the husband was obliged to be absent from his home for long periods, while his family was left unprovided for, as well as in a natural desire to maintain the ancestral property undiminished. That the Sinhalese of this time acquiesced in polyandry and rejected polygamy, cannot but be regarded as a significant indication of their standard of sexual morality.

Wijaya Bahu when a young man had lived with one of his brothers as the associated husband of one wife, and three sons represented their common family. It now began to be whispered about that he proposed to override their just claims to the Throne in favour of Deva Raja Sinha, a son by a previous marriage of his second Queen, one of the Kirawella Princesses. Fearing that their lives were in danger the three brothers fled from Court, and the youngest of them, Mayadunna, making his way to Senkadagala, soon returned with an army and threatened Kotte, whereupon Wijaya Bahu was compelled to sue for peace.

The Princes now advanced to the Capital, and stationing the army outside the palace, entered it unattended and without suspicion. As they passed within the walls they were met by the young Deva Raja Sinha, then but seven years of age, who innocently informed Mayadunna that a body of soldiery was lying in wait to kill them. Turning on his heel and hurrying his two brothers in front of him, Mayadunna dashed through the palace gates and escaped to the army. Their line of action was quickly resolved upon. The King's army was known to be sympathetic, and soon the palace was being besieged by a fierce mob, assisted by the soldiers of the two armies. The gates were battered down and the crowd rushed to the *Antahpuraya* or Harem, to plunder the great treasures of the King. The coffers and chests were burst open; the magnificent gems and hoards of gold coin, the priceless silks and foreign stuffs, and the whole contents of the royal wardrobe, were tossed about from hand to hand. The King himself was left for the present unmolested, and allowed to escape to the upper storey where, with two of his wives, he barred himself in; at the same time strict orders were issued by beat of drum that no violence was to be offered to any citizen.

Night came on. A Council was summoned and formally decided that Wijaya Bahu should be put to death; but no Sinhalese would incur the odium of shedding royal blood. At last a stranger was found, and at his hand the King met his death within his own chamber. The next morning the Council assembled again and selected Bhuwaneka Bahu, the eldest of the three brothers, as a fitting person to succeed to the vacant Lion Throne, the nomination being received with acclamation by the expectant people, to whom in accordance with ancient custom, the selection was submitted for ratification.

Attended by the Great Officers of the Household, the King was ceremonially bathed and attired in the sixty-four regal ornaments, after which he was conveyed on the richly caparisoned State elephant to the Dalada Maligawa, where the religious rites were performed by the Chief Priests. Last of all he was escorted to the stone *Mandape* or platform, and presented to the people who prostrated themselves in obeisance before him three times, amidst the roll of drums and the chanting of hymns of praise. His formal investiture with the Sword of State was delayed for a short time while Mayadunna was suppressing all resistance, striking terror into the hearts of the disaffected by bestowing the villages of the rebellious nobles upon the low-caste cutters of grass for the elephants.[1]

No event, however, even the most trivial in the life of the Oriental, could take place till the fortunate hour had been ascertained. A King starting on a campaign would turn to his astrologer with the same anxiety with which a Roman general consulted the entrails of his birds. The pettiest and the most important doings, the beginning to build a house, the ploughing of a field, or the despatch of a proposal of marriage, were all controlled by the decision of the *Nekatiya*, the Learned in the Planets. It is a curious illustration of the interdependence created by the system of caste, that the actions of the highest were thus placed under the control of the members of one of the lowest castes. For the Nekatiya was of the caste of tomtom beaters. How the complicated system of mathematics which astrology involved came to be the special field of this caste, is a mystery; there is, however, a tradition that the knowledge was communicated to them by a Buddhist priest, who desired to humiliate an arrogant Brahmin.

An auspicious hour was therefore selected, and the new King was escorted to the gaily-decorated *Mandape* together with the five Insignia of Royalty,[2] and placed under the *Chatra* of Dominion on a seat prepared in accordance with all the ancient rites. A beautiful virgin of the Royal Caste then poured on his head the sacred water of the Ganges, brought from the remotest point accessible to man, where it emerges from the everlasting snows, out of a milk-white chank with its whorls twisted to the left,[3] which she held aloft in both her hands. The Household Brahmin and a Goigama Minister[4] followed in turn, the former employing a chank fashioned in silver, and the latter one of gold. Each of the three concluded by exhorting the King to rule in accordance with the Ten Royal Virtues,[5] and to protect the caste he or she represented, vowing allegiance and fealty to him, but at the same time imprecating a curse on him should he be found wanting. The Crown was then placed upon the King's head, and the Sword of State fastened to his side by a nobleman of the Royal caste. When this was accomplished the King drew the sword from its scabbard and plunged it into a vase full of powdered sandal wood; after which, carrying it unsheathed in his hand, he was conveyed in procession round the Capital, mounted on his State Elephant, while the rejoicing populace shouted "Live, O live, Great King."

By the advice of his Minister Illangakon the King created two Principalities for his brothers, Rayigam Korale being allotted by *Sannas* to the elder, Para Raja Sinha; and Sitawaka, from the neighbourhood of Kotte as far as the mountain ranges of the Uda Rata, to the gallant Mayadunna.

In the meanwhile de Brito had completed his fortress, but upon the accession of King Dom Joao III to the throne of Portugal in 1521, it was decided that the expense of maintaining an outpost in Ceylon was not sufficiently compensated for by the revenue derived therefrom. The cruelty and quarrelsome disposition of the Portuguese officers also had destroyed their popularity among the Sinhalese; and when in 1524 the aged Dom Vasco da Gama was persuaded once more to return to India as Viceroy, he carried with him instructions to dismantle the fort at Colombo. This was accordingly done, the artillery and garrison being removed; whilst such commercial interests as the Portuguese still retained in Ceylon were left in the care of a certain Nuno Freyre de Andrade, who remained in the Island as Factor, under the protection of the Sinhalese King.

The abandonment of the fort which they had established at Calicut soon followed, in consequence of the hostility of the powerful Hindoo ruler of that place, who bore the proud title of Samorin, the Lord of the Ocean. His subjects included the fanatical Moplahs who were descended from the Arab settlers on the Malabar Coast, and who were the wealthiest inhabitants of the sea-board. The bulk of the sea borne trade with the Red Sea was in their hands, and consequently the bitterest hatred existed between them and the Portuguese. Their swift vessels now appeared in large numbers off the coasts of Ceylon, and the Portuguese had to flee for shelter to the Court of Bhuwaneka Bahu. His own relations with his brothers had soon become so strained that hostilities had broken out between them, and he begged the Portuguese to rebuild their abandoned fort, that they might be the better able to render him the protection which they had promised. Mayadunna on this side applied to the Samorin, who in 1528 sent him a small armament commanded by the two distinguished Moors, Pachchi Marikar and Cunhale Marikar of Calicut, and a third named Ali Ibrahim. The united forces laid siege to Kotte, but on the Portuguese sending assistance to Bhuwaneka Bahu from Goa, the Moors withdrew. This however did not bring hostilities to an end. Para Raja Sinha, or Rayigam Bandara as he was called after his principality, joined Mayadunna, whose successful conduct of a campaign against the Kanda Uda Rata added to their strength. Matters dragged on without any definite result till in October, 1536, Ali Ibrahim arrived at Colombo with a fresh contingent of four thousand men and Kotte was once again laid under siege; but as before the news that Portuguese assistance was on its way compelled the King's enemies to retire.

The following year a great armament of fifty-one vessels carrying eight thousand men and four hundred pieces of artillery was despatched by the Samorin to Ceylon, and Martin Affonco de Sousa, Captain Major of the Seas, hurried in pursuit. He overtook the fleet near Rameswaram, the sacred island which lies between Ceylon and the mainland. There was fought on the 29th of February, 1538, one of the fiercest battles in the history of the Portuguese in India, the forces of the Samorin being overwhelmingly defeated.

De Sousa now visited the delighted Bhuwaneka Bahu, by whom he was entertained in regal fashion, and who gave tangible expression to his gratitude by a loan of 45,000 cruzados[6] towards the expenses of the expedition. The death of Rayigam Bandara which followed shortly after served as an excuse to Mayadunna for seizing his brother's principality, in spite of the remonstrances of the King. The latter was anxiously considering the question of a successor. He had had by his principal Queen but one child, a daughter, who bore the beautiful name of Samudra Devi, the Queen of the Ocean. She was now given in marriage to a scion of the Royal family, Widiye Bandara, a tall swarthy young Prince with large fearless eyes. Mayadunna, whose hopes of succeeding to his brother's throne had been strong so long as the legal heir was an unmarried girl, now saw that the realisation of his wishes depended on his sword alone. His army was soon on the field, while the Samorin sent a fleet of sixteen vessels under Pachchi Marikar and his brother, to assist him by sea. Bhuwaneka Bahu once more applied to the Portuguese for help, but the appearance of the Turks before Diu [7] where Bahadur Shah of Gujarat had permitted them to erect a fort in 1535, compelled the new Viceroy, Dom Gracia de Noronha, to divert the assistance which was being prepared in response to this appeal. He sent a message begging the King to forgive him for using for his own purposes that assistance for which the other had paid. He assured him that no sooner should Diu be relieved than the promised force would be despatched, and expressed his appreciation of the generosity the King had displayed in the matter of the loan to de Sousa ; at the same time entreating him, as a friend and brother of the King of Portugal, to assist yet further with money at this hour of sore peril.

Disappointed as he was, Bhuwaneka Bahu immediately despatched three thousand gold Portuguezes [8] with an apology for his inability to send a larger sum, expressing at the same time a hope that the Viceroy would not forget to help him as soon as his own troubles were terminated. The Viceroy, delighted at such generosity, gave profuse expression to his gratitude—albeit the loan was never repaid.

By the end of March 1539 the prospects of the Portuguese had so much improved that the veteran Miguel Ferreira, now past seventy years of age, was able to set out for Ceylon. His arrival brought about an entire change in the situation ; Mayadunna promptly withdrew to within his own territory, and once more Kotte was saved.

A great military reception was accorded to Ferreira, but the King had found his friends more intolerable than his enemies, and poured out to him all his grievances against the Factor, relating further how he was exposed to open insult and obloquy at his hands, and ending with the demand that he should be removed from his office at once and sent to the Viceroy to be dealt with. Ferreira was much embarrassed at this unexpected turn and suggested that the matter should be referred to the Viceroy, as he had no authority to do anything but fight the King's enemies. The King, however, was so indignant at the treatment which he had received, that he passionately declared that he would rather lose his Kingdom than tolerate the presence of such a man at his Court: Ferreira and his men could go back if they liked. Matters appeared to be at a deadlock; but the next day Ferreira had another interview with the King, and with great tact persuaded him not to abandon the proposed campaign. He was finally won over, and expressed his determination to take part in the expedition in person.

The preparations were soon made, and three hundred Portuguese with 18,000 *Hewayo*, or Lascarins, as the Sinhalese troops were called by the Portuguese, took the field. For two days they advanced ravaging the country, a Mudaliyar being sent on ahead to Mayadunna at Sitawaka with a message from Ferreira calling on him to surrender the Moors. Ferreira swore by Nazareth, his favourite oath, that should the mission end in failure Mayadunna's capital should be burnt, and he himself taken in chains to receive his reward at the hands of the Viceroy.

Mayadunna in reply pointed out how dishonourable it would be for him to surrender men who had taken shelter with him, but begged for two days in which to arrange some settlement ; the two days passed without anything being done, but a night attack on the allied forces brought matters to a crisis. Mayadunna laid the blame on the Moors, and the King on Ferreira's indignant remonstrance insisted that they should be surrendered. In reply he was informed that they had escaped. Orders had already been issued to march on Sitawaka, when a body of men were seen approaching the camp. A hostile demonstration was feared, and the Portuguese opened fire on them before it was discovered that they were 200 low caste Paduwo[9] who were bringing in the heads of the offending Moors, including those of their gallant commanders. Some say that they were done to death on the orders of Mayadunna, and others that they were killed by the villagers who resented their overbearing conduct ; the truth will never be known. The King's demand had been satisfied and there was nothing more left to do but to return to Kotte.

A peace which was faithfully observed till 1547 was now concluded between the two brothers. Mayadunna surrendered to the King all the territory he had conquered, paying a heavy war indemnity and swearing never again to take up arms against his Suzerain. Bhuwaneka Bahu in his joy at this success rewarded the soldiers of the armada, and presented the officers with jewels and precious stones. To the Government at Goa he despatched a large quantity of cinnamon, together with a loan of 30,000 cruzados. The offending Factor, whilst on his way to India in chains to stand his trial, met with a violent death at the hands of robbers.

The question of a successor to the throne could no longer be deferred. Samudra Devi had borne two children, Dharmapala and Wijayapala, and the elder of the two was selected by his grandfather as his heir. In view of the attitude of Mayadunna it was resolved to place the infant Prince, who had been entrusted to the custody of his father's brother Tammita Sembahap Perumal, under the protection of Dom Joao III. A beautiful image of the child was prepared; the head was of ivory and gold, and the body of silver, while in the hand the figure carried a jewelled crown studded with the finest gems of Ceylon. The whole was placed in a rich coffer and despatched to Portugal in the care of a Brahmin Minister named Panditer, who reached Lisbon after a tedious voyage about August 1541.

By the King's command all the Fidalgos who were at Court attended the landing of the Sinhalese, who were attired in crimson *Cabayas*[10]. Escorted by two Marquises they were driven in a State coach to the Palace, where after a ceremonious exchange of greetings the Sinhalese delivered the presents they had brought with them, and handed to the King a palm-leaf scroll from Bhuwaneka Bahu. Therein, after the usual compliments, he requested the King of Portugal to recognise Dharmapala as heir to his Kingdom, and to receive him under his protection. Should the request be granted Bhuwaneka Bahu pledged himself to continue the payment of the subsidy as before, and to allow Dom Joao to retain the places which had been assigned to him, on condition of his undertaking their defence.

The arrival of the embassy was a source of much gratification to the Portuguese, whose vanity was flattered by this tangible recognition of the far-reaching extent of their Empire. The Coronation of the image was celebrated with all the stately pomp and ceremonial of the Portuguese Court, and the day was observed as a holiday throughout the country, with bull-fights and other festivities. A formal confirmation of the Act was drawn up, and the following *Alvara* proclaimed:

DOM JOHAM &c.

To all to whom these presents shall come: Whereas Buhanegabaho. King of Ceilam, has sent me word by his Ambassador *Panditer* of the great confidence which he has in

Taomapala Pandarym his grandson, being his daughter's son, that after his own decease he will be fit to rule and govern his kingdom and protect his subjects and vassals with all justice, and will preserve inviolate the true friendship which exists between us, as it is his great desire that all his heirs and successors should observe the same,

And whereas he has requested me to be pleased to ordain that at his demise his aforesaid grandson should succeed to and inherit his kingdom;

And whereas I have considered that it is the custom for sons to succeed their fathers in the aforesaid kingdom, and that the aforesaid Tammapala Pandarym is his grandson, being his daughter's son, and that there is no other son or grandson of the aforesaid King save he alone, wherefore by the aforesaid custom the aforesaid kingdom pertains to him of right,

And whereas it is my earnest desire in this matter to please the aforesaid King of Ceyllam as well for the great good-will I bear towards him as for the high kindness which he has always willingly displayed in all matters relating to my interests which have arisen, and it is my hope that the aforesaid his grandson will likewise for all time cherish, maintain and preserve this our friendship, and will be grateful to me and will merit all this great kindness at my hands,

And for various other just causes me thereunto moving:

I do by these presents ordain and it is my pleasure that at the death of the aforesaid Buhanegabaho, King of Ceillam, he the aforesaid Tammapalla Pandarym his grandson should succeed to and inherit the aforesaid kingdom and be the King thereof as and in the like manner that his aforesaid grandsire does at this day hold and possess the same without question, let, or hindrance of any kind soever.

Wherefore I do issue my command in such wise to my Captain-Major and Governor in the parts of India, to the Comptroller of my Treasury, and to all and several my other Captains, officers and persons to whom these presents are shown or to whom knowledge is conveyed thereof, that they do hold the aforesaid Tammapalla Pandarym as true and lawful heir to the aforesaid Kingdom of Ceyllam, and that at the decease of the aforesaid King his grandsire, they permit him to inherit and succeed thereto, and for such purpose render him all support and assistance he may desire, and protect him from all those who attempt to impede or oppose the same; for such is my pleasure, and it is to the advantage of my service.

In confirmation whereof I have commanded that these presents do issue signed by my hand and sealed with my leaden seal and registered at my Chancellary.

Given at the City of Allmeirym this XII day of March: thus done PERO FERNANDEZ

In the year of the birth of our Lord Jesus Christ one thousand and five hundred and forty-three.

Ordinances were also promulgated regulating trade transactions between the Portuguese and the Sinhalese. The former were declared liable to render the same dues on goods purchased as any other nation. The extortion and violence of their merchants were provided against: they were forbidden to fell the timber-trees of the Sinhalese for purposes of ship-building, or to construct ships without the licence of the King of Ceylon and of the Governor of India. Regulations were moreover drawn up with regard to the purchase of lands by Portuguese settlers, and the conversion of slaves to Christianity; and at the special request of Bhuwaneka Bahu six Franciscans, with Frey Joao de Villa de Conde as their Superior, were despatched to Ceylon to preach the Gospel among his subjects.

Upon the return of the Sinhalese ambassador to India, Martin Affonco de Sousa, who was now Governor, fitted out two galliots to convey him to his own country, at the same time charging him with a courteous message to his friend the King, assuring him that he had never forgotten the kindness which he had received at the Royal hands when Captain Major of the Seas. The spear which he had once grasped, he protested, was still as keen if required in the King's defence. The result of the mission was very gratifying to the King, who testified to his appreciation in that practical manner which he knew to commend itself to the Portuguese, by including with his letter of thanks to the Governor a quittance for a sum of 50,000 cruzados out of the debt due to him from the King of Portugal.

But the despatch of the embassy led to further complications. According to the constitution of the Sinhalese monarchy, the occupant of the Throne had necessarily to be of the Royal Caste. Not only so, but he had to be a member of that division of it which called itself the *Suriya Wansa* and claimed descent from the Sun—a claim which recalls the story of the Quest of the Golden Fleece. As the Royal Caste was in Ceylon found untainted only in the reigning family, it had been customary to obtain from South India the Queens who were to perpetuate the succession. Such a Queen was popularly known as the *Ran Doliya,* or Golden Vehicle. In the case of the King the prevailing rule of monogamy was relaxed, and he was permitted, if he so desired, to have in addition two or three junior wives of the Goi Wansa, and to these was applied the designation of *Yakada Doliya,* or Iron Vehicle.

At this time Bhuwaneka Bahu had by his *Yakada Doli* two sons who had cherished high expectations on their own account, and were bitterly disappointed at his choice of Dharmapala to succeed him on the throne. To pacify them he proposed that they should conquer for themselves the Kanda Uda Rata and Jaffna, while at the same time there were ominous rumours that Mayadunna proposed to support his claim by a display of force. Under the circumstances Bhuwaneka Bahu made representations at Goa, begging the Governor to interfere to prevent the outbreak of a war which would ruin the hopes of his grandson, and further requesting his assistance in conquering the Kingdoms which he proposed to give to his two discontented sons. He himself undertook to bear all expenses likely to be incurred in the attempt.

The application was a tempting one, and on the 12th of August 1543 de Sousa set out from Goa with a fleet of thirty-six vessels. Misfortune attended the expedition from the start. Storms scattered the ships about the Indian Ocean, and the Governor himself was glad to take shelter in Neduntivo,[11] a small island off the Coast of Jaffna. From there negotiations however were opened with Chaga Raja, the reigning chieftain at Nallur, the capital of Jaffna, who was finally bullied into an agreement whereby he promised to pay a yearly tribute of 5000 xerafims,[12] and two tusked elephants: of this tribute he was required to deliver two instalments in advance. He was on the other hand allowed to retain a large number of the cannon which he had taken from wrecked Portuguese vessels, on payment of their value. After these achievements the Governor returned to Cochin.

In the meanwhile an important development was taking place in Europe. The spread of Classical learning, the extension of maritime enterprise, and the views advanced by Luther and others who thought with him, compelled the Church to take stock of her position and to adopt vigorous action for the maintenance of her lofty claims. In 1534 Ignatius of Loyala founded the Society of Jesus at Paris, and two years later the Inquisition was established. Dom Joao III supported the cause of the Church with a zeal which was fanatical, and in the very year in which Bhuwaneka Bahu's ambassador to his Court set sail from Ceylon, presided over the first *Auto da Fe* held in Portugal. Bhuwaneka Bahu therefore acted with much political shrewdness when he applied for Missionaries to be sent to his country, though he himself had no intention of adopting the new religion. Buddhism, perhaps not the least intellectual of religions, disdained the idea of spiritual rivalry, and treated with genial liberality all who attempted to minister to the higher cravings of mankind. With the King's encouragement Churches were soon erected in the fishing villages of the south-western coast, while de Conde took up his residence at Court, where he was placed in charge of the education of Dharmapala.

In October 1542 Francis Xavier arrived in India, and the story of his conversion of the Parawas, who mainly supplied the divers for the Indian Pearl Fishery, and who possessed at the time a nominal Christianity, the price of their being rescued from the oppression of their Moorish rulers, is well known. A wave of enthusiasm swept all heathen practises from the country, idols were destroyed with every mark of ignominy, instruction in the Faith was rapidly organised, and whole villages were baptised daily. A convert of Xavier, who had adopted his name, was sent to carry on the good work among the kindred people at Manar, the sandy Island which, lying between Ceylon and Adam's Bridge, controlled the approach by sea to Jaffna from the South. The disciple proved worthy of his teacher, and crowds flocked to join the Church of Christ. No doubt the converts in their ardour for their new faith showed, like their kinsfolk in India, an excess of zeal; at any rate the Hindu priests found it necessary to report to Nallur the danger which threatened the country from the spread of these new ideas. Chaga Raja adopted prompt measures to nip the movement in the bud, and five thousand troops sent by him landed at Manar and put all the converts and their teacher to the sword. Xavier threw himself with his fiery energy into the preparations for avenging their death, but all his efforts were nullified by the wreck of a treasure ship off the coast of the Jaffna Peninsula. The King, in the exercise of the right claimed by several of the Indian Rajas, seized its rich cargo of gold and silk stuffs, and to persuade him to yield this up became the chief preoccupation of the authorities; so busily engaged were they in coaxing the Raja into a complacent mood, that all idea of a punitive expedition had to be abandoned.

Dom Joao de Castro succeeded de Sousa in September 1545, and was called upon to deal with the application of Bhuwaneka Bahu in respect of his two sons, who had arrived at Goa with ample treasure from their father to purchase help. The Council was quite prepared to assist them, for if the Princes were successful they were ready to declare themselves vassals ot Portugal. But at this juncture a severe epidemic of smallpox broke out and among the victims were the two Princes, who died within a month of each other. They were interred with royal honours in the Convent of St. Francisco.

On the 18th of March 1546 the King of Portugal despatched a remarkable letter to his Viceroy. After bewailing the idol-worship which prevailed in certain parts of India subject to Portuguese authority, he continued: "We charge you to discover all the idols by means of diligent officers, to reduce them to fragments and utterly to consume them, in whatsoever place they may be found, proclaiming rigorous penalties against such persons as shall dare to engrave, cast, sculpture, limn, paint or bring to light any figure in metal, bronze, wood, clay or any other substance, or shall introduce them from foreign parts; and against those who shall celebrate in public or in private any festivities which have any Gentile taint, or shall abet them, or shall conceal the Brahmins, the pestilential enemies of the name of of Christ." While emphasizing the necessity of severe punishment he added: "And because the Gentiles submit themselves to the yoke of the Gospel not alone through their conviction of the purity of the Faith and for that they are sustained by the hope of Eternal Life, they should also be encouraged with some temporal favours, such as greatly mollify the hearts of those who receive them; and therefore you should earnestly set yourself to see that the new Christians from this time forward do obtain and enjoy all exemptions and freedom from tribute, and moreover that they hold the privileges and offices of honour which up till now the Gentiles have been wont to possess."

He also directed that if the King of Jaffna had not been suitably punished for his persecution of the Christians, action should be taken against him without delay, so that the displeasure of the King of Portugal against those who ventured to interfere with the conversion of the heathen might be made plain to all.

NOTES TO CHAPTER III

1. This was a social degradation which was probably more feared than the punishment of death. The practice was not unfrequently resorted to by Raja Sinha II in the seventeenth century.

2. These were the White Shield, the Pearl Umbrella, the Golden Sword, the Chamara or Tail of the great Thibetan Yak, and the Golden Shoes. The Crown merely ranked among the sixty-four Royal Ornaments.

3. Shells of the genus *Turbinella*, which are collected in large quantities off the north-west coast of Ceylon, and exported to India, where they are sawn and used as ornaments. The larger shells are perforated and used as trumpets at Hindu temples. The spiral goes normally to the right ; left-handed shells are extremely rare. Vishnu is always represented with a chank in his hand.

4 The system of caste obtaining in Ceylon recognised three high castes—the Royal, the Priestly or Brahmin, and the Grahapati or Goigama. The first two were represented only by the frequent arrivals from India ; these by intermarriage soon disappeared within the Goigama caste, and had to be replaced for religious and ceremonial purposes by fresh importations.

5. Including Liberality, Piety, Lenity, Moderation, the sense of Honour, the spirit of Mercy, &c.

6. A *cruzado* of gold, worth 420 reis, was issued by Albuquerque in 1510. A *re* in 1513 was worth. 268d, and by 1600 it had depreciated to 16d. Ten *reis* = a Sinhalese gold *fanam*. Dr. Garcia de Orta accompanied de Sousa on this expedition as his physician. He settled in India, where in 1563 he published his *Colloquios* on the Simples and Drugs of India.

7. Under the command of Solyman Bashaw, the Governor of Cairo. This expedition had been despatched by the Grand Turk at the request of the King of Cambay.

8. The *Portuguez* was a large Portuguese gold coin, displaying on the reverse the Cross of the Order of Christ, and worth 15 *xerafims*, at 300 *reis* the *xerafim*. A *Portuguez* was thus the equivalent of 450 Sinhalese *fanams* of gold.

9. These are said to be the descendants of the Pandiyan prisoners of war, and were attached to the Royal villages where they cultivated the King's fields. In peace

time they acted as palanquin bearers, and with the introduction of gunpowder they were entrusted with the conveyance of the small cannon. The Portuguese historian de Couto has left an unamiable description of them . . . "a caste of Chingalas cruel in the extreme, so that when they capture an enemy they immediately cut off his ears and lips."

10. *Cabaya,* a word originally Asiatic, received by the Portuguese from the Arabs, and brought back with them to India. It was applied to the long tunic which was worn by the better classes of India, and which was frequently presented by the Portuguese to Indian Rajas. The *Cabaya* is still a portion of the uniform of a Sinhalese Mudaliyar.

11. A small island twenty miles south-west of Jaffna. The Portuguese subsequently named it *das Vacas,* and the Dutch who followed them renamed it Delft.

12. This name, representing the Arabic *Ashrafi,* was applied by the Portuguese to a silver coin of the value of 300-360 *reis.*

CHAPTER IV

The negotiations which were carried on in connection with the claims of the two Kotte Princes reveal this work of conversion in a pitiful light. Everyone realised that the Portuguese King was fervently anxious for the spread of Christianity, and the conversion of his future subjects was the chief thing that each aspirant to Kingly power held out to the Portuguese as the price of their military assistance. A friar acted as intermediary between the authorities at Goa and the Uda Rata monarch, while no less an agent than Xavier himself undertook a similar mission at Lisbon on behalf of the Jaffna King's brother and rival. For war was in the air and Kotte, Sitawaka, Senkadagala and Nallur were all eagerly bidding for Portuguese assistance; the authorities at Goa, however, were too intent on securing what profit they could from all the four competitors to give a definite undertaking to any one of them. Nevertheless towards the end of 1547 they despatched a small force of a hundred men under the command of Antonio Moniz Barretto, apparently leaving it to him to decide after inquiry on the spot, in which scale the weight of the Portuguese sword was to be thrown. Barretto's position was an embarrassing one, and in the maze of intrigue he did not know in whom it was safe to place confidence. He at length decided in favour of Bhuwaneka Bahu, and a large body of men set out on the road to Sitawaka.

Mayadunna on being informed of the approaching danger, abandoned his capital and retired to the stronghold of Deraniyagala, leaving his palace prepared for the reception of the King, with lighted lamps as for a welcome guest. Sitawaka was occupied by the royal army, and in a few days the Portuguese advanced into the Uda Rata; but the opposition they encountered was so severe, that Barretto was compelled to set fire to his baggage and turn in flight. The Sinhalese were soon in full chase, and pursued the Portuguese with such terrible vigour through the dense forests, that by the time the unfortunate expedition was able to reach Mayadunna's territory, nearly half the Portuguese had been killed, while of the rest there was not one that had not received some hurt.

Mayadunna was quick to take advantage of the turn affairs had taken ; by his orders the men were carefully attended to, and boats were provided for the conveyance of those whose wounds prevented their continuing their march to Colombo. He also utilised the opportunity to poison the mind of Barretto against Bhuwaneka Bahu, hinting that the King was privy to what had taken place.

On reaching Colombo Barretto sent a message to Bhuwaneka Bahu reminding him of the conversation which he had had with Xavier, and subsequently waited on the King to discuss with him the question of his conversion. Unfortunately he was more of a soldier than a priest ; his whole theme consisted of the awful terrors of hell, and these he painted in such terrifying colours that the King, appalled, inquired whether he had been through them in person. This so offended Barretto that, forgetting in whose presence he was, he dashed his hat on the floor and turning on his heel, walked away, leaving the King sorrowfully to reflect how dreadful must be the nature of the Christian hell since the souls which went there had to undergo the tortures which Barretto had described. The latter refused to accept some presents which the King sent after him, and sailed away without even bidding him farewell.

Meanwhile the shrewd Mayadunna had realised that it suited his purpose very much better to win the confidence of the Portuguese and to estrange them from his brother, than to enter on a war the end of which none could foresee. He had already created a good impression on Barretto, and he followed this up by a secret communication to the Factor to warn him that the King was plotting the destruction of the Factory; the substantial presents with which the message was accompanied, as well as the scoffs of Widiye Bandara at the boasted valour of the Portuguese, went far to convince them that Mayadunna, and not Bhuwaneka Bahu, was their true friend.

At the end of August 1550 the new Viceroy, Dom Affonco de Noronha, was driven by storms whilst on his way to Goa into the harbour of Colombo. He had already heard of the evil reports against the King, who was again at war with Mayadunna. The Franciscan de Condé had returned to Europe the previous year, disappointed in his efforts to convert Bhuwaneka Bahu, and Xavier himself had written representing Bhuwaneka Bahu as the bitter enemy of Christianity and unworthy of the protection of the Portuguese. Anxious to clear himself of these suspicions, the King sent two Mudaliyars to call on the Viceroy with a valuable present of gems; the present was accepted, but the arrogant nobleman let it be clearly seen that he regarded the failure of the King to appear in person as a slight to his own dignity. To add to the King's distress Mayadunna himself appeared on the scene, accompanied it was whispered not so much by men as by money-bags, and he went away leaving the Viceroy very favourably impressed. The King now sent a further present of 15,000 pardaos [1] in cash for the Viceroy, with some valuable jewels for the Queen of Portugal, and an interview was arranged at the Franciscan

Convent of St. Antonio : but the vanity of the Portuguese was not easily soothed, and the Viceroy was so overbearing in his behaviour that the King, seeing the suspicion with which he was treated, turned his back and returned to Kotte, swearing that only his respect for the King of Portugal prevented his ordering the immediate destruction of the Factory. He sent an imperious message to the Viceroy commanding him to leave his dominions forthwith, and this the latter, though he longed to avenge the humiliation, was compelled to do, for his forces were not sufficient to make success certain.

Five months later Bhuwaneka Bahu, who was suffering from the effects of recurring attacks of fever, withdrew to Kelaniya on the pleasant banks of the Kelani Ganga, to recruit. One day at noon as he appeared at the window of the palace which overlooked the spot where, according to tradition, the Buddha himself had bathed in the stream, he was shot through the head by Antonio de Barcelos, the mulatto slave of the Viceroy, who had stayed behind when his master sailed away. The King fell mortally wounded, and in spite of all the remedies which were applied he died within three hours. The Portuguese themselves appear to have had little doubt as to who was responsible for this dastardly act ; but, to quote the *Rajawaliya,* [2] "Some say that this hurt was done of set purpose, others that it was done unwittingly : God alone knoweth which is true."

The administration of their eastern settlements by the Portuguese had, as revealed in the letters of St. Francis Xavier, degenerated into an outrage on the good name of Christian Europe. His consuming desire for the rapid acquisition of wealth swept away from the mind of the official all consideration of the duty which he owed to his God and to his King. No scruple of honour was allowed to interfere with the contemptuous breaking of the word plighted to the Indian Raja who had welcomed the foreigner to his territory. The limitless avarice which could convert Portuguese gentlemen into procurers who entrapped village girls into the brothels from which they derived a considerable income, was only equalled by their horrible lust and peculiar callousness with regard to the infliction of physical pain on others. The real obstruction to the progress of St. Francis' work arose from the acts of his countrymen. "I feel strongly inclined," he wrote on the 24th of March 1544 "to be off and have done with it. For why should we waste more time here among men who are utterly regardless of any consideration of justice, and who never care a straw at the cost of what damage to religion or to the State they indulge their own passions ?" [3]

All this, however, was only the reflection of the change which had come about in Portugal itself. For fifty years the East had been pouring her wealth by the shipload into that small country, till her Ruler was the richest King in Europe. The countryside was abandoned to African slaves, while the peasantry flocked into the seaports to share in the profits of the Eastern trade. That trade was a Royal monopoly, for it had to be maintained by means of armies and fleets. The noblemen of the great houses whose scions had fought so gallantly for their King, still rallied round him, but now in the character of sycophants whose sole desire was the acquisition of wealth, whatever might be the nature of the means employed to secure it. Each year the crowded Indian fleet bore away the more enterprising, and very few of them lived to return to their native land. Moreover, the large number of emigrants who were continually sailing for Brazil, still further reduced a population which hardly numbered a million souls when Portugal began her career of conquest. In the struggle for gold, however, no statesman could spare the time to reflect on the result which this incessant drain of her men was bound to produce in Portugal before many years had passed.

Ceylon was soon to supply a shameful illustration of the truth of Xavier's words. The youthful Dharmapala had been proclaimed King immediately upon the death of his grandfather, and his father Widiye Bandara had been nominated Regent during his minority. Early in October the Viceroy, de Noronha, arrived at Colombo with the largest Portuguese army which had yet visited the Island. His declared object was to settle the affairs of the country, and three thousand soldiers had been got ready to assist him in this self-imposed task. The greatest excitement prevailed when his fleet of over seventy vessels was seen approaching the harbour; but the excitement was changed to amazement when five hundred soldiers under the command of the Viceroy's own son occupied the Capital and arrested all the higher officials of the Household. An inquisition was held as to the whereabouts of the Royal Treasure, the unfortunate officials being freely tortured to compel them to disclose the hiding-places. Not satisfied with the results of his search, the Viceroy proceeded to ransack the Palace itself, seizing everything of value, iucluding even the King's golden spittoons.

A meeting was now summoned to discuss the steps to be taken to meet the danger which threatened from Mayadunna. The Viceroy demanded 200,000 pardaos as the price of the Portuguese assistance. Half of this sum was to be paid at once, while the plunder of Sitawaka was to be equally divided between the Kings of Ceylon and Portugal. Eighty thousand pardaos were forthcoming, and then the 3000 Portuguese together with the same number of Sinhalese took the field. Driving back the outposts guarding the road which ran by the side of the Kelaniya river, they approached the Capital, which they found abandoned. Mayadunna had withdrawn to Deraniyagala, leaving behind him at Sitawaka a Portuguese with a letter addressed to the Viceroy. He had heard, he wrote, that the Viceroy was coming with a very large body of men, and as there was not room for all of them, he had arranged to vacate the place in good time so that the Portuguese should not be incommoded. Mayadunna added that he had also heard that the Viceroy was anxious for precious stones; he and his people had therefore decided to leave him the stones of their city; if he aimed higher he could follow them to the mountains where Mayadunna was awaiting him with his treasure.

The city, built on either side of the Sitawaka Ganga, was of considerable size. On the southern bank, between the river and the rapid Getahetta Ela, a stream still so famous for its precious stones, on an eminence which was approached by twenty wide steps, with three gates on each side, rose the royal palace. On the northern bank facing the palace, where the broad river hurried past in a wide curve, was the beautiful Bhairawa Kovil, an exquisite temple of carved granite. The city was entered and sacked and the whole of the palace dug up in a fruitless search for treasure. The temple was robbed of all its valuable contents, its images and fittings of gold and silver being seized upon by the Viceroy. When, however, the young King begged him to fulfil his share of the contract and to send a few hundred Portuguese in pursuit of Mayadunna, he was met by a demand for the immediate payment of the 20,000 pardaos still due. This sum the King was unable to raise, whereupon the Viceroy, refusing to share the plunder with the King as had been promised, retired with it to the Coast. "Had the Indian broken his word with the Christian, he had been a barbarian. I know not what a Christian is, that breaks his with the barbarian. Perhaps wiser men know," is the comment of Fariay Sousa[4] on this transaction.

Returning to Kotte the Portuguese hastened to make the most profitable use they could of their now limited time. The wretched inhabitants were treated as if they belonged to some conquered town, being exposed to the violence of the lustful and needy soldiery. Men were killed to rob them of their bracelets and earrings; and women were ravished till none dared to show herself in public. Widiye Bandara, burning as he was with indignation, was helpless to resist and escaped from the Capital, while Sembahap Perumal was nominated in his place. A pressing message was sent to the King urging on him the desirability of his turning Christian; but the King had had enough of the affection of Christians and of the honour of Portuguese noblemen; he returned an evasive reply declaring that it would be impolitic for him to take so unpopular a step while the attitude of Mayadunna remained what it was. He was, however, willing to consult the wishes of the Viceroy to this extent: he gave into his care an infant child, a son of the late King, to be taken to Goa and brought up as a Christian,[5] and with this the Viceroy's religious zeal had to be satisfied.

He still, however, pressed for the payment of the 20,000 pardaos which in spite of his gross violation of his contract he claimed as due to him. When the King declared his inability to meet this demand, the Viceroy, as the final act in his career of shame, seized the person of Sembahap Perumal and sent him on board one of the Portuguese vessels, as a hostage for the payment of the money. The Regent having failed to obtain the required sum from his friends, sold his own golden girdle and paid the Viceroy 5000 pardaos; for the balance he gave his promissory note made payable within a year. This transaction concluded, the Viceroy, having convinced himself that there was nothing to be squeezed from anyone, sailed away. Well might Xavier express his amazement at the inflexions which the word "to rob" was capable of receiving in the mouths of Portuguese officials.

With the departure of the Viceroy Widiye Bandara came back into power. The Factor was put to death, the conversion of the Sinhalese was forbidden, and several of the priests were driven to seek shelter in the forests.

It is indeed the boast of the Sinhalese that force has never been employed by them in those fields where reason alone should prevail. No Hypatia has stained their country with her blood ; no Smithfield has darkened their serene sky with its murky clouds. Buddhism, alone of the great religions which Asia has produced, has displayed a real spirit of tolerance. Temples were erected to the Hindu deities by monarchs who were staunch upholders of the Dharma. Buddhist temples still provide for the religious exercises of the Mohammedan tenants living in the villages belonging to them. It was in this spirit that Bhuwaneka Bahu had applied for Christian missionaries to be sent to his country, and it was in the same spirit that his subjects had received them into their midst. But at this juncture the arrogance of the Portuguese, culminating in the treachery of the Viceroy, produced a reaction directed against the religion which the conduct of the latter had so grossly maligned. De Noronha, however, on his return to Goa found himself too busily employed with the Turks, who again laid siege to Ormuz, to attend to matters in Ceylon; he had therefore to content himself with sending conciliatory messages to Widiye Bandara, who was glad to be left undisturbed.

De Noronha had in fact lost an opportunity of establishing the supremacy of Portugal over the entire

Island such as never presented itself again in the course of the next hundred years of warfare. The forces of Kotte were at his disposal, and neither Sitawaka nor Senkadagala was in a position to offer more than a feeble resistance. The Sinhalese had not yet acquired that familiarity with the use of fire-arms which was soon to make them so formidable among their wilds, while the Portuguese still employed protective armour, against which the missiles of the Sinhalese were of little avail. That opportunity had been lost through lust of gold, but the helpless condition of Dharmapala, threatened as he was by the ambitions of Mayadunna, made it desirable that the Portuguese should have their own head-quarters in the Island, rather than continue as the dependents of the Sinhalese King. Accordingly Dom Pedro Mascarenhas, who succeeded de Noronha in 1554, turned his attention to the abandoned fort of Colombo, and in November of the same year he despatched Dom Duarte de Eca to Ceylon, with five hundred soldiers and all the necessaries for building it anew. This time it was designed on a larger scale than had been proposed by de Albergaria, and included the area subsequently occupied by the walls of Colombo. The lagoon which almost encircled the new settlement appears to have been now dammed, and formed the main defence of the position which rapidly grew in importance. Outside the fortifications there sprang up the palm groves and delightful gardens where the Portuguese had their villas and occupied the period of peace in a round of pleasure. In later years the settlement aspired to the dignity and privileges of a *Cidade*, and employed as its arms the gridiron of the Saint after whom de Almeida had named the headland.

De Eca had also received secret orders to arrest Widiye Bandara, whose hostility towards the Portuguese had grown more and more pronounced.

This was treacherously done and the Prince thrown into a dungeon where he was kept in heavy chains, while Samudra Devi fled to Rayigama. By the powerful influence of gold she soon caused a tunnel to be opened into the Prince's dungeon, by means of which he effected his escape, and joining the Princess retired with her to Pelenda, amidst the lofty mountains in the extreme limits of the Pasdun Korale. From there he began his career of vengeance. Crowds flocked to his standard, the coast towns were ravaged, the Churches which had been built in them by the Franciscans were razed to the ground, and the Portuguese, one and all, put to the sword. Unfortunately the Princess died about this time, whereupon Mayadunna gave his own widowed daughter to Widiye Bandara for wife. But the hopes of an alliance thus created were destroyed by the harsh manner in which he treated her, and the irritated father turned to the Portuguese, with whom in August 1555 he entered into a treaty.

In accordance with this the Sitawaka army, commanded by the youngest son of Mayadunna, Tikiri Rajjuru Bandara, a boy of thirteen, with whom was associated Wikramasinha Mudiyanse, the bravest of his father's Generals, advanced to the Kalu Ganga, and was joined at Kalutara by the Portuguese contingent of three hundred men. After crossing the limpid waters of the Pelen Ganga the allied forces were met and attacked by Widiye Bandara, who after a hard-fought battle was forced to flee, abandoning his wife and treasures to the conquerors. The Princess was sent on elephant-back to Sitawaka, while two miserable days were spent in destroying the entrenchments which guarded Widiye Bandara's stronghold. The soldiers were encamped in the midst of rank grass and marshy pools infested with myriads of leeches, that horrible curse of the wet zone. Clothes afforded no protection against their fine needle-like bodies; satiated they dropped in streams of blood from the eyelids and ears of the men, and had to be plucked out of their very gums as they ate their food. Rest was out of the question, for the voracious animals swarmed on all sides in ever-increasing numbers. The task was hurriedly completed, and then Tikiri Rajjuru Bandara started in pursuit of his brother-in-law, who at length found refuge within the Uda Rata, where he was welcomed by Karalliyadda Bandara, who had revolted against his father Wikrama Bahu, and had succeeded in wresting the power from him.

Widiye Bandara without delay raised another army and descended into the Four Korales, whereupon Tikiri Rajjuru Bandara advanced into the district and forced him to withdraw by night to within the mountain barrier, whither he was conveyed on the back of a man in the curious fashion which the Russian traveller Athanasius Nikitin had described in the previous century, and of which Sindbad has left us an account in his story of the Old Man of the Sea. The Uda Rata army, demoralised by the desertion of its leader, fled after a short resistance and was pursued with great slaughter, the victors with one accord saluting their boy-General on the field of battle by the name of *Raja Sinha*, the Lion King, a name destined for many years to come to cause the blood of the Portuguese in Ceylon to run cold.

Mayadunna now called upon Karalliyadda to drive out Widiye Bandara, who took shelter with Edirimanna Surya Raja at Devamedda. Six miles from where the precious Danta Dhatu had lain enshrined in the massive base of Etu Gala, to the left of the road from Kurunegala to Puttalam, begin the forest-clad heights of the Natagane Range. Parallel with them runs a second range, which beginning with the sinuous outline of the Anda Gala, reaches its highest point in the pallid austerity of the Yakdessa crag, where the hapless Kuweni had invoked the curse of heaven on her faithless lover Wijayo. A sudden depression of the Natagane range, running north and south, reveals a deeper hollow of a few acres in extent, in which lay Mudukonda Pola, the stronghold of the Raja. To the north lies the great plain stretching in the direction of Puttalam, its monotony interrupted at intervals by the isolated hills which rise abruptly from the level of the surrounding country. A massive ring of stone encloses the great hollow, and here and there large caves afford a dry and secure retreat, while artificial piles of stone helped to strengthen the natural depressions in this majestic rampart. The approach from the village of Kirimune lies over rugged ground closed in by enormous boulders, the entrance to the stronghold being effected through a tunnel formed by a rock rising to a height of nearly 100 feet and resting against the great mass by its side.

Such was Mudukonda Pola, the retreat to which the refugee was welcomed by his kinsman; but the restless Widiye Bandara was not satisfied. He basely plotted the murder of his host, and seized on the Government of the Seven Korales. The horror-stricken inhabitants appealed to the rulers of Kotte and Sitawaka, and their joint armies supported by a few Portuguese took the field. Widiye Bandara's forces were hurled back, and he himself, realising that fortune had turned against him, collected what he could of his treasures and escaped to Kalpitiya, whence he took ship to Jaffna. The Sinhalese Kings were accustomed to carry about their persons a model of the Tooth Relic set in gems and gold, and such a model had accompanied the Prince through all the tribulations to which he had been exposed at the hands of the Portuguese. His last desperate throw had failed, but as he fled he still clung to the precious object as the most cherished of all his possessions.

On his arrival at Jaffna Widiye Bandara was kindly received by its ruler, who promised him assistance against his enemies, and caused a great festival to be celebrated at his temple at Nallur. There a sad tragedy occurred. The accidental explosion of some powder alarmed Widiye Bandara, and he immediately drew his sword. A fight ensued between the Sinhalese and the Tamils within the sacred precincts; a young noble threw himself in front of his Prince, and sixty Tamils it is said fell victims to his sword before he himself was stretched in death at his master's feet. Widiye Bandara and his son Wijayapala were among the slain, and all his treasures including the model of the Tooth, fell into the hands of the Tamil King.

So ended the wars and troubles of this strange character, of whom de Couto[6] truly remarks: "whom the Captain of Colombo persecuted. If he came to bite, it was because they worried him."

With the disappearance of Widiye Bandara, the adherents of the Kotte dynasty found themselves discredited and without a capable leader. Sembahap Perumal had the previous year, as a consequence of an intrigue between Mayadunna and the Portuguese, been banished to Goa, where fortunately for him his friend Francisco Barretto was Governor. Barretto gave him a warm welcome, and before long succeeded in persuading him that it was to his advantage, both spiritual and temporal, to go through the rite of baptism. This he accordingly did, adopting at the same time the name of his sponsor, the Governor. He shortly afterwards returned to Ceylon, accompanied by de Conde, and took up his position as the chief of the King's subjects; but, though gentle and cultured and with much quiet worldly wisdom, his was not that type of character of which the country stood in such urgent need, if the nationality of the Sinhalese was to be saved from destruction. The action of Bhuwaneka Bahu in placing his infant heir in the hands of the Franciscans, however much it may speak for his liberality of mind, has not added to his reputation for political sagacity. The results of such a course of training in the case of a youth threatened by powerful enemies, could not be long in showing themselves. There was a feeling of nervous uneasiness in the air, and it began to be whispered about from mouth to mouth, though no one ventured to say it aloud, that the gold finial of the Dalada Maligawa would never again reflect the mysterious five-hued aura' of the Buddha, for the Danta Dhatu no longer rested beneath its shadow.

It was not till some years afterwards that the details of the story became known. Hiripitiye Diyawadana Nilame was the great nobleman who was entrusted with the custody of the relic, and to him warning was conveyed in a vision of the night. He dreamt that a venerable figure appeared before him and addressed him in a strange jingling verse of Sinhalese and Tamil. He was greatly distressed in mind, and after much consideration interpreted the jingle for himself as follows: "My love for Kotte is no more. Begone with the Tooth into the Middle Kingdom." Taking advantage of a dark night he secreted the Relic in its smallest and loveliest ruby-encrusted case, within the folds of his waist-cloth, and plunging into the Diyawanna Oya swam across the stream. On reaching the further bank he made his way with all secrecy and expedition to Sitawaka and presented himself before the delighted Mayadunna, who almost at once set about erecting a magnificent Maligawa at Delgomuwa for the reception of the Relic: for he who holds the Danta Dhatu holds the sovereignty of Sri Lanka.

The year 1556 witnessed in Ceylon one of those strange out-bursts which the enthusiasm of Xavier had kindled so frequently among the fishing populations of South India. In this year the whole of the allied caste occupying the sea coast to the south of Colombo, a community of 70,000 souls in all, took refuge within the fold of the Catholic Church. "For this I give much praise unto Our Lord," wrote King Dom Joao III on the 20th of March 1557 to the Custodio of the Franciscans, "and I much commend to you that so far as in you lies you labour that there may not be lacking the means necessary for obtaining the fulfilment to be expected from such a beginning."

His gratification would have been even more intense had he lived long enough to receive the letter containing the news of his own conversion which his *protege* despatched to him in the same year. Dharmapala was baptised with the name of Dom Joao Periya Bandara, while his Queen, who was baptised at the same time, took the name of Dona Catherina, after the Queen of Portugal. Dharmapala's letter to the King contained further an appeal for protection against Mayadunna. The Queen Mother and the Cardinal Dom Henrique, who were acting as Regents during the minority of the infant Dom Sebastiao, while thanking the Lord Who had illuminated Dharmapala in his darkness, assured him that instructions would be issued to the Viceroy to protect his interests. The Pope also, who had been busy forming an alliance with the Grand Turk, the heretics of Germany, and the Most Christian King of France, to wage war on the Most Catholic King of Spain, found time to send the Royal Convert his Apostolic Benediction, and to recommend him to the special protection of the King of Portugal.

From the political standpoint few actions could have surpassed in folly the conversion of Dharmapala. As the *Raja Ratnakare* says: "This Kingdom can never be governed by a King who is not of the religion of Buddha." None the less, however distasteful the action of the King might have been to the overwhelming majority of his subjects, it is possible that the liberality of Buddhism would have condoned the error, if the King had kept his convictions to himself. Unfortunately the Church was in a peculiarly aggressive mood; Dom Joao III was a pronounced fanatic, whose policy was controlled by ecclesiastical advisers, and his zeal animated the Franciscans, who saw in Dharmapala a divinely appointed instrument for the conversion of the whole of Ceylon. The enthusiasm of the convert equalled that of the teachers who for fifteen years had striven to lead him within the fold; and his thank-offering consisted of a *Sannas* by which he transferred to them the Dalada Maligawa,[8] the two great shrines at Kelaniya, and all the temple revenues in the Island, for the maintenance of the Colleges which they proposed to found.

Had it been possible for the Franciscans to take advantage of the grant of Dharmapla to its full extent, it would have meant the destruction of the only organisation which existed for the spiritual and intellectual education of the people. It is difficult for a religious association to enjoy a position of influence for any considerable length of time without deteriorating from its original simplicity and virtue; but the Buddhist priesthood had probably suffered less in this respect than the bulk of the similar associations which the world has seen. It is true that Buddhism looked on the distinctions of caste with some degree of disfavour; but in the sixteenth century the priesthood was closed except to those of the highest caste. Vowed to poverty and chastity, its members received semi-royal honours from the people, as with their yellow robe so draped as to expose the right arm and chest, and veiling their faces with a fan, they went from door to door silently begging for their one simple daily meal.

In every group of villages there rose the *Vihara*, small and retired, or as sometimes with a towering snowy-white dagoba and imposing gateway.[3] The Sinhalese had a keen eye for the beauties of Nature, and all their poets give expression in their songs to that appreciation. Every commanding spot was utilised for the purposes of worship. Beneath it would be the great tank, the very source of life for the village—a hundred acres of lotus—pink and white, with here and there blue—scenting the air with its rich and wholesome fragrance for a mile around. The water-fowl would splash lazily in the cool of the evening, confident in the security which no one would disturb. And as the great full moon rose in the heavens, etherealising everything with its radiance, the villagers would come forth joyously with their offerings of sweet-smelling flowers—men and women and children all dressed in spotless white—to renew their vows as before the *Bo* tree at Anuradha Pura. That was the one innocent break from his round of toil in the life of the villager; for he did not touch intoxicants, and had no tavern where he could meet his fellows of an evening.

Every morning the children would troop to the *Pansala*, where the priest resided, to be taught their letters; for love of learning has always been inherent in the Oriental. There they would be taught, without fee or payment, to trace the characters of the alphabet on sand till they knew enough to be entrusted with an iron style wherewith to inscribe sentences, like strings of rounded pearls, on strips of palm-leaf. As they advanced in years they learned to compose verse, with the same sedulous care with which Hexameters are fashioned at Oxford or Cambridge. The great institutions at Totagamuwa and Keragala long maintained the traditions brought over from the Universities of India; and in the next century, though these institutions had ceased to exist, the learning to be found in Ceylon was still recognized by the Portuguese in India.[10]

Dharmapala was but a helpless puppet in the hands of his spiritual advisers, who now applied themselves with reckless ardour to the task of pulling down the structure which it had taken twenty centuries to erect. It is impossible to entertain any doubt as to the genuineness of the feeling which animated the now triumphant missionaries, or the absolute conviction under which they acted; unfortunately their impulses were the result not of reasoned belief but of impassioned ignorance. Vasco da Gama had worshipped at Hindu shrines under the idea that he had discovered a new branch of the Catholic Church; but the missionary could see in Buddhism nothing but the abhorrent creation of the devil. He did not stop to inquire what were the principles which were taught by its Sages, nor what the ideals after which its lofty philosophy struggled; Buddhism was not Christianity, and since by Christianity alone could souls escape damnation and hell fire, it was his duty to God to destory Buddhism by every means in his power. He did not ask whether the people were prepared to receive his new wine, or whether the destruction of their ancient beliefs might not mean the destruction of all spiritual life; his every idea was centred on the one thought that Buddhism must be wiped out of existence. In these circumstances it is not surprising that the rash action of Dharmapala was viewed with the greatest alarm by his subjects. A few of his great nobles followed his example, and biblical names were soon the fashion in the Sinhalese Court, the highest dignitaries of which at the same time assumed the title of Dom ; whilst the language and manners of the Portuguese were rapidly adopted among those who desired to continue in favour with the power which controlled patronage. As a result of all this a cleavage and estrangement, more deadly than any that had ever risen out of the institution of caste, began to creep in among the Sinhalese.

NOTES TO CHAPTER IV

1. The *pardao* was originally a golden coin from the native mints of West India; and the name, which is a corruption of the Sanskrit *pratapa*, was subsequently applied to a Portuguese silver coin of degenerating value, and nominally of 370 reis.

2. This work, which appears to have been compiled towards the end of the XVIIth century, is the best Sinhalese authority for the Portuguese period in Ceylon.

3. The Jesuit, Emanuel de Morales, writing from Colombo on the 28th of November 1552, has left the following account of his countrymen in Ceylon: "The most wicked vices reigned supreme in the Island, and men were given to lewdness and to lust ... There were more women of bad life than honest matrons. In fact women were worse than men in this regard, and these vices had become so habitual that they did not even seem to look upon them as sins."—*The Ceylon Antiquary*, I., 223.

4. His work, *Asia Portuguesa*, is in Spanish, and was published in three volumes at Lisbon, in 1666-1675.

5. He was baptised as Dom João and was sent to Lisbon, where under the name of the Prince of Ceylao he was a popular figure at Court, and received the precedence of a Conde. He later returned to Goa and married a Portuguese lady.

6. Diogo de Couto, born at Lisbon in 1543, appointed Guardian of the Torre do Tombo in 1595; died in India on 10th December 1616.

7. The five-hued effulgence which was believed to emanate from the body of the Buddha. Regarding this Dr. John Davy, M. D., F. R. S., brother of Sir Humphrey Davy, who was in Ceylon from 1816 till 1820, has written the following:

"There is a pecular phenomenon occasionally seen in the heaven in the Interior that is deserving of notice. In January 1820 it was witnessed in Kandy, and by European gentlemen as well as by natives. One of the former, a most respectable individual in whose account I could put the firmest reliance, described it to me as an appearance of rays or beams of light in motion, intersecting one another, faintly resembling the northern lights. It occurred when the atmosphere was clear, in the middle of the day . . . The natives call it *Boodhoo rais.*"

8. The Church of the Holy Sepulchre took the place of the Maligawa, and the bell of the Church, with its Latin invocation to the Virgin, is to-day a prominent feature in the Pettah of Colombo.

9. Father Morales has the following regarding the Temples. "Some of these are more splendid than the most splendid Churches of Lisbon, though the buildings are not so high nor so beautiful, yet everything seems covered with pure gold. I once entered a pagoda which impressed me more than anything I had seen in Portugal or Castille, in both of which I have seen many a magnificent building." Cey. Ant. I. 224.

10. It is difficult to say what was the condition of female education in Ceylon at this time, but the Kusa Jataka (see Index) makes it clear that fifty years later highborn ladies were able to read with ease Sanskrit and Pali, in addition to their own language.

CHAPTER V

Mayadunna was quick to take advantage of the mistake which his grand-nephew had committed ; he now presented himself as the champion of the national faith, and laid claim to the Lion Throne on the ground of the apostasy of the present occupant. Serious rioting occurred within the Capital itself, and the King was stoned by an excited mob, which only dispersed when the Portuguese opened fire upon it. Thirty Buddhist priests, whose persons were regarded as sacro-sanct, were arrested and punished, and this unprecedented act of sacrilege filled the people with such horror that several of the most prominent inhabitants of Kotte fled to Sitawaka ; while Mayadunna threw his armies into the great Province or Disawani of Matara, which extended from the neighbourhood of Kotte to the Walawe Ganga. So serious was the outlook that the veteran Affonco Pereira was hurriedly despatched from Goa to the assistance of Dharmapala, and only his vigorous exertions saved the Capital from the armies of Mayadunna.

In May 1559 Dom Jorge de Meneses Baroche succeeded him in the command, and was able to drive back a small army which was advancing under Wikramasinha Mudaliyar. Raja Sinha, however, hastened up in person and a powerful body of expert target-men, supported by elephants and cavalry and the bravest soldiers of Aturugiri Korale and Koratota, were hurled at the Portuguese. The great tract of low land lying between Mulleriyawa and Kaduwela, twelve miles from Colombo, which is yearly enriched by the alluvial deposits left by the Kelani Ganga when swollen with the monsoon rains, was this day the scene of a terrible fight. Raja Sinha himself attacked the Portuguese in front, while the Koratota and Hewagama Arachchis took them in the rear. The carnage was terrible, but though the Sinhalese were mown down by the firearms of their opponents, they still pressed on reckless of life, clinging to the tails of the elephants in their efforts to get within striking distance of the enemy. In the thickest of the fight was to be seen Raja Sinha on his horse, commanding, exhorting, encouraging his men by word and deed. "The battle was like a show of fireworks and the smoke from the discharge of the muskets resembled mists in early *Duruta.*[1] Blood flowed like water on the field of Mulleriyawa. The Portuguese were attacked in such wise that not one foot could they retire."

At last the Portuguese turned in flight. De Meneses seized the Banner of Christ which they were abandoning and tried to rally his men round it, but his voice was lost in the din of the battle. Raja Sinha, perceiving that victory was in his grasp, pursued them vigorously as they fled across the field towards a narrow passage in the line of their retreat. This they found already occupied by the Sinhalese who had blocked the way by cutting down trees, and here as they laboured desperately to clear the road they were brought to a stand. The war elephants were now thundering down upon them, and one of the beasts rushed at de Meneses with uplifted trunk as he again tried to rally his men, but a fortunate shot turned it back and he had time to escape. The elephant Viradareya—the Mighty of Strength— hurled the Ensign Luis de Lacerda through the air and captured the Banner of Christ, but still the Portuguese fought on with teeth and nails, for their powder was now exhausted. Their complete destruction seemed assured, when a soldier fired a *berco*[2] which they were abandoning right into the midst of the men who crowded round the passage, with fearful effect. The Sinhalese opened out their ranks and gave the Portuguese an opportunity of reaching the river and getting on board the vessels which were waiting there. Only a demoralised and weary handful succeeded in reaching the camp, where de Meneses threw himself on the ground, cursing himself in the depth of his despair.

Raja Sinha now erected strong forts at Kaduwela and Rakgaha Watta, to control the roads from Colombo, and the Portuguese, who had obtained reinforcements from India, determined to re-establish their lost prestige by an attack on the latter. The result was disastrous, and once again their demoralised men turned and fled, hotly pursued right up to the suburbs of Colombo by Wikramasinha, who returned in triumph on the back of a Portuguese prisoner. A fresh army was ready in India, but the Portuguese, instead of concentrating their energies on the urgent task of reducing Mayadunna, wasted their forces in a futile endeavour to punish the Raja of Jaffna. The Viceroy himself, the princely Dom Constantino de Braganza, led a great expedition against him in October 1560, and returned after securing little beyond the Tooth which had been found with Widiye Bandara. The price paid for this, in men and treasure, was very heavy, and the King of Pegu was willing to ransom it for a large amount. The Viceroy's Councillors urged that the King's offer should be accepted, but de Braganza, in deference to the wishes of his clerical advisers, directed that the alleged relic should be reduced to powder and burnt, and the ashes cast into the sea.

In the meanwhile Raja Sinha was unfalteringly pressing on his course. Guerilla bands following each other in quick succession, ravaged the rich and populous district which fed the Capital. Their rapidity of movement bewildered the Portuguese, whose energies were wasted in warding off the threats aimed alternately at Kotte and Colombo. More than once they were driven back in headlong flight, and it was soon clear that they were helpless to afford any effective protection to Dharmapala's subjects. Indeed so closely was Kotte blockaded, that after devouring the King's elephants, the Portuguese were forced to have recourse to cannibalism ; while their anxieties were greatly increased by the disaffection which prevailed within the walls, where there was an influential section which favoured surrender. But the leaders held grimly on till at last Raja Sinha's men returned to Sitawaka. The relief however was not for long, and in October 1564 he appeared once again with his army before the walls of Kotte, and proceeded to lay it under close siege, till on the 12th of February 1565 a determined attempt was made to carry the place by storm. Raja Sinha in person commanded the attack at Periya Kotte, and after a fierce conflict some of his men succeeded in crossing the water on bamboo rafts and effecting an entrance. But at last by efforts which were superhuman —for the Portuguese declared that the Virgin and St. Joseph were seen fighting in their ranks— the defenders within the walls succeeded in forcing them to withdraw. The Portuguese had in the meantime been negotiating with Karalliyadda, who now made a timely demonstration on the borders of Sitawaka, and thus compelled Raja Sinha, disappointed though he was, to hurry to meet this danger.

The Indian Government now decided that the continued maintenance of Kotte as the Metropolis was detrimental to the interests of the Portuguese, as it only served to divert their forces. The position of Colombo on the coast where it could always be reached from India, pointed to it as more suitable for the seat of the central authority. Diogo de Melo Coutinho was therefore sent as Captain of Colombo with orders to dismantle Jayawardhana Kotte and to transfer the Court, population, and artillery to Colombo. This was done in July 1565, to the great grief of the Sinhalese. Their ancient Capital was abandoned to the wild beasts, and a hundred years later elephants were being hunted on the site of its ruined palaces. Its granite columns have been removed to beautify the country houses of Dutch officials, or to buttress tottering bridges on the public roads ; and today the villager stealthily digs up the cabook stones over which his forefathers so freely shed their blood, to make a foundation for his fragile hut[3].

The kingdom of Kotte now ceased to exist, and Mayadunna was the undisputed lord of all the Sinhalese country except the Kanda Uda Rata and the area dominated by the guns of the Colombo Fort. A strong garrison at Wattala prevented the Portuguese from moving northward across the Kelani Ganga. Another at Nagalagama, almost within sight of the Fort, made impossible any movement in the direction of Sitawaka. A third force on the great plain of Mapane to the South of Colombo cut them off from Matara. The Portuguese were helpless, and it was only by the exertions of the Mudaliyars who still followed the fortunes of Dharmapala that they were kept supplied with provisions. From time to time a raiding expedition swept the food from the neighbouring villages into the Fort, but Raja Sinha was too busy reorganising for a great undertaking his father's military forces to allow himself to be disturbed by them.

In 1568 Dom Sebastião, though only in his fifteenth year, was declared to be of age and took over the administration from the Cardinal. The growing power of the Mohammedans, who three years previously, in 1565, had destroyed the Hindu Empire of Vijayanagara, was distracting the attention of the authorities at Goa, and they were unable to spare any assistance for Colombo. In 1570 a Mohammedan army laid siege to Goa itself, and it was only after ten months of the fiercest struggle that the invaders were compelled to retire. A series of Captains succeeded one another at Colombo, but not one of them was able to take any effective action. Colombo offered little opportunity for building up a reputation or amassing a fortune, and the Captains tried to make up for their disappointment by begging for loans from the unfortunate Dharmapala.

At length in 1574 Diogo de Melo arrived with a sufficient force to enable him to take the field, and swiftly-moving bodies were soon ravaging every village which had a temple with a reputation for wealth, and which could be reached without fear of being intercepted by Mayadunna's commanders. The famous shrine at Kelaniya was destroyed; the port of Negumbo was plundered; the garrison at Nagalagama was driven out; and the coast towns of Kalutara and Beruwala devastated. In the course of the following year one plundering expedition pushed its way as far south as Weligama. Another force sent out with a similar object ravaged the district of Chilaw, after which it made its way to the ancient and revered shrine of Munnessaram, one of the five *Isparam* or Residences of Siva in Ceylon. This temple is said to have been founded by Rama Chandra, the Avatar of Vishnu, himself, after the defeat of Ravana. Its *Lingam,* the emblem of the God, was a great cylinder of stone of the height of a man, and like the Diana of the Ephesians, was believed to have fallen from heaven. Numerous inscriptions there bore testimony to the wealth which the devotion of successive Kings had dedicated to its service, and its separate domain comprised 62 villages to which it gave its name. Much plunder was anticipated and the Portuguese pressed on eagerly. The Sinhalese force which blocked the way was driven back with the loss of its commander, and the temple sacked.

Laden with spoil the Portuguese turned back towards Colombo. Mapane was devastated with relentless fury, and the beautiful Vihare at Horana destroyed. An attempt was also made to surprise the Dewale[4] at Nawagomuwa, where a festival was being celebrated; but one of Raja Sinha's Arachchis seized the road and frustrated it, though the gallant Arachchi himself and three hundred of his men sacrificed their lives in the struggle.

In the meantime a horrible incident had occurred at Colombo. An attempt had been made to poison Dharmapala, while he sat at dinner with the Captain, by drugging his wine. On tasting it the King had fallen to the ground, and though restoratives were hastily applied and his life was saved, he remained toothless and a stammerer. There can be little doubt that the Captain had been bribed to destroy the King. Familiar though the Portuguese were both with bribery and with poisoning, the popular clamour which this shameful attempt against the unfortunate monarch evoked was so pronounced, that in October 1577 the Viceroy was compelled to remove De Melo from office and to order an inquiry. The Captain was despatched to Goa under arrest ; but on the way, harassed by anxiety and illness, goaded to despair by the pangs of a conscience which tormented him, and haunted by the fear of a shameful death, the unhappy man breathed his last, ending pitifully what had been a brilliant career.

Mayadunna was now feeling the weight of his years. He realised that the military operations against the Portuguese necessitated more activity of body than he was capable of, and in Raja Sinha he found a general who could be relied on efficiently to fill his place. Adopting the self-sacrificing custom which had long been in usage amongst the Sinhalese Kings, he in May 1578 with the consent of his subjects renounced the throne in favour of his son.

On the 4th of August of this same year was fought the great battle of Alcacer Quibir in Morocco, in which the dreamy and youthful Dom Sebastiao fell together with 9000 of his men, while 8000 more remained prisoners in the hands of the victorious Moors. This defeat proved a death-blow to the imperial aspirations of Portugal, and indeed the end of her own independence was not far off. Dom Sebastiao was succeeded by his uncle the Cardinal Dom Henrique, a feeble old man and a fanatical religionist of sixty-five, who had to be supported up the steps of the throne which he was destined to occupy but for a few brief months.

Raja Sinha lost no time in putting his newly acquired authority to the test. In the following year he laid siege to Colombo with a large army, but in spite of all his efforts, the garrison successfully maintained their resistance till in February 1581 Matthias de Alboquerque, subsequently Viceroy of India, arrived with a large force and compelled him to withdraw. On his way back to Sitawaka Raja Sinha received the news of the death of Mayadunna at the age of eighty years, and thus at length found himself unhampered in the execution of his plans for the entire subjugation of the Kingdom of Kotte.

Meanwhile an event of the most serious import had taken place in Colombo. On the 12th of August 1580 Dharmapala had, on the advice of the Franciscans, executed a deed of gift by which, after setting forth his own title to the Throne, and recounting how the hostility of Mayadunna and Raja Sinha had robbed him of everything save Colombo, he made over all his claims to Dom Henrique. This was perhaps the one shrewd act of this unhappy King during the long years of his nominal reign. Dom Henrique himself had, however, died seven months before, and with him had ended the great House of Aviz. Very little remained out of the Kingdom which that House had built up. The Treasury was empty; the public service was seething with peculation and corruption; and the drain towards India and Brazil of the country's manhood, culminating in the loss of the flower of what still remained in the fatal battle of Alcacer Quibir, had so affected the population, that few were left except slaves, priests and beggars. The Crown of Portugal fell to Philip II of Spain, who on the 15th of April 1581 swore to the conditions which were meant to preserve the individuality and maintain the interests of Portugal, and was proclaimed King as Philip I. Under these conditions Portugal was to have a Viceroy who was to be a native of the country. All offices within the Kingdom and the Indian trade were reserved to the Portuguese, while the revenue was to be kept distinct from that of Spain and spent for the benefit of Portugal only. Thus began the Sixty Years' Captivity, as the period of the Spanish domination of Portugal was called. Meanwhile Raja Sinha had turned his attention to the Uda Rata, and in 1582 thirty thousand veterans of the Portuguese wars appeared before Balane, the mountain stronghold which commands the gate of the central plateau. Karalliyadda's army, which was supported by a few Portuguese, was driven back after a sanguinary struggle, and the capital was occupied, Wirasundara Mudiyanse being placed in charge of it. Karalliyadda himself fled to Trincomalee where together with most of his family he fell a victim to an outbreak of smallpox, his infant daughter, who was at the time but one year old, being left in the care of his nephew Jama Sinha Bandar, who made his way to Jaffna and sought protection from the Tamil King.

Wirasundara, however, was not satisfied with his position and seized an early opportunity to revolt; but his treachery was met with treachery and he was trapped to his death, while the punishment inflicted on the rebellious districts was both swift and severe. The Sitawaka army rapidly overran the country, disarming all the disaffected, and reducing a large number of the inhabitants to slavery. The remainder were compelled to render service without payment, and were put to the most arduous labours in erecting the earthworks of Raja Sinha's fortifications, so that for several years to come there was no fear of any hostile movement from that quarter. Wirasundara's son Konappu fled to Colombo where he was hospitably received by Dharmapala, who gave him the daughter of Sembahap Perumal in marriage.

A few years of uneasy peace followed, while Raja Sinha was busily engaged in strengthening his position, by removing with unhesitating resolution all disaffected persons from his path. In 1583 Joao Correa de Brito succeeded Manoel de Sousa as Captain in Colombo, and on the 4th of November of the same year Dharmapala executed another instrument, ratifying in favour of King Philip the donation of 1580, and disinheriting all his kinsmen who should after his death lay claim to the Throne. Upon the completion of the instrument the populace was summoned to the palace, where the document was explained to them and they were invited to appoint proctors authorised to approve of the King's nomination. Three such were elected, and they on behalf of the King's subjects accepted Philip II as the heir of Dharmapala, waiving all the right vested in the people to nominate and elect a King on the death of the occupant of the Throne.

Raja Sinha's aims were, however, well known and his armies were even then hovering about and cutting off supplies. The condition of the garrison was wretched in the extreme, and so scarce had food become that the soldiers could with difficulty be restrained from abandoning their posts. Their wages were allowed to fall into arrears, and they had hardly the necessary clothes with which to cover their nakedness. The remittances received from Goa were irregular in arrival, and were conveyed at great risk in consequence of the pirates who infested the Indian waters. Meanwhile Raja Sinha's position was daily becoming stronger; he had achieved some measure of sea power, and more than once his vessels made descents on Manar. To meet the growing menace from Raja Sinha, the Portuguese hit upon the expedient of attempting to create disaffection at Court. Some of the Royal Princes were inveigled into a treasonable correspondence with the object of raising a revolt against the King; strange to say the priests, who had till now found staunch supporters in Mayadunna and Raja Sinha, were also attracted into the conspiracy. Fortunately, however, the plot was discovered in time. The guilty parties were punished with terrible severity. The Princes were put to death, one of them committing suicide by taking poison; while the Chief Priest was stoned and cut in pieces. Tradition indeed says that this last and his followers were buried up to their necks in the earth, and had their heads ploughed off.

It was this treachery which embittered Raja Sinha against Buddhism and made him virulently hostile to the priesthood. They found him "like unto a serpent full of poison when it is beaten with a stick... He embraced heresy and became like unto a thorn in the path of Continued Existence."[5]

Many of the priests disrobed themselves and others fled to the Uda Rata, while the King deprived the more important temples of the villages from which they derived their revenues. An even more severe blow was dealt when he proceeded to remove the Buddhists from the control of one of the most venerated spots in the East, the Sacred Foot Print.

As the voyager approaches the Island from Europe, the most prominent feature which catches his eye at early dawn is the graceful Peak of Samanala Kanda, rising 7352 feet above the level of the sea over the billowy masses of snow-white clouds. On its summit may be seen a depression fashioned roughly like a human foot, and long before the Sinhalese race arrived in the Island, this, the Sri Pada, was an object of worship among innumerable human beings. The Hindus saw in it the impress of Siva; the Buddhists declared that Gautama himself left this for his perpetual memorial; while the Arabs worshipped it as the foot print of Adam, who found consolation in Ceylon for the loss of Paradise. Thousands of pilgrims climbed the steep ascent every March and April, being assisted on their way by the iron chains which Marco Polo says had been presented to the shrine by Alexander the Great. Many nationalities and many religions met at the summit, towards which the neighbouring peaks appeared to bow in reverence, and there celebrated their rites in peace and friendship. This august shrine the indignant Raja Sinha now placed in the charge of the ash-daubed Indian fakirs; even today the priests have not forgiven him this insult.

Raja Sinha was now at the height of his power, and the Sinhalese everywhere, except the handful round the walls of Colombo who still remained faithful to Dharmapala, acknowledged him as their King. All eyes were turned on Sitawaka, and for the first time since the death of Sri Rahula patriotism and pride in the doings of their race brought forward a poet, in the person of Alagiyawanna Mukewetti.

A prose literature, consisting mainly of Commentaries on the Buddhist Scriptures, existed among the Sinhalese before the beginning of the Christian Era, and to this were later added some historical works which were made use of by Mahanamo in the compilation of his *Mahawansa*. This last was written in Pali, a language which holds among the Buddhist priesthood the same position as that which latin occupies in the Church of Rome. King Buddhadasa in the fourth century composed a medical treatise in Sanskrit, and King Kumaradas two centuries Later was the author of a poetical work in the same language. It is known that several poets, whose productions were held in esteem, lived about the period of this latter King; but none of their works survive to-day, though there are good examples of the prose of the time.

The three hundred and fifty years which followed the accession to the Throne of Parakrama Bahu the Great, were adorned by the works of a series of writers several of whom have always been considered, and can justly claim to be, of the first rank. The most prominent among them were priests, as was natural in a state of civilisation where every temple was also a school; but even they did not confine themselves to religion and philosophy, as might have been expected from their dissociation from worldly interests; the history, medicine and poetry of the country have been enriched by their contribution. The reward of literary merit was in the hands not of a reading public, but of the King, and the necessary encouragement was not lacking. Pandita Parakrama Bahu was more than a Sinhalese Maecenas; he was himself a scholar whose religious Commentaries still hold as high a rank as his poetic works.

Literature reached its high water mark in the productions of Sri Rahula. He was the chief exponent of the use of rhyme, which in his day began to displace the blank verse which had hitherto been the fashion. The greatness of his literary influence is proved by the numbers of his countrymen who still adopt his poems as their model, and to every Sinhalese his *Kaviya Sekara* is what it calls itself, the Crown of Song.

It is not unusual for Europeans to sneer at the poetry of the Sinhalese; and yet it is not possible to point to one European who can be accepted as a competent critic. Certain blemishes are indeed obvious, but they are not such as to destroy the excellences; and for perfect melody of sound, beauty of imagery, richness of language, and intense appreciation of Nature, the *Kaviya Sekara* is difficult to surpass. Sinhalese poetry has not yet been placed before the Western world; is it too much to hope that one of the Universities of the West will some day train the Sinhalese youth who will adequately interpret his countrymen in the English tongue?

Sri Rahula and his group of brilliant contemporaries—for he was only the most brilliant of a brilliant group—were all dead at the time of the arrival of the Portuguese, and the first seventy-five years of the sixteenth century proved singularly barren in literary results. It is not surprising that during this unhappy period of internecine warfare, when the power of the Sinhalese was being steadily destroyed and foreign influence was gaining the ascendency at the Court, there was little to fire the imagination of the man of letters. The triumphs of Raja Sinha, however, struck a responsive chord in the breast of Alagiyawanna, the cultured son of the learned Dharmadwaja Pandita. The learning of the son, indeed, has secured for him a reputation outside his native country such as the father never enjoyed;

his name was well-known in India when in the middle of the XVIIth century Jean Baptiste Tavernier, Baron of Aubonne, went to sell his diamonds and pearls at the Court of the great Mogul.

The *Sevul Sandesaya* was probably the earliest of Alagiyawanna's works; and though it shows no originality of conception, and is a polished specimen of composition rather than a poem, yet it is of great value for the glimpse it affords of the Court of Raja Sinha as it presented itself to one who had access to it. The poet is at Sitawaka , and sends his message or *Sandesaya* to the God who was worshipped at Saparagamuwa, invoking his protection for the religion of Buddha, and for the King, his Council and his army. The message is entrusted to the *Sevula* or cock, and the opportunity is taken to describe the sights which meet the messenger's eye as it proceeds on its way. Raja Sinha himself is shown on his throne, giving audience to ambassadors from foreign Courts. "Glory, Liberality and Truth he cherished ; second to them he held his life." The ambassadors display presents of silk and camphor and musk, sandalwood and pearl, while the Court bards sing the King's praises. Beautiful maidens stand behind the throne and fan the King with the Royal fan, the tail of the great Himalayan Yak ; the Princes, victors in many a fight, and the gallant warriors of India who have lent their swords to the King, make obeisance at his feet, and are followed by the Ministers, "who watch over the people as over their own eyes, skilled in law to decide all tangled suits." In the courtyard are assembled the choicest of the royal troops, and the Wanniyan chiefs, who rule the wild country between the Uda Rata and the Jaffna Kingdom, are present with their tribute of elephants. The Bhairawa Kovil has been repaired after the devastation of 1551, and in its great hall, the walls of which are frescoed in rich colours with scenes from the Ramayana, the dancing women move their graceful limbs to the rhythm of the Tamil music. In the main street or *Vitiya* is the Court House, where justice is administered "without affection or ill-will, ignorance or fear." There is also a quarter of the city devoted to music and dancing halls, and other recreations for the people, and in its neighbourhood are the royal elephant stalls, and a great caravanserai erected for the use of the public by Wikramasinha Mudiyanse.

Ceylon was a small field in which to train a General to meet the finest troops of Europe, for Portugal had sent her very best to the East. Yet the native talent of the Sinhalese Chief and the whole resources of Sinhalese civilisation were to be matched against the science of the West, in a struggle which was to decide whether Oriental or Occidental was to be supreme in Ceylon. An armed camp was established at Biyagama, ten miles from Colombo. The forts at Nagalagama, Kaduwela and Rakgahawatta protected it against any surprise attack from Colombo, and the broad Kelani River which flowed past it not only provided a safe and easy means of getting in touch with the enemy, but also served to bring to it materials of war in unlimited quantity. The services of every feudal tenant throughout the country were requisitioned. Ingots of the finest steel poured in from the villages of the Yamanoo whose service it was to smelt the ore. Relays of smiths toiled to convert these into crowbars and axes, armed with which the woodcutters proceeded to the forest-clad mountain slopes adjoining the stream, down to the bed of which the great logs which they felled were dragged by two thousand of the King's elephants. There the logs were lashed together into immense rafts on a foundation of thousands of the buoyant golden-coloured bamboos which grew by the water's edge, and secured by great lengths of stout cane.

These rafts travelled rapidly down stream till they reached Biyagama, where they were moored unbroken to the bank.

The 1900 royal villages also sent their whole store of rice on the backs of the transport oxen which it was part of their service to maintain. Stacks of the dried branches of the Palmyra palm were prepared to serve as tents. Four hundred blacksmiths were employed in the manufacture of billhooks, mattocks, and, not least important, a vast quantity of arrow-heads. The carpenters too were busy fashioning the timbers for the stockades and the ponderous siege engines. A hundred and fifty pieces of bronze artillery were cast, the majority of them *gingals* supported on a light wooden frame consisting of two legs in front, and a long curved handle behind; and such as a pair of men could carry. Matchlocks also were prepared in large numbers; for the Sinhalese, as the Portuguese writers admit, soon excelled their teachers in the manufacture of these weapons. All hand-guns were fired with match-cord, for flint is not found in the Island. The animal accumulations of ages, fetched from the caves of Uwa, were utilised to obtain a supply of saltpetre, while sulphur was imported from Persia. Leaden bullets were cast in abundance, and an application was sent to Achim, the King of which country was at this time waging war on the Portuguese in Malacca, for further supplies of ammunition. The services of every Malay, Kaffir, and renegade Portuguese who could be secured to serve the artillery were purchased, while a select body of expert Indian warriors was collected as the personal guard of the King. The enthusiasm of Raja Sinha was infectious, and few Sinhalese to whom the summons came were found wanting. Not all in the great crowd which assembled at Biyagama were fighters; but every member of it knew how to handle an axe or a spade with skill, and there was plenty of trench work to be done.

NOTES TO CHAPTER V

1. The Sinhalese month corresponding to December-January.

2. In 1525 among the guns used by the Portuguese were Nags, Falcons, Camels, Lions, Serpents, Basilisks, Savages, Culverins, Bombards, Pedreiros, Spheres, Roqueiros, Passamuros, Mortars and Bercos.

3. It is distressing to think that while the Ceylon Government was spending lakhs of rupees in maintaining a Museum and an Archaeological Department, the very foundations of Dharmapala's Palace were being dug up and sold for building material within six miles of Colombo.

4. *Dewala* is a temple of the Hindu deities who are recognised by the Buddhists.

5. Mahawansa.

CHAPTER VI

It was not unnatural that the Portuguese should view these preparations with the deepest apprehension. De Brito accordingly sent an embassy with rich presents to the King, who was persuaded to agree to a short truce, which was prolonged by an attempt to poison him which just failed of success. Urgent appeals for assistance were meanwhile sent to Goa, and everything possible with the means at the disposal of the Portuguese was done to strengthen the fortifications of Colombo. All the plantations outside the walls which were likely to afford cover to the enemy were felled, use being made of the timber in the fortifications.

On the North the town was protected by a rampart. The bastion of S. Thome, which stood at the north-western corner, was in a dilapidated condition; and another bastion, named after S. Joao, was built at a spot closer to the Bay. This bastion was thirty feet high, and was connected with the Bay by a stout wall. The central bastion of S. Estevao, which was the most important on that side of the town, was mounted with the best artillery the defenders possessed, so as to command the neck of land between the Lake and the sea. Across this neck of land there ran a moat, and between the moat and the ramparts a strong palisade was now constructed, to which was secured, to prevent the elephants from pulling out the beams, a row of unwieldy *pada* boats used for transporting heavy cargo on the river. Towers and sentry boxes were erected at intervals on the top of the wall which ended at the bastion of S. Sebastiao. Beyond that point the main defence consisted of the water of the lake, along the bank of which there was

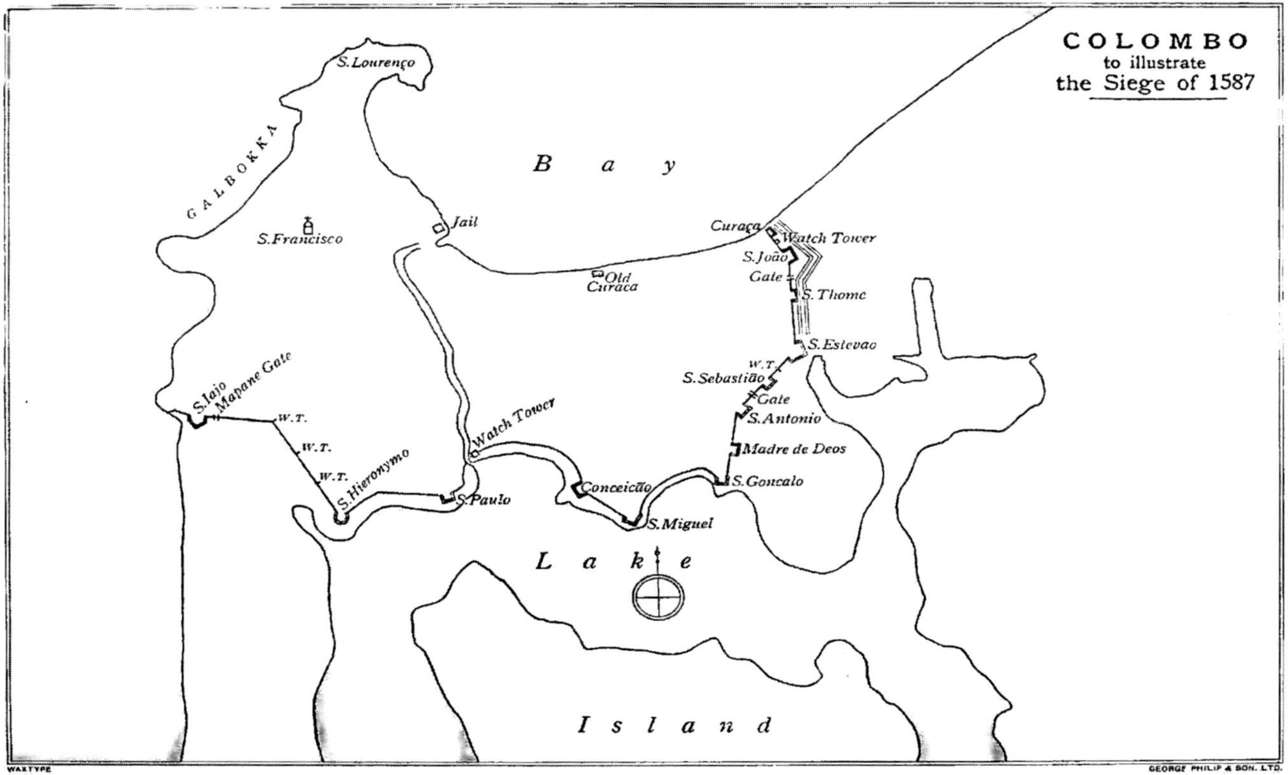

COLOMBO
to illustrate
the Siege of 1587

also a low wall strengthened by the bastions of S. Goncalo, S. Miguel, Nossa Senhora de Conceicao and others.

At last Raja Sinha was ready, and a great army estimated at 50,000 men took the field. It was whispered, and probably not without reason, that human sacrifices had been offered to the awful divinities who control the destinies of war. [1] It is at least certain that images of gold were lavishly bestowed on their temples throughout the country, to secure their blessing on this undertaking. Crossing the Kelani river the Sitawaka army reached Demata Goda on the 4th of July 1587 and proceeded to entrench itself. The camp was soon strengthened by a broad moat and palisades, after which Raja Sinha resumed work upon the canal for draining the lake, which had been left unfinished at the conclusion of the last siege. This was pressed on till a layer of stone was reached which defied all the efforts of the Sinhalese engineers. Raja Sinha was however equal to the occasion; vinegar and sour milk were poured upon the rock, after which it was heated by means of large fires which were steadily maintained till the whole was pulverised. [2] In twenty days the canal had reached the lake, notwithstanding the desperate resistance of the garrison, who watched with terror as the level of the water gradually sank, till at last the armed boats maintained by the Portuguese on the Lake had to be beached.

Raja Sinha now laid his plans for his first great assault on Colombo.

Before dawn on the 4th of August the Sinhalese advanced to the walls. Three Mudaliyars commanded the three companies of elephants which went in the van to attack the bastions of S. Miguel, S. Goncalo, and S. Francisco. Behind the elephants came spearmen, the targe-bearers, the archers, and last of all the matchlock men. On the Lake, in which there still remained a little water, several rafts were placed, and so secured together as to form a floating platform which was loaded with men. The various detachments crept up to their posts in deep silence, betrayed only by their matches, which showed like a swarm of fireflies in the gloom.

The alarm was raised; and as Raja Sinha's drums roared back their hoarse answer to the cries of the Portuguese, the Sinhalese dashed towards the walls with a shout, and planting their ladders began to clamber up them with amazing agility, while a body of sappers two thousand strong set to work to open a breach. But it was only for a moment. Volley after volley crashed out from above against the surging mass of the attackers, creating terrible havoc; and the cries and lamentations of the women and children in the crowded streets within increased the confusion. Soon too the elephants came up and began to tear down the walls with their trunks. Hand grenades were hurled at the elephants' heads, reinforcements were hurried to the rescue, and missiles of every kind were brought to bear on the soldiery thronging beneath the wall. Nevertheless the Sinhalese did not flinch, and de Brito, seeing how critical was the situation, dashed into the midst shouting out his name to encourage his men.

At S. Goncalo the pressure was even greater. The arrows and the fire which the Sinhalese poured in through the embrasures could at length be faced no longer, and the Portuguese retired, scorched by the flame and blinded by the smoke. But even as the Sinhalese crowded up the ladders the Portuguese returned, and as each man reached the coping of the rampart, presented their spears at his breast. Where the Sinhalese succeeded in thrusting aside the spears, they were met by the swords of the defenders, which inflicted terrible wounds on their bare bodies. But as one fell another took his place, and the fight went on till the bastion became one blaze of fire. Once again the Portuguese drew back; once again the flame was extinguished, and they returned to continue the struggle, guided by the light of the cressets which the forethought of their leaders had caused to be prepared.

Time after time the elephants were hurled against the walls; time after time they had to retire before the grenades and bullets, their shrill screams rousing terror in every heart even in the midst of that fearful din of battle. So for a full hour the assault lasted, till at last the Sitawaka men, exhausted with their efforts, fell back a distance of twenty paces.

Furious at this failure, Raja Sinha who was directing the operations gave the signal, five beats of the drum, for the whole army to engage. The men of his own guard, armed with breast-plates, head-pieces and morrions, and wielding their two-handed swords, charged recklessly towards the walls and the bastion of S. Goncalo, crying aloud their names and cutting down the spears of the Portuguese. At the same time the elephants once more advanced, and seized the artillery which was being discharged against them. So encumbered with corpses was the ground that the movements of the living were impeded. It was a titanic struggle. Sinhalese and foreigner alike, clasping each other in a close embrace, went whirling down to death, till at last on the bastions of S. Goncalo and S. Miguel the Standard of Raja Sinha was triumphantly unfurled over that appalling scene of blood and carnage.

A feeling little short of despair now came over the garrison; but de Brito himself remained undaunted. Every available man was hurried to the spot, and once more the struggle was renewed, and the Sinhalese army forced to retire before the splendid defence of the Portuguese. Again it rallied, and for the third time by the imperious command of Raja Sinha threw itself against the walls; again the brave Sinhalese, reckless of their lives, charged up to the very mouths of the Portuguese cannon; but the task was now recognised as an impossible one, and Raja Sinha in profound disappointment gave the signal for withdrawal. Colombo had been all but won, but the bravest troops of Europe stood behind the walls and guns which the bare-bodied Sinhalese had with such desperate valour tried to carry.

Then the day dawned—"which was for our people a joy as great as comes, when the day breaks clear and serene, to those that in some storm thought themselves lost in the darkness of the night.[3]"

Raja Sinha now betook himself once more to the tedious labour of a siege. The stockades were pushed up close under the walls, and at their corners wooden bastions were erected of a height sufficient to command those of the Fort. To meet this menace a lofty wooden platform on which guns were mounted was erected on S. Miguel, and deep trenches were opened to prevent the elephants from approaching the walls. At the same time urgent messages were sent to India entreating help, and stating that the garrison was at the last extremity. On the 20th of August another assault was attempted, under cover of which the Sinhalese vessels sailed out and tried to set fire to the magazine situated on the high ground to the West of the Fort; but once again the Portuguese by desperate efforts succeeded in driving the enemy back. Three days later five vessels conveying men and munitions arrived from Cochin, and these were followed shortly afterwards by other vessels from the settlement of S. Thome and from Goa, reinforcements which raised the number of the Portuguese available for actual fighting to nearly a thousand.

It was known that Raja Sinha was preparing a series of mines, but no information could be obtained of their whereabouts. A fortunate accident, however, led Thome de Sousa, who was in command at S. Joao, to discover a slit in the timbering of the mud wall which ran from S. Sebastiao along the shore of the lake, and peeping through this he descried opposite to him the mouth of a mine. The Captain was summoned in haste and a warm reception prepared for the Sinhalese. The wall was rapidly hollowed out to receive a *camello*, a thin curtain which could be pushed down at the critical moment being left on the outside. The gun itself was heavily charged with ball and stones. When everything was ready a few Lascarins were sent outside to serve as a bait, and before long the Sinhalese were thronging from every side, while the mine was filled with a closely packed crowd of men who poured out into the ditch. Seated astride the gun de Sousa watched through the slit for his opportunity. When at length the ditch was full of men, the *camello* was run out, breaking down the curtain by its own weight, and fired right into the mouth of the mine. The plan had been cleverly laid, and the effect of the cannonade was terrible. From end to end of the mine the stones and bullets swept, and not one out of the dense crowd within escaped alive. So great indeed was the havoc caused, that the King had the mine filled in over the bodies as they lay.

On the 4th of October eighteen Sinhalese ships appeared off Colombo and engaged the Portuguese vessels in the harbour, which were under the command of Thome de Sousa, now Captain Major of the Sea. Though the Sinhalese were unaccustomed to this kind of warfare, they maintained a gallant struggle, grappling with the enemy with great boldness, and it was only after four of their ships had been lost to them that they were forced to retreat. The Viceroy meanwhile spared no pains to collect what assistance he could in India for the relief of the beleaguered garrison. On the 4th of December a further body of a hundred and fifty soldiers with stores reached Colombo, bringing with them the welcome news that a great expedition was in preparation, and that Manoel de Sousa Coutinho, whose defence of Colombo during the last siege had greatly enhanced his reputation, had been nominated for the command. This expedition was to be joined at Colombo by the fleet from Malacca, and the whole armament, comprising the greater part of the forces at the disposal of the Portuguese Government in India, was to make the attempt finally to drive Raja Sinha from before Colombo. He on his side made more than one desperate assault on the Fort, but his efforts were in vain, for the increased numbers of the Portugese had added greatly to their *morale.* Albeit plague had broken out within the crowded city, where the natural consequences of the prolonged confinement of a large population within a limited area had been aggravated by an excessive drought, lasting over a year, followed by the heavy rains of the north-east Monsoon. So numerous were the deaths that it was suspected that the wells from which the drinking water was obtained had been poisoned.

News of the preparations which were being made to relieve Colombo now reached Raja Sinha, and he realised that further delay would be fatal to the success of his projects. Accordingly, on the 10th of January 1588 an attempt, so carefully planned that the Sinhalese were not discovered till they had actually begun to ascend their scaling-ladders opposite S. Estevao, was made to carry the walls by surprise. Like the former attempts, however, it ended in failure. There followed a three days' bombardment of the bastions of S. Goncalo and S. Miguel, against which Raja Sinha had massed all his heavy artillery, including guns which threw iron balls weighing forty-four pounds. The way having been prepared, a fierce assault was delivered on the 27th. The great war elephants were brought up to S. Goncalo, and a desperate attempt was made to batter down the walls. So fierce was the struggle that a wild rumour spread that the Sinhalese had entered the fort; but the rumour proved to be false, and after two hours' fighting they were compelled to draw' back.

The Portuguese now found themselves strong enough to assume the offensive, and Thome de Sousa sallied out of the harbour with ten vessels, bent on the congenial task of ravaging the southern coast. Kosgoda was burnt to the ground, and Madampe, verdant amidst the pleasant waters of its lake, was soon converted into a blackened waste. Near Madampe was the monastery where Sri Rahula had composed those melodious strains which are the delightful heritage of every Sinhalese, and the *dewale* of the mysterious Weragoda Deviyo, merchant-prince and divinity, whose golden treasures, lost in the seas, are still in stormy weather tossed up by the waves on the shores of Sinigama. Having reduced these to shapeless ruins, the expedition hurried on, past the rich temple village of Hikkaduwa and the haunted shores of Ratgama, to devote three days to sacking the ports of Galle and Weligama. Matara and Mirissa shared the same fate, after which the Portuguese re-embarked to proceed to the neighbouring Dewale of Dewundara.

This famous shrine, founded according to tradition in the year 790 A. D. in honour of a Red Sandalwood Image of Vishnu, was inferior in sanctity to the temple at Trincomalee alone. Its great roof of copper gilt flashing far out to sea served as a landmark for the mariners of every nation who sailed the Indian waters, and many a pious offering betokened their acknowledgment of the protecting influence of the Divinity. The glory of this City of God' had penetrated even to distant China, and numerous stone inscriptions at the spot testified to the devout zeal of the Emperors of that great country. Nearly 250 years before, Ibn Batuta the Moorish traveller had visited the shrine and had found there a thousand Brahmins serving as the Ministers of the God. Kings too had vied with one another in beautifying the place and adding to its wealth, and its annual Fair ranked amongst the most important in the East. The vast precincts of the temple, where dwelt the attendants of the God, resembled a small town; the skill of its silversmiths, a special colony imported from the neighbouring continent, shed lustre on the art of the entire Disawani of Matara; and every night 500 women danced and sang before the Image.

Greedy for the plunder of this rich temple, the Portuguese sailed thither, in spite of the tempestuous seas which the god appeared to have sent for the protection of his shrine. There was little or no opposition to their landing, and the city and temple were found deserted. The images, of which there were over a thousand, were soon broken to pieces; the processional car of the god, a great lacquered and gilt structure of seven stages, was reduced to ashes; the store houses, which were found to be full of all manner of wealth, were sacked; cows were slaughtered at the holiest shrines; and then the great building itself was razed to the ground.

This done, the marauders, well satisfied with the result of their expedition, sailed back to Colombo. A Church with columns of stone subsequently occupied the site of the descrted temple.

On the 18th of February the long looked-for flotilla of Manoel de Sousa Coutinho appeared befor

Colombo, and was greeted with a joyful salute from all the guns of the Fort. The vessels from Malacca were also beginning to arrive, and Raja Sinha realised that he could no longer maintain his present position. Three Sinhalese officers presented themselves before the gates, and were received in audience by the Council. They had come from their King with a request for a short truce to enable him to attend a festival at his Capital; but before the audience was concluded the alarm was raised that the King was striking his camp. Consternation prevailed on every hand and the city was thrown into a state of uproar, while the Council, having first sent out spies to ascertain what was actually taking place, began hurriedly to discuss the situation.

It was now nine o'clock on the night of Saturday the 21st of February. Immense flames were seen to burst from the Sinhalese lines, were Raja Sinha had set fire to his wooden stockades. But the Captains were afraid to move till the report of the spies should be received. Diogo de Silva, however, having been sent out with his Lascarins by the gate Sao Joao, the few Sinhalese who were in sight retired before him, whereupon the whole army poured out of the gates, the van being led by Manoel de Sousa in person. Wijayakon Mudaliyar, who commanded the rearguard of the Sinhalese army, fell back as the Portuguese advanced till he reached the Dematagoda bridge, which he ordered to be pulled down. The Portuguese pressed forward to thwart his intention, but were met by so furious a fire that they were driven back. De Sousa now hurried up with all his men and Wijayakon retreated to the Kelani Ganga, the difficulty of the intervening ground hampering the movements of the Portuguese.

The city was saved, and the gratitude of all found expression in an outpouring of thanks to the Almighty. Raja Sinha had done gallantly and well,[5] but neither his iron will nor the devoted courage of his men could avail against the walls and artillery of Colombo, so long as the sea remained open to the Portuguese. As it was, the siege had strained every resource of Portuguese India, and swift vessels were soon speeding over the ocean to carry the joyful news throughout the East.

Raja Sinha's last marvellous efforts had reduced him to exhaustion, and the Portuguese were thankful for the ensuing interval of rest. The country too was getting restless under the strain of these never-ending campaigns, and the severity of the King's rule. Konappu, who had risen into prominence during the siege, had in some way fallen foul of the authorities in Colombo and been banished to Goa, whither Jama Sinha Bandara, who had embraced Christianity under the name of Dom Philip, had preceded him. A deed of gift by which the latter conveyed to the Portuguese the Kingdom of the Uda Rata which he hoped to reconquer, in case he or his son Dom Joao should die without male heirs, overcame the hesitation of the Government, and a small army was placed at his disposal. Konappu, whose reputation had been greatly increased by his success in a duel with a swash-buckling Captain at Goa, joined him. Dom Philip landed on the Northern coast and advanced unopposed to Senkadagala. There he was proclaimed King, but died within a few weeks after a short illness. This was a contingency which had not been anticipated. The Sinhalese hesitated to accept at so critical a time a child as their King, and the Portuguese decided to withdraw with the young Prince before the country should be roused to oppose them. They were allowed to return unmolested to Manar, whence Dom Joao was sent to the College of the Magi at Goa[6].

Konappu meanwhile had remained behind to organise the movement against Raja Sinha, and so successful was he that the Sitawaka garrisons were soon driven out of the mountains. The Portuguese at Colombo were however once again in a condition bordering upon anarchy, and could do nothing in his support. In 1591 indeed Andre Furtado de Mendoca, who subsequently rose to be the most prominent Portuguese General in the East, invaded Jaffna and set up a new King at Nallur; but this did not influence the trend of events in the South. The Generals whom Raja Sinha sent to the Uda Rata were unable to cope with the popular movement, and in 1593 the King himself took the field on what proved to be his last campaign.

His efforts met with no greater success than those of his Generals, while at the same time sickness broke out in his camp. "The power of my Merits," declared the weary King, "has declined".[7] Placing the Perumal[8] Aritta Kivendu in charge, he retired to his pleasaunce at Petangoda. Whilst he was there a bamboo splinter ran into his foot and caused blood-poisoning. Grave symptoms soon began to show themselves, and the royal barge was summoned to convey the King to Sitawaka. Down the broad Kelaniya the barge glided and turned into its swift tributary stream, the Sitawaka Ganga, the oarsmen toiling against the current to bring their King once again to his royal city. Not a word escaped Raja Sinha's lips; he lay there buried in thought, reviewing the life which he had so gallantly spent for the country that he loved. When at length the barge took a sharp turn and ran its prow up on to the white sand of Kikili Bittera Wella, Ra Sin Deviyo was dead.

"Verily," says the clerical writer of the Mahawansa, to whom the memory of Raja Sinha was distasteful because of the antagonism which he had displayed towards Buddhism in the latter years of his reign, "this sinner did rule with a strong arm."

Thus "in the one thousand five hundred and fourteenth year of the Saka King, on Wednesday the Full Moon day of the month Medindina, under the asterism Site, Raja Sinha Maha Raja who had brought the Island of Sri Lanka under one Canopy of Dominion, departed this life and went to Kailasa."[9]

A few rough stones still mark the spot where the last great King of the Sinhalese race was cremated; and even to-day, deified as the Ganegoda Deviyo, he compels by the terror of his name the worship of his countrymen. [10]

Raja Surya, a grandson of the late King, succeeded to the throne, but before long a palace intrigue resulted in his assassination, and the youthful Nikapitiya Bandara was proclaimed King in his stead, though the chief power remained in the hands of the Perumal. This remarkable man had originally come from India as a Fakir or religious mendicant, but his talents had quickly been recognised by Raja Sinha, at whose hands he received rapid promotion. He now enhanced his reputation by meeting and overthrowing the Mudaliyar Diogo de Silva, who had advanced with an army from Colombo. The Mudaliyar himself was killed, but the Perumal's brilliant victory nearly proved his undoing, for it emboldened him to solicit the hand of the sister of Nikapitiya Bandara in marriage, a development which the Sinhalese nobles viewed with disfavour.

Lampoons reminiscent of the pilgrim's wallet which he had once worn were soon in the mouths of all, and the Perumal in alarm, and believing his life to be in danger, moved with the army to Menikkadawara, whence he secretly opened a treasonable correspondence with Pedro Homem Pereira, the Captain at Colombo, undertaking to reconquer the Kingdom of Kotte for Dharamapala, and that of

Sitawaka for himself, within twelve months. The Portuguese agreed to assist him, and he assumed the royal designation of Jayawira Bandara: but upon the advance of an army commanded by Illangakon Mudaliyar from Sitawaka his chief officers deserted him, and he himself was glad to escape with a small guard of 200 men and twenty-six of his elephants to Colombo, where, prostrating himself before Dharmapala, he reasserted his determination to carry out his share of the undertaking.

By way of making good his word he captured the important outpost of Kaduwela, whereupon reinforcements were hurried across from Goa, and the whole of the Portuguese force took the field. The garrisons of Rakgaha Watta and Malwana were driven back and the main body of the Sitawaka army defeated at Gurubewila, after which the victorious Jayawira occupied Sitawaka with little or no resistance, the bulk of the great treasure of Raja Sinha falling into his hands. Nikapitiya Bandara, [11] who had escaped to the mountains, was pursued and captured. This done, Jayawira swooped down upon the Matara Disawani, and soon had nearly the whole of the Kingdom of Kotte in his power. He was now *de facto* King of Sitawaka, and such was the power of his gold that the Portuguese almost to a man were soon in his train—it was indeed asserted that only twelve of them were left to guard Colombo.

The ease and rapidity with which Jayawira had fulfilled his promise made the Portuguese open their eyes. Dharmapala, now once more master of the Kingdom which his grandfather had left to him, and legal overlord of the country, was well on in years, and there was little probability of his having children to succeed him on the throne. In accordance with the donation which he had executed, his rights would, in the event of his leaving no heirs, vest in the King of Portugal. The beautiful land they had coveted so long was in fine in the grasp of the Portuguese. The climate of Ceylon fitted it admirably for colonisation, whilst its wealth in elephants, cinnamon, pearls and gems, made it a desirable possession for any nation. It was, moreover, the natural centre of the rich traffic with the Southern Seas; and so long as the Portuguese were supreme at sea, its insular position would render its defence against all possible enemies no difficult matter. Could it be that Ceylon was destined to be the scene of the fulfilment of Alboquerque's dream—that in Ceylon would be established a second Portuguese nation which should hold sway over the whole of India?

Such were the thoughts which presented themselves to the Viceroy and his Council when they met to discuss the situation, and under their influence they decided to conquer Ceylon, and to place on the throne of the Uda Rata Dona Catherina, the young daughter of Karalliyadda, with a Portuguese for her husband, expelling Konappu who at present ruled under the name of Wimala Dharma Surya. The Council further unanimously resolved to entrust the execution of its plans to Pedro de Sousa, who had recently distinguished himself by a successful campaign in Malacca.

The decision was a momentous one, and fraught with consequences more disastrous to the continued existence of the Portuguese Empire in the East than its authors could have contemplated, marking as it did the beginning of a new policy of aggression and territorial occupation in Ceylon. Hitherto the arms of the Portuguese had been used only in defence of the Kingdom of Kotte. That Kingdom they realised would soon belong to them, and the temptation to seize what appeared an easy opportunity to reduce the entire country, proved too much for their judgment. In their ardour and the pride engendered by their military achievements, it did not occur to them that there might be serious obstacles in the way of success. They did not stop to consider that the powerful army which Dom Constantino de Braganza had taken to Jaffna had failed to impose a foreign yoke on the unwarlike Tamil, and that too in a country the nature of which presented no special difficulties from the military point of view. Further, a Portuguese army could not carry on an effective campaign in the Island without the assistance of native levies, especially when the theatre of operations consisted of so wild and rugged a country as the Uda Rata. It was one thing to rely on such levies to aid in asserting the suzerainty of Dharmapala; it was quite another to expect them to assist in depriving their fellow-countrymen of their freedom. An appeal framed on these grounds would at most obtain a half-hearted response from the men of Kotte, while it would nerve the men of the Uda Rata to a desperate resistance.

Moreover, they did not take into account the condition of affairs in Portugal. Her subjection to Spain had brought her into undesired collision with the enemies of the latter, and the loss of the formidable squadron which she had been obliged to contribute to the Invincible Armada in 1588 had destroyed her naval power. In this very year Philip II had closed the port of Lisbon to his rebellious subjects in Holland, and the shrewd merchants of that country were preparing to wrest from Portugal her Eastern trade. Effectually to maintain their position and protect their commerce, the Portuguese required an uninterrupted stream of reinforcements from the mother country. From the Cape to Japan they tried to monopolise the entire trade, laying their hands not only on what was of real importance, but even on such petty matters as rice and coconuts. A series of factories would have sufficed to secure to them everything that was of value, but their reckless greed —as was inevitable—roused violent opposition, and the factories were soon converted into forts. Scattered as these were at wide intervals along the sea-coast, they could with difficulty render one another assistance in case of need. In consequence they were always in danger from neighbours whose hostility they had earned, and absorbed a number of men out of all proportion to the profits which they yielded. Nor could the scattered garrisons be efficiently supervised from the seat of Government. Each of the petty commanders was allowed to do much as he wished, with the result that their evil practices ruined the good name of Portugal, and intensified the feeling of hostility which prevailed on every side.

The first care of a Captain when he arrived at his station was not to correct abuses and to attend to the military duties of his post, but to ascertain what sources of income his predecessor enjoyed, and to devise fresh means of acquiring wealth rapidly. Their attitude towards the neighbouring potentates was marked by an overbearing arrogance which was far from conducive to the existence of friendly feelings, and forcible repression left a bitter feeling of resentment which necessitated increased military expenditure. The folly of each Captain had to be paid for at the expense of the State, and every day the difficulty of procuring sufficient men for the garrisons was more acutely felt.

NOTES TO CHAPTER VI

1. There is reason to think that such sacrifices did take place on a hill overlooking the beautiful town of Kandy a little more than a hundred years ago.

2. Compare what Hannibal did when he crossed the Alps.

3. De Couto, x. 10. 2.

4. This is the meaning of Devi Nuwara, of which the modern Dewundara is a corruption. A fine lighthouse now serves to guide mariners round this, the most southerly point of the Island.

5. Antonio Teixeira, who left Ceylon for Goa this same year, 1588, has this of the Sinhalese: "To conclude with the Chingalas, they are naturally inclin'd to the Exercise of Arms, in which they have, and still do perform incredible Feats, some of which I have seen."

6. After fifteen years spent at the College in the study of Latin and Divinity, Dom Joao was sent to Lisbon, where a pension was allowed to him out of the Indian Treasury. He was subsequently created a Grandee of Spain, with a seat on the Bench of Bishops and the privilege of remaining covered in the Royal Presence—"A prerogative so illustrious in itself, and so admirable in its effects, that it alone suffices to stamp its peculiar character on the dignity of the grandee," says Dr. Salazary Mendoza.

   The Prince died in 1642 and his tomb may be seen at the Oratory which he established at Telheira, in the suburbs of Lisbon. He left two illegitimate daughters by a Portuguese lady.

7. This refers to a well-known Buddhist doctrine. In the Russo-Japanese war the successes of the Japanese army were similarly ascribed to the Merits of the Emperor.

8. The word Perumal is a Dravidian title and was frequently bestowed by the Sinhalese Kings upon the higher Indian officers of the Court. The honorific, as was usually the case with Sinhalese titles, was placed after and not before the personal name.

9. This quotation is from the Rajavaliya. The exact date of the death is 8th March 1593, the Saka Era commencing with the Christian year 79-80.

10. Deification in the East is analogous to canonisation in the West, though probably it is Fear more often than Love which amongst Orientals leads to Worship. A high-born Sinhalese who was executed by the British Government for rebellion in 1818 is now a god.

11. Nikapitiya was baptised with the name of Dom Philip and accompanied his kinsman Dom Joao to Lisbon. He died in 1608 at the University of Coimbra, where he was being trained to fill a Bishopric.

CHAPTER VII

Such was the state of affairs when the Viceroy's Council resolved upon the new policy. "The Island of Ceilao," wrote de Couto, "amongst our discoveries, proved to the State what Carthage was to Rome. Little by little she consumed men and artillery to so great an amount, that she alone has used up in her wars more than all our other conquests in the East.[1]" Such a contingency, however, did not present itself to the Council. Raja Sinha had swept through the Kanda Uda Rata ; his great Kingdom had crumbled before the sword of Jayawira ; surely the Uda Rata alone could not resist the might of the Portuguese arms ? Such was their reasoning, and by the end of April 1594 six hundred of the finest troops that could be found in India had started for Ceylon under de Sousa, now appointed General Conquistador. Orders were sent to the Captain at Manar to despatch the Princess under escort to join the army of the Conquistador, while De Sousa himself with Jayawira and his nine thousand Lascarins advanced from Colombo to Menikkadawara. He had, however, failed to give sufficient consideration to the difficulties of the task which he had undertaken, the possibilities of delay, and the importance of making careful arrangements for provisioning his army. Headstrong and self-willed, he neither sought the advice of others nor gave them an opportunity of tendering it. At Menikkadawara, where the heavy rains of the south-west Monsoon necessitated a fortnight's delay, he was joined by the Princess. The narrow pass of Balane was found abandoned, and the Portuguese marched unopposed to the Mahaweli Ganga, while Wimala Dharma disappeared into the great forests on the Eastern side of the Island.

These forests have always been the shelter of a race of people known as the Veddahs or Hunters, who were as much of a puzzle in the days of the Portuguese as they are at the present hour. They represent probably the pre-Aryan aborigines, and were regarded by the Sinhalese as being of high caste. Though under-sized, they were expert in the use of the bow. Some of them had reached a certain degree of civilisation, but the majority had no fixed abode, and lived entirely on the produce of the forest and the results of the chase. They stored their meat in hollows of trees, where it was preserved by being covered with wild honey. Their language was not understood by the Sinhalese, with whom nevertheless they maintained a crude form of barter. Arrowheads and axes being their chief needs, they would obtain them by hanging up in the course of the night at the house of the village smith a model, cut out of a leaf, of what they required. In due time the finished article would be hung up at the same spot, where the Veddah would in return leave such remuneration as he thought the labour demanded. Backward as were these people, they were among the most trusted servants of the King, and in times of dire peril it was to the *Vedi Rata* or country of the Veddahs, that the Royal Family and treasure were sent for safety.

The Portuguese occupied the abandoned palace, placing a close guard over the Princess ; a Portuguese lady, four Franciscans, and a Jesuit were her only attendants, and no Sinhalese was allowed to have access to her. No greater mistake could have been committed. Such extraordinary conduct aroused the suspicions of the Sinhalese and inflamed their resentment. They feared that their country was being conquered not for the benefit of their native Princess, but for some outsider, and their innate hatred of foreign control asserted itself. Before long every man in the neighbourhood had disappeared to swell the ranks of Wimala Dharma.

Negotiations were now openly begun for the marriage of the Princess with Francisco de Silva Arcelaos, who, in addition to his other qualifications, had the reputation of being the tallest and handsomest Portuguese in India; but to the great disappointment of the General nothing came of this and de Silva returned to Manar.

Matters were not going smoothly with the Portuguese. Bands of Sinhalese were seen prowling about in the surrounding woods and mountains, and at night their signals could be clearly heard from the camp. Foraging parties were continually harassed and stragglers shot at. Every day the difficulty of obtaining provisions increased, and there were whispered suspicions as to the good faith of Jayawira. A palm leaf scroll purporting to have come from him and detailing a plot to set fire to the camp and to fall upon the Portuguese in the ensuing confusion, was produced before the General, who on the strength of it determined to put him to death. The details are obscure, but all the accounts are agreed as to the folly and injustice of the plan, and the bloodthirsty violence with which it was executed. Jayawira was invited to meet the General, and on making his appearance was confronted with the incriminating scroll; but before he could utter a word of comment the General snatched from him the golden dagger which he carried at his waist, and stabbed him three times to the heart, so that he fell down dead on the spot; whereupon the soldiery outside, learning of what had occcurred, fell to killing every one of his

Indian followers whom they could find in the camp. Then followed the agreeable task of plundering the murdered man's treasurers. The delight of the Portuguese, however, did not last long; for when morning dawned it was found that the experienced Lascarins of Jayawira had disappeared. Joy gave way to dismay, and everyone cursed the wanton rashness of the self-willed General. The great peril in which they stood was clear to all. The whole country was in arms against them; no one would sell them provisions; and at the most they could only hold out for a couple of days.

A body of 150 Portuguese and some Lascarins, who were sent out to forage, having been cut in pieces with one man alone surviving to tell the tale, the General decided to retire at dawn to Balane. By seven o'clock the vanguard of the Sinhalese army, prominent among whom were the Lascarins of Jayawira who were burning to avenge their Chief, had come in sight, and before long mountain, hill and valley were swarming with them. As they came within range they opened fire, and soon a terrible battle was raging. Each time that the Portuguese van rushed forward, the enemy recoiled, only to close in again the next moment in ever-increasing numbers. Fighting its way step by step through the narrow defiles, and with its leader killed, the van struggled on, without guides, till it was surrounded in the marsh of Danture and cut to pieces. The centre which guarded the Princess was dispersed after three hours of hard fighting; but the rear—its flank protected by a mounain—still maintained the contest. When at last the darkness of night brought some pause in the struggle, the ammunition had run short and the General himself had received no less than eight wounds. At daybreak but two hundred and twenty survivors remained, every one of whom had been wounded. Further resistance was hopeless, and they surrendered at discretion.

Wimala Dharma's victory was now complete. Dona Catherina, the admitted heiress of the Kanda Uda Rata, was a prisoner in his hands, and on the following day he led her in triumph together with the long train of his Portuguese captives, to take her place as his principal Queen in the ruined Palace at Senkadagala. By the King's orders de Sousa's wounds were carefully tended, but he soon succumbed to them, having first personally entrusted to his conqueror his youthful son, who three years later was set at liberty.

In one stern but just act of reprisal did Wimala Dharma indulge. A ghastly train of fifty Portuguese staggered into Colombo holding each other by the hand. Their ears were clipped to resemble those of the village cur; there was but one eye left to every five of them; and they had been so mutilated as to prevent their propagating their kind. Thus did he proclaim the resentment of the Sinhalese towards those who had outraged and violated their women. The remainder of the prisoners were treated with kindness; they were healed of their wounds and then employed in rebuilding the palace and fortifications of Wimala Dharma's capital.

This victory, won on the 6th of October 1594, was a magnificent achievement. The tactical skill which the experienced eye of Raja Sinha had detected in Konappu Bandara, had now reached its fruition. Many another brilliant stroke was Wimala Dharma fated to deal at the power of the Portuguese, but on this his first success he ever looked back with pride. Throughout his life the head of the Portuguese General, the first of the Conquistadors, wrought in silver, adorned his feet[2].

The intense jealousy which so frequently marred the relations of Portuguese officials towards one another, had restrained Pereira from giving de Sousa that loyal support which the latter had a right to expect. The former was still at Sitawaka, brooding over his disappointment at not being appointed to command the expedition, when the first vague rumours of the peril in which the General and his army stood—those rumours which were so soon to be confirmed by the arrival of a refugee noseless and wounded, with the terrible story of the disaster—reached him. The grief which ensued was universal and overwhelming, but the danger was too close at hand to permit of time being spent in unavailing regrets. Within a few hours the Portuguese were in full retreat towards Colombo, taking with them five elephants laden with the treasure of Raja Sinha, under the charge of Samarakon Rala, a Sinhalese noble who had embraced Christianity.

On Christmas Eve of this year Dom Jeronymo de Azavedo arrived at Colombo as successor to de Sousa, and eight days later the army, accompanied by Dharmapala in person, set out for Sitawaka. The ferocity of the reprisals with which the new General struck terror into the country as he cautiously advanced, was ominous of the principles which guided him during his eighteen years in Ceylon. Upon the army reaching the desolate capital of Raja Sinha, the ruined palace was hastily repaired for the reception of the King, and Samarakon was recalled from Galle, where he had been engaged in erecting a fort, and selected to take charge of the operations against Wimala Dharma; but his progress was slow, and he suffered more than one reverse in the execution of his difficult task.

It had by this time become clear to the Portuguese that the new policy of aggression had brought them into a position of the gravest peril. The scanty supplies both of men and money which were sent over from India, only served to enable them to cling precariously to the little that remained in their hands, at a cost which was wholly disproportionate to the results achieved. They realised, moreover, that Wimala Dharma might prove a more formidable opponent than Raja Sinha had ever been. His long residence amongst the Portuguese had made him fully aware of their circumstances, and they believed with reason that he was but patiently waiting till they had exhausted themselves in futile endeavours, to make himself master of the entire Island. Further, the already small Portuguese garrison was being reduced by disease and the lack of proper food. The hardships of the campaign against Wimala Dharma were well-nigh insupportable, and the troops were on the verge of mutiny. The success of Domingos Correa against the Prince of Uwa, who supported Wimala Dharma, secured a brief respite; but it proved to be only the lull before the storm, and every Portuguese heart was chilled when one morning in November the whisper ran round, that Correa had on the 17th of the month raised the standard of revolt against his master Dharmapala, and crowned himself King.

The meteoric career of this young man—for he was still under thirty years of age — was but typical of many in the tumultuous times which were soon to follow. The son of Edirille Arachchi, Dharmapala's Interpreter, he was, like his father, a Christian by religion. Alboquerque, the mother of whose only son was a negress, had recognised that Portugal by herself would prove unequal to the task of supplying the men whom the East demanded from her, and he deliberately set about creating a new Portuguese nation in Asia. Like Alexander the Great at Susa, he encouraged inter-marriage, and had obtained the sanction of Dom Manuel to the custom of permitting this as a special reward in the case of men of good character and exceptional services, for whom dowries were provided out of the conquered territory.

The same policy had for some time been followed in Ceylon, and the Sinhalese; who freely inter-married with the Indian races, were prepared at this period to view the innovation, if not with equanimity, at least without repugnance. Edirille Arachchi's own daughter and his two nieces were married to Portuguese husbands, and this fact increased the friendliness with which his son was regarded among the Portuguese, and caused honours to be conferred on him with a liberal hand.

There was nothing among the Sinhalese corresponding to the European Orders of Chivalry. It was not customary to group eminent men together under the emblem of a garden weed, or a household utensil. Distinguished service was rewarded by the gift of gold chains, jewels, or swords of honour, gifts which, as in the case of the Insignia of the European Orders, had to be returned to the King on the death of the recipient. A village would also be assigned to the favoured individual, either for a limited period or for ever, so that he, and in the latter case his descendants, might have a sufficient revenue, and be able to command the services of the tenants of that village for the better maintenance of their dignity. These villages were assigned with due consideration of the restrictions imposed by the rules of caste, and the grant itself was either engraved on a sheet of copper, or written on a strip of palm leaf, and authenticated by the letter *Sri*,—which stood for the Royal signature. Forgery of such a signature was punishable with death. The grantee of a village was known as the *Rala*, or Lord, of that village, and like other high-born men was never addressed by his own personal name but always by an honorific ; as Robert Knox[1] who spent twenty years of his life as a prisoner among them, has said : "It is an affront and shame to them to be called by those (personal) names, which they say is to be like unto dogs."

More than the gift of jewels and lands, the token of royal favour which was most highly prized among the Sinhalese was the grant of an honorific name. This also would be selected in accordance with the merits of the recipient, whether his distinction lay in some feat of arms, in great scholarship, or in some rare product of his handicraft. When such a name was conferred, the King with his own hand bound a thin frontlet of gold by means of a silken band to the forehead of the individual whom he sought to distinguish. In the case of humbler persons less costly materials would be employed, and an officer would be delegated to perform the task.

Domingos Correa was the personal name which, according to European custom, had been conferred on Edirille Arachchi's son at his baptism. As a youth he was known by his father's name and rank ; but his meritorious services had earned him promotion to the higher rank of Mudaliyar, and for his recent distinguished success against the forces of Wimala Dharma, the honorific of Wikramasinha· had been conferred on him, and he took his place as the first subject of Dharmapala. These accumulated favours, however, had failed to stifle in him the craving for a royal name, and on this fateful morning, in the presence of an army of seven thousand men, he assumed the title of Edirille Bandara.

Fully alive to the danger which threatened the King, the General hastened in person to Gurubewila and ordered the garrisons at Menikkadawara and Ruwanella to concentrate on Sitawaka—an order which was carried out only after excessive toil, for the whole district as far as Colombo was already in a seriously disturbed state, and the roads everywhere were blocked with trees and other hastily improvised barricades. At length after fifteen days the want of provisions began to be felt, for none were to be procured in the surrounding country, which was now seething with revolt. The King's position was one of such grave peril that orders were sent to evacuate Sitawaka and to escort him to Gurubewila. Everything in the city which could be of use to the enemy was burnt, and jars and earthen vessels full of poisoned comfits were left behind, together with casks of powder skilfully concealed under cloth, and so disposed as to take fire on the approach of the enemy to plunder them. The garrison, consisting of about three hundred Portuguese, then set out for Gurubewila and pushed on steadily for a whole day, clearing the road as it advanced and subject to constant harassment from the Sinhalese. As evening drew on a determined rush was made by the latter, headed by their elephants. Repeated volleys barely checked the attack; nearly every one of the officers was wounded, and no fewer than twenty-three of the little force were left on the field.

At last in the dead of night they reached Gurubewila. Here once again they encountered famine. For two weeks the soldiers did not have more than a plate of rice gruel each a day. So close was the blockade that not a drop of water could be obtained from the river without serious risk. The beleaguered garrison therefore decided that it was better to face the swords of the enemy than the certainty of death by starvation. Having confessed and partaken of the Sacrament, the Portuguese started from Gurubewila, the munitions being carried by elephants. The General, although ailing, went on foot; while the King and Queen were borne along in palanquins. Avoiding the usual road, which was infested by the enemy, they struck off southward into the Rayigam Korale, which had so far manifested no symptoms of disaffection. Correa immediately crossed the Kelaniya and proceeded to block the roads. The Portuguese were compelled to move step by step, cutting a path for themselves with their axes held in one hand, while the other grasped musket and pike in readiness for an attack. From every side the Sinhalese poured in upon them. The Captain in command of the rear was so badly wounded that he died within a short time ; one company of thirty men was all but annihilated, while a stalwart Sinhalese rushed at the Ensign and dragged away the standard from his grasp.

For three days and three nights the Portuguese were allowed no respite for sleep or food, and then a fierce attack was launched against the rear, while Correa himself supported by twelve elephants fell on the van and hurled it back on the centre, where the General had taken up his position. In the eagerness of pursuit friend and foe, living and dead, were rolled one over the other. One hundred and thirty-four Portuguese had been stretched in death, one hundred and eighteen were wounded, and only one hundred and twelve remained to resist the enemy, when fortunately for them, Correa himself sustained a serious hurt, whereupon his men retired.

The General had now his opportunity. Giving the signal on the two trumpets and the one drum which still remained to him—for everything else was gone—he rallied the survivors ; then, as night came on, abandoning the dead and such of the living as were helpless from their wounds, he crossed the river and continued the retreat. Iddagoda Rala, however, took Correa's place and with untiring tenacity kept up the pursuit, till he succeeded in hemming them in not far from the desecrated temple of Horana.

The last hopeless struggle for life had come, and the weary soldiers fought with a reckless valour which aroused wonder among the Sinhalese, who opened out their ranks and harassed them with their muskets. Many had already fallen, and of the survivors the greater number were wounded, when at the far end of a vast rice field there appeared the glint of steel. At the sight of what they supposed to be an addition to the forces of Correa, the hands of the Portuguese, whose ammunition was nearly exhausted, dropped momentarily to their sides. The Sinhalese also, seeing in the advancing body of men the army of Samarakon Rala, the powerful nobleman whose assistance Edirille Rala had attempted to secure, stayed their attack till he could join them. Nor had they long to wait, for Dom Diogo, the brother of Samarakon, at the head of the five hundred Christian Tupasses[5] of Colombo who formed the advanced guard of his army, charged into their midst with such impetuosity, that Iddagoda Rala himself was killed in the first onset, his head being cut off and carried away on the point of a lance, to be laid at the feet of the King whom he had betrayed. The main body under Samarakon now came in sight and the rebels drew back. Whether joy or grief prevailed at this miraculous deliverance, it were difficult to say. The exhausted remnant of the Portuguese, who for three days had been sustained mainly by hope, were now able to rest and eat. On the following day they returned to Colombo taking the King with them, not fifty out of the whole number being unwounded.

Edirille Rala now sought refuge with Wimala Dharma, who formally made over to him the Kingdoms of Kotte and Sitawaka. Their two armies soon took the field, but the arrival of fresh forces from India enabled de Azavedo to reoccupy Malwana, while Samarakon began the construction of a fort at Uduwara in the Rayigam Korale. In the hope of surprising the latter Edirille Rala made a forced march with an army of five thousand men, but was repulsed with heavy loss by Samarakon, who had been forewarned and was ready for him.

Had Samarakon been able to follow in pursuit, the matter could have been brought to a conclusion then and there, for Wimala Dharma was too far away to assist. So swollen was the river with the recent floods that it was impossible to cross it, though not a few were drowned in the attempt. Edirille Rala concealed himself among the extensive marshes in the neighbourhood, till at length after three days hunger compelled him to enter the hut of an old woman to beg for a little food. To her he revealed his identity, and the woman, aware of the heavy price which had been set upon his head, and urged by her poverty, sent a secret message to Samarakon to tell him of the whereabouts of his foe. He was soon arrested and brought before the Mudaliyar, who received him with all courtesy and ordered that his wounds should be attended to, at the same time communicating the welcome news to the General, who was now at Kalutara.

Strange thoughts must have welled in the breast of de Azavedo. He, the haughty Portuguese, in whose military prowess his King had placed so much hope, had been compelled to save his life by ignominious flight before an ill-armed Sinhalese rabble inspired by the courage and directed by the skill of his own favourite. How eagerly therefore must he have scanned the water from the foot of Kalutara Hill—once the site of a lovely temple, now prostituted by the foreigner to the uses of a fort—as three days later the boat of Samarakon appeared in the far distance,—as it seemed, immediately beneath the graceful pinnacle of the sacred Peak. Thousands crowded the bank as the barge, in which was to be seen the slenderly built Sinhalese Mudaliyar by the side of his distinguished prisoner, drew near. One last heave of the great oars by which the boat was steered brought it to the landing-place. It had scarcely touched the shore when a strange thing happened. The terrible General Conquistador was seen to rush to the water's edge, followed by the Captain of Colombo and two other officers ; seizing the Mudaliyar, they raised him on their shoulders and carried him in triumph to the General's tent, amidst a thousand *vivas* from the Portuguese, and a demonstration of delight from the Sinhalese crowded around.

The prisoner was now brought before the General and sharply questioned, but gave his answers with great coolness. His fate was soon decided upon, and the General returned to Colombo, taking the prisoner with him in massive chains. The execution was delayed forty days till the 14th of July, in the hope that Edirille Rala might be induced to reveal the place where his treasure was concealed. At last the day arrived. A theatre, fitted with such marks of mourning as his rank demanded, had been erected in the most public spot in the city. Thither he was led, and after expressing in a few words his sorrow for the evil he had wrought, paid the penalty of his treason.

The death of Edirille Rala was the signal for fresh excesses on the part of the Portuguese officials. Dharmapala was helpless in their hands, and de Azavedo and Thome de Sousa, who was now the Captain of Colombo, exchanged the cringing sycophancy which they had hitherto employed to obtain money from him, for open brutality and violence. The King estimated the revenue which his domains should yield him at nine hundred thousand cruzados in addition to which he looked for a further thirty thousand cruzados from the Customs duties. All this should have been available for military expenditure, but was as a matter of fact embezzled in every direction. By appointing his own creatures as Factors and Secretaries, de Azavedo soon brought this revenue under his own control, and no receipts were given save where it suited his plans. The trade in areca nut, which was expected to yield as much as the Customs, de Azavedo and de Sousa kept exclusively to themselves. The King protested against this interference with his Treasury, and urged that the revenue should be deposited in a chest to be lodged at the Franciscan Convent: this chest was to be locked with three keys, to be held severally by the representatives of himself and of the King of Portugal, and by the Guardian of the Franciscans, and disbursements were to be made only on the orders of his Council and in his own presence. He insisted that the large revenue which he was entitled to receive in kind from the royal tenants should, according to custom, be handed over to him personally and stored as ordered by his Council. He, moreover, emphasized the fact that the privileges granted to private parties in respect of his ports did not imply a waiver of his royal dues on exports. Further to protect himself (for he found that the Captains of Colombo were acting as if they were themselves sovereign) he proposed the appointment of a select "Cabinet" which could assist him in the work of Government, and which he suggested should consist of a Sinhalese nominated by himself, a Portuguese nominated by the King of Portugal, and a Franciscan: orders issued by this "Cabinet" were not to be questioned by anyone.

In addition to these proposals Dharmapala appealed to King Philip to safeguard the dignity of his Royal Person; and indeed it was whispered about that personal violence had been resorted to in order to wring concessions from him. He further begged for a Portuguese Secretary and a Captain of the Guard in whom he could have confidence and who should not be in any way connected with the Captain of Colombo, adding that they should be of such social standing as not to bring discredit on his Court. The insolence and the lawlessness of the Christians who had grown up with the Portuguese had in fact attained such dimensions, that special action was required to keep them under control. Moreover, the General was for ever interfering with the sentences passed by the King, and the Viceroy was unwilling to exert his authority and check his subordinate; Dharmapala therefore asked for experienced judges who would be able to give him assistance in the administration of justice. The reckless manner also in which valuable fruit trees were felled for the purposes of shipbuilding had for many years been a cause of complaint, and Dharmapala once again urged that the Portuguese officials should be forbidden to build vessels in the country at all.

Moreover, King Philip received credible information that his own ships were employed by de Azavedo more in his private trading concerns than in conveying military stores. For eight years it had not been possible to obtain any profit from the gem-yielding lands, but it was now reported that the General was making preparations to exploit them on his own behalf, and this in spite of the fact that the royal prerogative over the gems was so jealously guarded, that no pit could be opened without the special order of the King himself. Vague rumours were current about a ruby of the size of a small hen's egg, which was said to have been dishonestly put out of the way with the connivance of de Azavedo and de Sousa; and King Philip, who was very anxious that every attempt should be made to secure this rare gem for himself, sent instructions in this sense to the Viceroy. The Franciscans openly complained that torture was being employed to extract money from the wretched inhabitants of the Island; one woman who was pregnant with child died under the brutal treatment to which she was subjected by de Sousa, who extorted from her three hundred gold *Portuguezes.* It is not surprising that the Sinhalese Buddhists viewed with suspicion a religion the professed champions of which could be guilty of such conduct, and that the work of conversion was seriously hampered.

It was, however, in vain that King Philip expressed his strong dissatisfaction at the reports which reached him, and insisted that Dharmapala should be treated with every consideration. The Viceroy was negligent, and the local authorities ignored the censures passed on their conduct. In the meantime, on the 27th of May 1597, Dharmapala himself died. Though harassed, robbed and even poisoned by the Portuguese sojourners within his gates ; at one time maltreated and insulted by their Generals and Captains, at another slavishly fawned upon and caressed, as either course in turn was considered the more likely to secure the gold they lusted for ; with his subjects estranged from him by his apostasy from the ancient religion of his forefathers, and the reality of power snatched from him by his own kinsmen at the point of the sword ; he yet bore himself to the end with the contemptuous patience and dignity which befitted the last of the Kings of Lanka.

"The Most High Prince Dom Joam, by the Grace of God King of Ceilam, Perea Pandar", was interred in the Convent of Sao Francisco with all the state and solemnity which the condition of the country could afford and his lofty position demanded. For the first and last time a Sinhalese King was committed to the earth with Christian rites, and solemn Masses were sung for the repose of his weary soul.[6]

NOTES TO CHAPTER VII

1. Ceilao, que des que descubrimos aquella Ilha foi sempre ao Estado da India outra Cartago a Roma. Porque pouco e pouco foi consumindo em despezas, gente, e artilheria tanto, que ella so tem gastado com suas guerras mais, que todas as outras conquistas deste Oriente.—*De Couto.*

2. In the form of a *Virakkala* or anklet such as was worn by warriors.

3. 1659-1679. His Historical Relation, printed in London in 1681, is the most accurate description of village life in Ceylon, in the English language.

4. This means The Victorious Lion.

5. The offspring of mixed Portuguese and Sinhalese origin, who formed the trading class.

6. The fact has reluctantly to be recorded that it was left to the British Government to permit the destruction of the tomb.

CHAPTER VIII

No sooner had the grave closed on Dharmapala's mortal remains, than the Portuguese authorities took action to carry into effect the donation of his Kingdom which he had made. A Convention was summoned to meet on the 29th of September at Malwana, a pleasant village on the banks of the Kelani Ganga, whither the people were invited to send two delegates from each Korale to take the oath of allegiance to the King of Portugal. The delegates duly assembled, and after two days spent in negotiations agreed to recognise Dom Philip II as their King, provided that the Portuguese officials would guarantee on his behalf that the laws and customs of the Sinhalese should be maintained inviolate for ever. The required guarantee was given, whereupon the delegates selected eight representatives to take the necessary oath. All of them, judging from their names, were Christians; and five of them were noblemen of the late King's Court, and bore the jealously guarded title of Dom. These eight knelt round a table, and placing their hands on a Missal took the oath promising faithfulness, loyalty and vassalage to the King of Portugal and his successors on the Throne. The Captain General thereupon delivered the Royal Standard of Portugal into the hands of Dom Antao, the chief man amongst the Sinhalese nobles, and headed by this the whole assembly went in procession through the principal streets proclaiming the accession of the new King.

Situated as the Sinhalese were, the change of dynasty was not a matter of great moment. There was one thing which they recognised as being greater than the King, Custom; and this the Portuguese had guaranteed that they would preserve and respect. Philip II was to them but a name, and in their eyes the real successor of Dharmapala was Dom Jeronymo de Azavedo, who was known as the King of Malwana, from the village which he now selected as his headquarters. To him the honours due to Royalty were paid; he was saluted with prostrations, and the White Shield and Parasol of Sovereignty accompained him in his progresses through the country.

Thanks to the brilliant achievements of Jayawira, almost the whole of the territory originally administered directly from Kotte was now under the control of the Portuguese. This territory was divided into four great Provinces or *Disawani.* The most important of these was that of Matara, lying, as has already been pointed out, along the sea coast from Kotte to the Walawe Ganga, and including the most fertile portions of the ancient Ruhuna. Immediately to the North of this lay Saparagamuwa, which skirted the mountains of the Kanda Uda Rata and terminated in the same river, the Walawe Ganga. Beyond the Kelani Ganga was the Province of the Four Korales, through which ran the road to Senkadagala, and which was to be the scene of fierce struggles during the next forty years; and North again of the Four Korales, and bordering the sea on the West, lay the Seven Korales, which stretched into the great forests of the Anuradhapura district. These three last-named Provinces represented roughly the Maya Rata, exclusive of the mountain plateau. Over each Disawani was placed a great noble with the title of *Disawa,* who was responsible for its revenue, and for the administration both judicial and military. Under him were numerous grades of officials, terminating in the village headmen or

Mayorals, as the Portuguese called them. The Disawa of Matara took rank immediately after the General, and was entitled to have a white shield with a crimson centre borne before him. Samarakon, while he was in charge of this Province, maintained a force of 12,000 men from among its warlike inhabitants.

The policy of aggression so disastrously inaugurated by the expedition of de Sousa was to be carried on till 1638 relentlessly, and with a vigour which was tempered only by the incapacity of the Government at Lisbon to furnish the necessary men and material. The lines which separated the two parties in the long-drawn-out struggle were no longer blurred as they had been while Dharmapala lived. His standard of the Lion and the Sun had now betaken itself to Senkadagala, and never again floated over Colombo ; for the Sinhalese Buddhists needed a Sinhalese King, and it was the banner of Christ which led the Portuguese to battle.

The attitude of hostility towards the Buddhist priesthood which Raja Sinha had adopted during the last few years of his reign, had resulted in there being hardly a priest left in the country whose Ordination could not be called in question. This circumstance caused much distress, and Wimala Dharma's attempt to remedy it greatly increased his popularity and strengthened his hold on the people. In 1475 an embassy, sent by King Ramadhipathi of Pegu, had taken back with it to that country a body of priests ordained in the sacerdotal succession which was derived immediately from the disciples of Gautama, and which had been preserved unbroken in Ceylon. Wimala Dharma now sent an embassy to fetch a Chapter to re-establish that succession in Ceylon. This mission was successful, and in 1597 an Ordination was held in the neighbourhood of the Capital, to the great satisfaction of the people. About the same time also the Danta Dhatu, which had been removed from Delgamuwa to safeguard it from the advancing Portuguese army, was solemnly installed at Senkadagala, a three-storied edifice with a finial of gold and gems being erected within the Palace grounds for its reception. As a crowning act of piety Wimala Dharma personally went on a pilgrimage to worship the Footprint on the Peak of Samanala Kanda. On his return he had a replica of the Footprint engraved on stone and set up near the Palace. The pilgrimage was now a journey of much hazard and danger, and his grateful subjects came together from all parts to worship at this model, each one bringing with him what he could out of his scanty resources, for the repair and maintenance of the desecrated temples.

Simao Correa, brother of Edirille Rala, had been anxiously awaiting an opportunity of proving to Wimala Dharma that the favour with which the latter had received him was not unmerited; he now came with an army down the Idelgashinna Pass, which rising to a height of 4700 feet is the only means of approaching Uwa from the South; and crossing the extreme eastern limit of Saparagamuwa entrenched himself strongly on some rising ground near Katuwana, so as to threaten Matara. Samarakon hurried up to check the movement, and was soon joined by a further contingent of 2000 men from Colombo, under the command of Simao Pinhao, a Portuguese who for an act of piracy had been banished to Ceylon, where he had won for himself a great reputation in the hostilities which had been carried on in 1591 against the King of Jaffna. He was now thirty-five years of age, wiry of body and of immense strength, with a large round head made all the more striking by the blindness of one eye. Such was the prestige he enjoyed, that he was considered worthy to be rewarded with the hand of

Dona Maria Perera, the grand-daughter of Raja Sinha, and he had succeeded Edirille Rala in the chief command over the Lascarins.

A brilliant victory on the 25th of September drove Correa back within the mountains, and obtained for Samarakon the coveted insignia of the military Order of Christ, with the grant of a village yielding 500 pardaos a year. Correa's movement southwards was, however, only part of a larger plan, and simultaneously a second force had descended westward down the Balane Pass into the Four Korales, and established itself at Iddamalpane, in the midst of the rugged country through which the road runs to Senkadagala. An attempt to surprise this camp proved so disastrous a failure, that the whole of the Four Korales up to within a league of Malwana rose in arms. Pinhao hurried to the rescue, and in his absence, to add to the confusion, Affonco Moro, who was entrusted with the task of provisioning the forces engaged in the Saparagamuwa frontier and who had become infatuated with a Sinhalese woman, deserted to Wimala Dharma. Pinhao found himself unable to advance beyond Attanagala, and in spite of the urgent requests of de Azavedo, the Indian authorities were too busy with their own wars to send assistance. The latter had already by his stern severity rendered himself odious among his soldiers. His rapacity had cast off all restraint since the death of Dharmapala, while his ferocious cruelty and utter indifference to suffering showed itself more and more as the resistance of the Sinhalese increased in obstinacy. By his orders little babes were spitted on his soldiers' pikes, or mashed to a pulp between mill-stones, while their mothers were compelled to witness the pitiful sight before they themselves were put to death. Men were thrown into the water to feed the crocodiles, which at length grew so tame that they came at a signal for the welcome feast.

It is strange that the imaginative Sinhalese have not selected to deify this thick-set swarthy Iberian, with his vicious hanging under-lip, as the incarnation of all the cruelty which man born from his mother's womb can devise; for generations at least they remembered his name with a shuddering horror.

In spite of all de Azavedo's skill and determination, the task seemed too difficult a one to be accomplished with the means he had at his disposal, and in disgust he applied to the Viceroy to be relieved of his duties. His request, however, could not be granted, and the exertions of Pinhao barely served to keep the foe in check, when, fortunately for the Portuguese, Correa reappeared with an army not far from Ruwanella, and, imitating in his turn the treachery of Jayawira, deserted to the General at Malwana.

To that harassed commander no visitor could have been more welcome, but the Inquisition, which had been established at Goa in 1560, had first to be satisfied as to the soundness of Correa's views on religion. So deep, however, were the signs of contrition and repentance which he displayed, that there was no difficulty in effecting a reconciliation with that Tribunal, and he returned with a Portuguese wife to Ceylon, there to prove himself a skilled pupil in the school of de Azavedo. Hostilities were now renewed with increasing energy, and all along the border raid and counter-raid followed each other in quick succession. Affonco Moro was surprised and put to death; Etgala Tota, which commanded the passage of the Maha Oya, was occupied; and by January 1599 a strong fort was erected at Menikkadawara, which was intended to be the head quarters for the proposed operations against the Uda Rata. The surrounding country was devastated till not a tree was left standing. Pusella Mudaliyar, a disappointed place-seeker, deserted to the

Portuguese and was so well received by them, that, to prove his gratitude, he erected a wooden enclosure which he was engaged in filling with heads of the Sinhalese whom he slaughtered, when he was seized and killed by the King's men. A more terrible punishment awaited his family.

The Sinhalese being Buddhists believe that death is but one incident in a chain of existence, and that it is followed by re-birth on a higher or lower plane, in accordance with the Merit of the previous life. For a nation holding such a belief death has few terrors, though the King alone was vested with the power of inflicting this penalty. There was, however, one punishment which the King could inflict which was in the eyes of his subjects more awful even than death. Whatever the services of an individual might be, the King could not confer on him a caste superior to that in which he was born ; but the King had the terrible power to make him an outcaste.

Here and there in Ceylon were, and are still, to be found small hamlets of a people named the *Rodi*—the people of the Dirt. Their hamlet was the *Kuppayama*, the Dirt Heap. They might not till the soil, nor cross running water, nor enter a place of worship. The roofs of their squalid huts could slope only in one direction, and almost their only occupation was begging, the proceeds of which would be eked out by what the women obtained by prostitution, or the men by thieving. Their touch was pollution, and they were obliged to leave the public path at sight of any other human being, lest there should be risk of contact with them. Their shadow falling on human food rendered it unfit for consumption. The only labour at which they were employed was to skin and bury the carcases of cattle which died in the fields, and from the hides so obtained they made the ropes used for securing elephants. The better to brand with infamy the treason of Pussella Mudaliyar, orders were issued that his wife should be seized and cast to these Rodi; but in mercy she was first taken to the riverside, and given the opportunity of drowning herself.

Success was not all with the Portuguese, and many serious reverses delayed their advance towards the Uda Rata. The banks of the Maha Oya have always had an evil reputation for sickness, and at one season of the year the fish caught in its waters are considered to be poisonous. Whether as the result of eating them, or, as is more probable, in consequence of an outbreak of malaria, sickness attacked the garrison at Etgalatota, and soon the hospital at Colombo was filled to overflowing. At the same time the men of the Seven Korales led by Manuel Gomes, an officer who had served under the Portuguese, devastated the coast from Chilaw to Negombo, destroying the Churches, putting the priests to death, and appropriating the sacred vessels. The Portuguese hurried in pursuit, but though they killed the villagers without mercy on the ground of their alleged complicity, they were unable to come up with Gomes. Simultaneously the Sinhalese attacked their outposts and put their garrisons to the sword. The whole district became a scene of pitiless warfare, till at length Gomes was ambushed and killed and some semblance of quiet restored, after the struggle had lasted till May 1601. Etgalatota was, however, abandoned.

The opportune arrival of some Portuguese troops strengthened the hands of de Azavedo, and by a series of rapid movements he advanced to Ganetenna, the fort which protected the entrance to the great Pass leading within the mountains. After twenty days the Sinhalese suddenly withdrew to their main fort at Balane which commanded the Pass from above, and the Portuguese hastened to occupy the stronghold they had vacated. The toil of eight years had once more brought them to the foot of the mountain wall.

Pinhao being now placed in charge of the operations, while de Azavedo busied himself in preparing a large force for the final reduction of the Sinhalese kingdom, Wimala Dharma entered into a secret correspondence with the former, offering to make him King of the Low Country if he would desert to him. Acting on de Azavedo's instructions, Pinhao appeared to acquiesce. It was agreed that the two parties to the discussions should exchange Commissioners before whom the King and Pinhao respectively were to take an oath to abide by their promise. De Azavedo's plan was to have the King stabbed to death at this interview.

The King, however, had lived too long among the Portuguese not to know the nature of the men with whom he was dealing. One morning Manuel Dias, who as a page had been captured at the defeat of de Sousa, and who had risen into great favour with the King, appeared in the Portuguese camp. Such were his professions that even the General was persuaded that in him had been found yet another providential tool for the carrying out of the plot against the King's life. The secret was disclosed to him, and he was promised high honours if he and his men would assist in the enterprise. This he agreed to do, swearing with the utmost fervour all the oaths which were demanded of him. He was then, to allay any suspicions, provided with two Portuguese banners and two heads, and allowed to return.

The fort of Balane crowned the loftiest peak of a high range of mountains. Nature had made the position one of almost impregnable strength, and art could do but little to add to its security. The entrance to the fort was at the base of the crag and lay beneath a bastion which commanded the approach up the mountain side. This approach was by a rugged and exposed path, and was narrow, steep and long. The adjoining mountains also were strongly held, and the whole position formed the key to the Sinhalese kingdom. The train being thus laid, the General made his dispositions with the utmost caution. Detachments were posted all along the road from Colombo, and sealed orders were given that on the momentous day all were to move on Ganetenna, so that if every thing went well, the whole Portuguese army might take part in the expected triumphal entry into Senkadagala. On the night of Easter the General himself set out to watch the explosion of this tremendous mine. Evil omens accompanied him on the road, where his men were set upon by a wild elephant with a fury which to their overstrung imaginations appeared to be diabolical. Two were killed and several were injured, and the General himself escaped with difficulty, for firearms appeared to take no effect on the raging monster.

In the meantime the unsuspecting Portuguese Commissioners were allowed to enter the fort of Balane, where they were quietly arrested, while the Sinhalese hurried down to lie in ambush outside the gate of the fort. The preconcerted signal was then given, and the Portuguese, confident of victory, prepared to sally out. Pinhao, however, was as keen-witted as the King, and insisted on waiting till the dawn. His advice prevailed, and before day broke three of the Lascarins who had accompanied the Commissioners came running in with the news of their arrest. The great *coup* had failed, and nothing now remained to be done but to send back the garrisons to their stations, while Wimala Dharma showed his gratitude to Dias by appointing him Maha or Chief Mudaliyar over the heads of all his Sinhalese officers.

Outside the Island events had in the meantime been moving rapidly. In 1598 Philip III of Spain had succeeded his father on the Throne of Portugal and with his reign began that decay, political and commercial, which continued into that of his successor and destroyed the greatness of the country with a rapidity which exceeded even that which had characterised its growth.

Three years earlier, in 1595, the Hollanders had despatched four of their vessels to the East. These ships penetrated as far as Bantam and returned home after an absence of two and a half years, a Factory having in 1597 been established in Java. Various Companies were soon on foot to secure the Eastern trade, and in 1602 their United East India Company was incorporated. On the 31st of May of that year Joris van Spilbergen, commanding two vessels of the Hollanders, appeared off the Eastern coast of Ceylon, and after some preliminary negotiations with the King set out on the 6th of July for the Court. A ceremonious reception was everywhere accorded to him, and as he approached the Capital messengers arrived hourly with inquiries after his health and presents from the King. On reaching the Mahaweli Ganga Spilbergen was met by Manuel Dias, who escorted him in procession to Senkadagala, at this time a small town of about 2500 inhabitants, the majority of whom were traders from South India. The same afternoon three saddled horses arrived from the palace with a summons for him to appear before the King. He was received with all the rigid formality of an Oriental Court, and after making his obeisance laid on the carpet for the royal inspection the presents which he had brought. These were then removed to within the Palace to be shown to the Household, while the King, who was dressed in white, rose and walked about conversing with Spilbergen and his companions, after which permission was at length given them to withdraw.

On the following day a second audience was accorded, at which the Hollander combined the shrewdness of the tradesman and the suavity of the courtier with such success, that the gratified King presented to him all the pepper and cinnamon in the Royal Stores, apologising for the smallness of the quantity and explaining that not only did he never trade in these articles, but that he had even caused the cinnamon trees to be destroyed, that they might not attract the Portuguese to his dominions. Daily interviews followed, for the King could not hear too much of this new people, their customs and their religion, and the entertainment of the visitors was concluded by a banquet at the Palace, at which everything was arranged in European fashion.

Eating does not occupy the same position with the Oriental that it does with the Western nations. As a necessity of the body, something to be ashamed of rather than otherwise, it is regulated soberly and discreetly. The Tropics have not those short days of winter confining men within doors, wherein the chief if not the only source of pleasure in ruder times was to gather round smoking joints of meat in the cheering warmth of a great log fire. The sun itself conveys to the body so much heat, that little has to be provided by man in the way of food. The Oriental, moreover, realised that meat was not essential for strength, for the strongest beast on earth, the elephant, eats no meat. The teachings of the Buddha against the taking of life had made the Sinhalese almost a race of vegetarians,[1] and such little meat as they did use was so prepared as entirely to remove all suggestion of blood. They had inherited the Hindu reverence for the cow, and none would eat beef save the outcaste. Fishing was carried on along the coast, and salted fish was used by all ; but the occupation itself was regarded with disfavour. Rice was the main article of food, although accompanied invariably by vegetables, of which an abundance could be found even in the forest, and which were cooked in a variety of ways. Numerous savouries stimulated the jaded appetite, and spices, which served both as a disinfectant and a digestive, were largely employed; as also was curd, for the value of whey was known to the East many centuries before Elie Metchnikoff had thought about it. The King took his meals alone, seated on a stool before a low table covered with a white cloth. On the table was laid a golden platter, over which was spread a tender plantain leaf taken unopened from the heart of a freshly-cut tree. Twenty or thirty dishes were usually prepared and brought to the King in the pans in which they were cooked, and whatever he selected was served to him with a ladle by a nobleman who had a muffler tied round his mouth. Ripe fruit of the choicest kinds, brought from localities which had a special reputation for them, completed the simple repast.

It was not, however, to a meal of this kind that Spilbergen was summoned, for the King had lived long enough among the Portuguese to understand the point of view of the European. Rich tapestries hung from the walls, and handsome Spanish chairs were ranged about the tables. At the conclusion of the banquet the Admiral presented Wimala Dharma with a portrait of Prince Maurice on his charger, which the King ordered to be hung up in his own room, that he might see it the more frequently. As a final and unique honour the Hollanders were permitted an interview with the Queen, who appeared in European dress. The main portion of the costume of a Sinhalese lady leaves the loom in the shape and size required for use, and depends for its charm not on the skill of the tailor, who occupies a very insignificant position in the scheme of society, but on the beauty of the material employed and the skill with which it is draped about the person. In honour, however, of the visitors, the Queen discarded for the occasion her long white cloth picked out with gold, and instead wore a dress cut according to the Portuguese fashion with which her residence at Manar had no doubt rendered her familiar.

However bitter may have been the hostilities which existed between Wimala Dharma and the Portuguese, both King and Queen had strong European sympathies. The same feeling prevailed among the courtiers, amongst whom were included not only refugees from the Low Country, but also Portuguese and Mesticos. The King welcomed anyone who could wield a good sword, and his Attapattu or bodyguard included Portuguese, Moors, and Kaffirs. Portuguese names were common among the nobility, and the language was as familiar to the King as his mother tongue. The Portuguese jacket and Portuguese cap or *barrete*, which, though distorted almost beyond recognition, still obtain in the Uda Rata, are a legacy bequeathed by Wimala Dharma. For a whole century Portuguese ideas moulded the fashions of the Court at Senkadagala, till they in turn gave way to the Dravidian influences which asserted themselves during the last century of its existence.

The visit of the Hollanders had been so acceptable to the King, that he declared with Oriental hyperbole that if the Prince Maurice desired to erect a fort in his dominions, he himself together with his Queen would assist in person in carrying the stones for the work ; adding that the name of his own kingdom was from that day forth Flanders.

When at length Spilbergen set out for the coast, he left behind him as one of his return presents for the gifts with which he had been loaded, two of the musicians who had accompanied him to the Court—a present greatly appreciated by Wimala Dharma, who had acquired a taste for Western music. Music indeed, as it is understood in the West, is not to be found in the East, and Ceylon was even more backward in that respect than India. The *Vina*, a primitive form of violin, was thought highly of, and there was also a small drum with a soft note which was used to accompany singing; but apart from these the majority of the instruments known to the Sinhalese were instruments of percussion, used to create sound rather than melody. For military purposes the drum is an unrivalled instrument, and in matters of ceremonial courtesy took the place which the cannon holds to-day among European nations. It was an essential element in the processions of the Hindu gods worshipped in Ceylon, and attached to each Dewale there were tenants whose duty it was to accompany their images with this mark of honour. Not least, in the medico-religious ceremonies of the Sinhalese (devil-dances, as they are called to-day), the aim of which was often to work the individual into a condition of ecstasy, the drum proved itself as effective an instrument as is, for a similar purpose, the band of the Salvation Army.

In the more temperate climates of the West dancing is indulged in not less for the pleasure of the performer than that of the spectator. Amongst Orientals, however, it has only the latter object. It was unheard-of for women to dance at all, except in the case of the outcaste Rodi who travelled from place to place dancing and tossing brazen trays in the air for the purpose of earning a scanty livelihood, or of those women who held their lands on the condition of performing a religious dance in the Dewales at the great festivals. There were, however, dancing men among the palace musicians who were trained to dance while accompanying themselves on the drum, and who would at the same time extemporise songs for hours on end on given themes, in the manner which prevailed among the Greeks of the time of Theocritus. Singing was indeed a source of great delight among the Sinhalese. As Ribeiro says, "Their singing is very soft and gives pleasure. Though we did not understand what they said, yet we used to leave off any occupation in which we were engaged to listen to them, for their verses were sonorous and the syllables well rounded."

A few months later, on the 28th of November, the Vice-Admiral Seebald de Weert arrived in command of another flotilla. He was hospitably received at the Court, and invited to assist in an assault on Colombo which the King was then contemplating. This he promised to do on condition of being properly recompensed for his trouble. On the 14th of January he sailed away for Achin taking with him a great quantity of cinnamon and pepper, a present from the King, who however assured him that "he himself was no merchant but a soldier, who thought neither of the building of houses nor of planting nor of anything else by which he should be able to make profit, but only of how he should protect his country."

NOTES TO CHAPTER VIII

1. "According to the exaggerated notions of their religion, they do dot kill anything that has life, not even venomous snakes. They eat no meat of any kind, neither flesh meat nor fish, even if they happen to be ravenously hungry." *Father Morales* in 1552.

CHAPTER IX

In the meantime de Azavedo was laying his plans for yet another attempt to capture the fortress of Balane; for he was confident that the superior numbers at his disposal and the demoralisation which he believed to have been created among the Sinhalese by the last few years of desperate struggle, would prevent a repetition of the misfortunes which had overwhelmed his predecessor. In January 1603 his army took the field and advanced to Ganetenna, whence roads were opened to the base of the mountain on which the Balane fort was built. Batteries were stationed on the adjoining heights, and a regular siege was organised; but such was the strength of the position that little progress was made. At length on the first of February a villager appeared in the Portuguese camp and offered to point out a secret path leading up to the stronghold. His offer was accepted, and a number of men were sent with him to surprise the place. Led by their guide they toiled through the night up a steep and precipitous track, and at daybreak reached the walls only to find that the Sinhalese had disappeared.

The exultant Portuguese occupied the fort and celebrated the event by a solemn service of thanksgiving. The lofty eminence whence so keen and vigilant a watch had been kept on the approach to the last refuge of the Sinhalese was now, after nine years of fiercely waged warfare, in their hands, and the richest portion of the Low Country of Ceylon lay stretched out at their feet, as if depicted on a map. Far away to the west could be seen the glitter of the sunlight reflected on the waves of the Indian Ocean; the perpendicular side of Nav Gala, crowned by the great slab which overhangs its base, together with the graceful and castellated mass of Utuwan Kanda, occupied the middle distance; while right below them were their forts of Ganetenna and Buddassagoda, with Attapitiya nestling beneath Dewanagala, itself overshadowed by the sombre grandeur of Ura Kanda and Batala Gala. They saw themselves in imagination masters of the whole of the beautiful island, and grumbled at the apathy of their General in not pressing home his victory.

De Azavedo, however, was suspicious; the mysterious disappearance of the Sinhalese made him uneasy, and he determined to wait for the arrival of the experienced Pinhao before taking any further action. Nor were his fears groundless, for on the fifth morning his Lascarins, without whom the Portuguese were helpless in the mountains, deserted in a body to the King. It seemed as though de Azavedo's army was after all to share the fate of de Sousa's. Messengers were secured by heavy bribes to warn the garrisons on the road to Colombo, and eighty picked men were told off to hold the passage by which the enemy was expected, whilst with anxious haste the Portuguese made their arrangements for the withdrawal. Dawn revealed the fact that the surrounding mountains and valleys were filled with hostile Sinhalese, whose drums and trumpets rent the air. The desperate efforts of the gallant eighty kept them at bay till midday, and at three o'clock in the afternoon the Portuguese began, with the deepest despondency, to evacuate the fortress, abandoning everything save the munitions of war. The Sinhalese swooped down like vultures to plunder the baggage, and were soon in hot pursuit, regardless of the terrible fire which was directed against them. The Portuguese were already two-thirds of the way down the mountain, when to their intense relief the banners of Pinhao, who was hurrying to their assistance, were seen in the distance, and by sunset they had succeeded in reaching the foot, though with the loss of nearly a hundred in killed and wounded. There a message was received from Samarakon urging an immediate retreat and warning the General that if he did not adopt this course, within three days there would not be a Portuguese alive in the Island, inasmuch as the whole country was in arms.

Samarakon himself had started with the utmost speed to the General's assistance. On the road a deputation waited on him and invited him to assume the Sinhalese Crown, assuring him that all were prepared to lay down their lives for him, and pointing out that never before had there been so favourable an opportunity of driving the Portuguese out of the country. Should he elect, however, to cast in his lot with the foreigner, they were unable to follow him, for they had already pledged themselves to strike a blow for the common liberty. It was a great temptation, but the noble Sinhalese scorned the idea of disloyalty to the heir of his late master, Dharmapala. He sent private information of what had occured to Pinhao, whilst informing the conspirators that Pinhao too was on their side, but that it had been decided not to take action before arriving at Sitawaka. He therefore begged them for the present to observe secresy in regard to their plans.

The Portuguese had by now reached Ganetenna, whence stage by stage they retreated to Sitawaka, the Sinhalese harassing them all the way just as Edirille Rala had done on their flight from Gurubewila. Three hundred Portuguese corpses marked the road when on the fifteenth day they crossed the broad

Kelani Ganga and reached Malwana. Here another horrible surprise awaited them, for the Sinhalese had already attacked and sacked the place, and nineteen grinning heads swinging from a tree greeted Dom Jeronimo de Azavedo as he returned to the palace to which his cruelties had given so evil a name. The Nestorian Christians from India, who were fighting side by side with the Portuguese, and who were rendered useless by the lack of the opium to which they were accustomed, had been cut down almost to a man.

For the second time de Azavedo, one of the most eminent of Portuguese warriors in the East, had been driven in headlong flight before the Sinhalese. The loss in men was serious, but the loss of prestige was more serious still, and its effects were to be seen for many years to come. Many of the officers and men who had taken part in the retreat, worn out with their exertions and finding themselves without a pardao, took the opportunity to desert to Colombo. To these last the General, who was anxiously laying his plans at Malwana, addressed on the 15th of March a letter, exhorting and commanding them to rally round him there, and adding "I await you here with a mat for my table, with bread and beef for dainties; that is all that the Sinhalese have left to me".

The appeal was not made in vain, and another army was already in the field when Anthony Baretto, one of Samarakon's servants who had risen to prominence during the retreat, deserted to the Sinhalese with a large body of troops, and moving skilfully in front of them blocked their advance. Before long every one of the outposts which had been occupied at such cost, and which were intended to protect the communications of a triumphant army operating in the Kanda Uda Rata, had fallen into the hands of the King, their garrisons being either put to the sword or distributed as prisoners among the royal villages. Of the conquests of Jayawira everything except Galle, which the personal influence of Samarakon kept for the Portuguese, was lost.

The walls of Colombo were in a ruinous state and everyone now set himself with desperate energy to the task of repairing them. Experience had, however, shown that it was almost impossible for the Sinhalese, who had no siege artillery, to wrest Colombo from the hands of the Portuguese so long as the sea remained open. If the Sinhalese had had but a few vessels with which to blockade the harbour, the Portuguese could scarce have avoided destruction.

It was a critical moment in the history of the Island, for on the 25th of April de Weert arrived at Batticaloa with the much-needed ships. On the first of June news was brought to the Hollanders that the King, who had a few days before captured Menikkadawara, was close at hand; whereupon de Weert went forward to meet him accompanied by all his officers and by two hundred of his men. Cordial greetings were exchanged with Wimala Dharma, after which they proceeded together to Sampanturai. There the majority of the Hollanders were dismissed with orders to return to their ships, but instead of doing so they went about the town and got drunk.

This, the ruling vice of the Hollanders, was to exercise so profound an influence upon the subsequent destiny of the Sinhalese race, that it is necessary at this point to indulge in a short digression with regard to it. The Portuguese, whatever the Kaffir troops they brought with them may have been, were very temperate, and two thousand years of Buddhism, with its prohibition of the use of intoxicants, had well-nigh made the Sinhalese a nation of total abstainers.[1] "Drunkenness they do greatly abhor," wrote Robert Knox, "neither are there many that do give themselves to it." A certain amount of spirits was distilled from coconut "toddy," the sap extracted from the inflorescence of the coconut palm before it has burst its sheath; but this was mainly for export. The high-caste man who touched the degrading stuff was socially disgraced, and the possibility of its use by women appears to have scarcely presented itself to the minds of the Sinhalese. Water was the universal drink except among one or two of the lower castes, who utilised for the purpose the toddy of some kinds of palms; and that craving for a stimulant or sedative which appears to be inherent in man was among the Sinhalese satisfied by the use of the betel leaf, which was obtained from a cultivated vine belonging to the pepper family. This was masticated, together with a slice of the astringent arecanut and a pinch of lime, by all classes and at all times, and occupied in the social life of the Sinhalese a position analogous to that of the pot of tea among the Japanese.

The betel leaf was what the maiden handed to her lover; it was the refreshment offered to every guest; it accompanied every invitation to take part in a harvesting or to attend a marriage; and it often concealed the bribe with which the petitioner sought an interview with the official. The nobleman on a journey would be accompanied by a long-haired page carrying a large embroidered betel-bag slung over his shoulder, while he himself held in his hand the richly chased box of gold or silver which contained the lime. This mild stimulant largely removed the desire for intoxicants, which madden the Oriental, and was thus a factor of no small importance in regulating the civic life of the country. The use of the betel leaf in place of alcohol rendered it possible to control the impulsive Sinhalese by a system of penal law which in its mildness was several centuries in advance of that which at the time prevailed in Europe ; and because drink was one of the contributory causes of the subsequent decline of the Sinhalese, the arrival of de Weert and his drunken myrmidons marks an epoch in the history of the country.

The exact details of the tragedy which followed are not known. The King, despite the annoyance he felt on learning that contrary to his express wishes the Portuguese prisoners captured in the neighbourhood of Batticaloa had been set at liberty, granted a formal audience to de Weert, whereat the latter pressed him to visit him on board ship. This, however, the King was not willing to do. The question of an attack on Galle was then discussed, and the King urgently requested the Hollanders to sail thither ; he himself, he said, must return to the Capital, where he had left the Queen alone. De Weert, who was under the influence of liquor, roundly declared that if the King could not visit his ships, he for his part would not sail to Galle, and concluded with a coarse remark regarding the Queen. The exasperated monarch haughtily turned his back upon the drunken sailor, bidding the attendant nobles to "Bind that dog." Four of them laid hands on him, whereupon, catching up his gun and shouting for assistance, he attempted to escape from the room. One of the nobles, however, seized him by the hair, while another drawing his sword struck off his head.

The King had not been a witness to the occurrence and was greatly distressed at the news; but the mischief could not be remedied, and it was decided that the best course, now that the leader was dead, was to kill all. Orders were given to this effect; the drunken Hollanders were hunted out of the houses, and over fifty of them were put to the sword though some escaped by swimming to the ships. One young man who was spared was taken into the King's service.

The news of these happenings, no less tragic than unexpected, produced consternation on board the ships; but the Hollanders were convinced that there had been some misunderstanding, and the following morning a Sinhalese was sent ashore with a letter. Shortly afterwards a curt epistle was received from the King. "He who drinks wine," wrote the latter, "is vile. God has wrought justice. If you desire peace, it is peace. If war, war."

A submissive reply was promptly despatched to the King who was already on his way back to his capital, and a fortnight later a messenger arrived from him with a letter in which he asserted that his attitude towards the Hollanders was still unchanged and invited them to assist him to capture Colombo and Galle. The negotiations, however, proved fruitless and on the 28th of July the fleet sailed away without having effected anything. The folly of a drunken Hollander had prevented the expulsion of the Portuguese from Ceylon.

Hostilities still dragged on. Samarakon, who had been sent to assist the Portuguese, was unable to effect anything, and de Azavedo, dissatisfied with the conduct of the great Sinhalese, had him arrested and sent in chains to Goa whence he never returned to his native land. No events of importance marked the remainder of the year, for the nations were too much exhausted for action; but early in 1604 the complexion of affairs was entirely altered by the death of Wimala Dharma. Continual exposure had wrought its effects on that frame of steel, and frequent attacks of fever warned him that he had not long to live. The weary King began to set his house in order. Summoning his Ministers to his chamber he presented to them the Regent during the minority of his son Astana Bandara, his cousin Senerat, who had doffed the robes of the priesthood, and called on them to promise him their support and allegiance. The aged chiefs stood silent, the tears flowing down their stern war-worn faces, while the Chief Minister made the required promise in the name of all. They then withdrew, and the still youthful Queen with her infant children were called in and solemnly entrusted to the care and protection of the Regent.

A mile to the North of the modern town of Kandy lies the hill of Asgiriya. The curious visitor who has the courage to approach it through its squalid surroundings will see little beside a small patch of bare grass, beyond which a few aged trees, with heavily-scented flowers of the colour of ivory, overshadow a small temple of massive stone. Beneath is the railway tunnel from which now and again rise puffs of sooty smoke; and close by stands a Christian school—symbolic, perhaps, of the possibility of revivifying a moribund race. It was on this spot that for centuries the rulers of Senkadagala were cremated.

Here a great pyre was raised, heaped with the richest spices of the East. Accompanied by the shrill wailing of fifes and the dreary roll of the funeral drums, the body was borne in slow procession followed by thousands who had known well that bearded face and tall figure. In a few hours nothing remained but a heap of ashes; though when they came to be removed, the heart—that brave heart which had ever throbbed responsive to the call of country—was found untouched by the fire.

A sigh of thankfulness rose up from Portuguese Asia as the Sword of State was transferred to the hesitating grasp of the ex-priest. A veil of obscurity now descended on events in the Uda Rata, which during the next seven years was but rarely lifted to permit of a glimpse of what was being carried on behind it. King Philip was thoroughly weary of the war. He suggested that a diversion might be effected among the Sinhalese by setting up as a rival claimant to the throne the Prince Dom Joao, who was still being educated at the College of the Kings at Goa, but his suggestion was not adopted. Instead, the Prince was shortly afterwards sent to Europe. The Viceroy for his part was busy preparing a great expedition intended to crush the rising power of the Hollanders in the Southern Seas, and he instructed de Azavedo to confine himself, till his return, to Colombo and Galle.

In the meantime bitter and by no means groundless complaints had begun to be heard on every side against the oppression and tyranny exercised by the Portuguese officials over the natives, who had been led to expect from them purer justice than that which they had received at the hands of their own Chiefs. The revenue derived from the pearl fishery was not properly accounted for, and munitions of war were being systematically smuggled into the enemy's country even from the Portuguese settlements in South India. Above all there was the haunting fear of the machinations of the Hollanders, whose ships had been already seen off the Western Coast, and who were known to be supplied with information by spies in Colombo.

With the death of Wimala Dharma, however, there came a change. The General reported to King Philip that the policy of concentration recommended by the Viceroy would have disastrous effects on the minds of the Sinhalese who still remained loyal to the Portuguese power, and that it would at the same time enable the Hollanders to obtain a footing in the Island. He was confident, he wrote, that the immediate addition of three hundred soldiers to his army would enable him to conquer Ceylon once for all. King Philip agreed. The work of conquest had already consumed so much blood and treasure that it was no longer possible to draw back. A strict inquiry was ordered into the conduct of the peccant officials, while instructions were issued that the despatch of vessels from the suspected ports should be closely supervised, and the coast from Manar to Galle blocked to prevent all external intercourse with the Sinhalese, who would thus be deprived of certain of the necessaries of life which the Island itself did not produce.

Of these not the least important was cloth, the bulk of what was used in Ceylon being imported from India. Secondly, there was opium which was consumed in great quantities by the Sinhalese, who found in it a powerful preventive against several of the diseases incidental to a hot and excessively damp country, though it does not appear that the abuse of the drug was common. The most pressing need of all, however, among the people of the highlands was salt, which was not found in their country and which was obtained mainly from the salt-pans beyond the Walawe Ganga, another source of supply being the Chilaw district, while a fair quantity came from Trincomalee and Jaffna. This local salt, which was conveyed to the Uda Rata on the backs of bullocks during the dry season, was usually obtained by the process of solar evaporation of the brine—a process which had been made use of in China for untold ages, and which was probably imported from that country. The demand, however, was greater than the supply, and had to be met by large shipments from South India. The Portuguese were of opinion that if the supply of these three commodities could be cut off for a period of three years the Sinhalese would be forced into submission, and King Philip ordered that every effort should be made to carry this plan into effect.

Orders were also given that the fortifications both of Galle and of Colombo should be strengthened without delay, for the former by its position as the most southerly port in this part of Asia was of the greatest value for the maintenance of the trade with the Southern Seas; and it was feared that the Hollanders would attempt to capture the place. The King was indeed anxious that a dockyard and arsenal should be constructed there, but was thwarted by the local authorities, who could not be induced to take the necessary action. The Customs duties, the revenues from Manar, and the tribute of several of the South Indian Princes were, however, placed at the disposal of the General for the purposes of the war; and the Bishop of Cochin,[2] under whose spiritual jurisdiction Ceylon had been placed, was invited to visit the Island no less to encourage the soldiers than to see that the natives were treated with justice and clemency by the officials, who were strictly prohibited from engaging directly or indirectly in mercantile pursuits.

Nor was Senerat the only foe; Satan had to be combated as well; for not only was the possession of a country of vast resources and of great importance to the Indian Dominion at stake, but also the souls of thirty thousand professing Christians, whose salvation would be in jeopardy should they fall into the hands of their infidel brethren, or into those of the heretical Hollanders. Amongst other things it was ordered that no Sinhalese should be baptised till he had been decently catechised and instructed, for the King had been informed that evil results had arisen from laxity on this point. Six years before his predecessor had given instructions that a larger number of priests should be sent to the Island, and that those who were engaged there, whether in education or in preaching the gospel, should render themselves thoroughly familiar with the native languages ; for preaching through the medium of an interpreter had not been found to be a success. Accordingly in April 1602 the Jesuits, who had been established for some time in India, sent a few of their members to begin work in Ceylon. They were, in spite of the opposition of the Franciscans, welcomed by de Azavedo, [3] whose own brother had been a very distinguished member of the Society. De Azavedo built for them at his own expense their *Casa* in Colombo, and assigned to them the sixty-two villages which had formed the domain of the Munnesseram Temple, together with some valuable royal villages. The Dominicans and the Augustinians soon afterwards followed, and an attempt was made to apportion the various spheres within which each of the Orders was to operate, though it was found in practice that this division was not adhered to.

Something more than missionary enthusiasm, however, was required if the power of the Portuguese was to be maintained in Ceylon, and this the political authorities at Goa were unable to supply ; for all available resources were diverted towards the expedition which in 1606 the Viceroy Dom Affonco de Castro led in person to the Southern Seas. With the Viceroy went Samarakon Rala, to whom the King had tried to make amends for the gross injustice which he had received at the hands of de Azavedo. Orders had been issued that the Sinhalese noble should be treated with every consideration, that all the property which had been taken from him should be restored, and that the requirements of himself and of his family should be amply provided for. He was even appointed Captain of Goa, a position which gave him a seat in the Viceroy's Council of State and of War[4]—a distinction such as probably has never during the next three hundred years, been conferred by a European Government on an Oriental.

The fleet which accompanied the Viceroy was the largest that ever set sail from Goa. A series of obstinately contested fights ended in the total failure of the Portuguese to achieve their object, and the Viceroy himself died of a broken heart at Malacca in June 1607. It was therefore out of the question to expect help from Goa, while, as the Councillors of Colombo wrote to inform the King, Ceylon was "eating up the State by the sackful." In the three years preceding 1609 only fifty men were received from India, and all that de Azavedo was able to do was to send two expeditions a year into the enemy's country to kill whomsoever they could and to bring back what food they could lay their hands on. Pinhao and Correa,[5] together with Dom Constantino Navaratna, a scion of the royal family who had succeeded Samarakon at Matara, usually headed these expeditions, but for which the Portuguese would have had little enough to eat.

The disappointment of de Azavedo found vent in an increase of ferocity, while the actions of the minor officials went unchecked, each assuming to himself such authority as he found convenient. The natives of the country were ground down under exactions of terrible severity; their venerated temples were ruthlessly destroyed on every side; and while the services of loyal men like Samarakon were so ill requited, renegades of the stamp of Correa were received with open arms, and promoted to positions of great power and responsibility. The fortifications of Colombo were so neglected that cattle could easily make their way over the walls; there was no hospital worthy of the name, and the soldiers were dying of hunger and privation, with their wages unpaid, and in clothes that were little better than raw hides. The Frenchman Pyrard de Laval, who visited the Island in 1608, has left it on record that the Portuguese soldiers were mostly criminals and exiles, and that only women of ill-fame were sent thither. What he adds is therefore the less surprising: that "the Sinhalese will not kill their Portuguese prisoners, but merely cut off their noses and send them back; for they say that they will not have their soil polluted by the bodies and blood of foreigners."

It was, on the other hand, a common occurrence for soldiers who had committed criminal offences to desert to the Sinhalese to avoid the consequences of their acts. To meet this difficulty Colombo had been created a sanctuary, in which capacity it was succeeded by Galle in 1610. The offender who took sanctuary could not be arrested except it were for *lese majeste*, false coining, or the murder of a sheriff or judge.

The twenty years prior to 1610 had cost twelve thousand Portuguese lives and half a million cruzados of treasure, but the end seemed to be further off than ever, a condition of things which the writer of a secret memorial on the subject addressed to King Philip finds no difficulty in explaining. "I assert that the ultimate reason is," he says, "that we Portuguese are evil Christians, with little fear of God."

Under such circumstances it is not surprising that the King should express his bitter disappointment at the failure of an undertaking which he had so much at heart. And yet a more favourable opportunity for finishing the work could hardly have been demanded, for in 1609—in which year also Senerat, who had married the widowed Queen and crushed all resistance, consolidated his position by assuming the Crown—a twelve years' truce had been concluded with the United Provinces, a truce which constituted a formal admission of the independence of the latter.

It was not, however, till 1611 that the Indian authorities were able to place seven hundred soldiers at the disposal of de Azavedo. In August of that year he took the field in person, and in spite of some resistance at the passage of the Mahaweli Ganga, occupied and burnt the capital, which was found deserted. After laying waste the countryside he returned to Colombo, leaving a garrison at Balane.

Ever since the death of Wimala Dharma, King Senerat had maintained a good understanding with the Hollanders; and on the 8th of March 1612 Marcellus de Boschouwer, their Under Factor, presented himself at the Sinhalese Court, armed with letters from the Estates General and Prince Maurice of Orange addressed to "The Most Illustrious and Most Noble Emperor of Ceylon, Our Beloved Brother in the Wars." So successful was his mission that on the 11th of May a treaty was entered into between the Sinhalese and the Hollanders by which the two contracting parties agreed to assist each other against the Portuguese, while the Hollanders were given permission to erect at Kottiyar on the east of the Island a fortress which would give them the control of the finest anchorage in the Indian Ocean. Commerce between the two races was to be unrestricted, each side, however, being subject to the exclusive criminal jurisdiction of its own officers. The King further ageed to confer on the Hollanders the monopoly of the trade in cinnamon, precious stones and pearls, though he reserved to himself the right to coin money. It was also provided that two Hollanders should have seats in his Council of war.

Such favour indeed did Boschouwer find with the King, that the latter could not be induced to permit him to return. The golden headband of a

Sinhalese dignitary was conferred upon him, and he took his place among the nobles of Senerat's Court with the name of Migamuwe Rala, from the seaport of Negumbo which was granted to him for his support.

NOTES TO CHAPTER IX

1. Three hundred years of European influence have brought about a change, and the revenue derived by Government out of the arrack and toddy trade for the year 1918-19 amounted to Rs. 9,265,315. To this must be added the revenue obtained from foreign spirits and cordials.

2. This bishopric was created by a Bull of Paul IV. dated 4 February 1557.

3. Writing to the Viceroy on 26th of November 1602 to thank him for sending the Jesuits, de Azavedo says: "Your lordship will have great merit before God our Lord for this work." Owing largely to de Azavedo's exertions the Jesuits were enabled in 1605 to open a College in Colombo, where the scions of the Sinhalese nobility were taught reading, writing, singing, divinity, *bons custumes* and Latin. See *Ceylon Antiquary, Vol. II.*

4. Under a Royal Order of 1604 this consisted of the Viceroy as President, the Chief Ecclesiastical Functionary, the Chancellor of the State, the Vedor da Fazenda, the Captain of Goa, and the Secretary of the State.

5. Hieronymus Gomez, writing on the 29th of December 1609, gives us the following account of an incident which took place on one of these expeditions. "Two hundred men, women and children were taken. Gathering them all into a field, Simon Correa, a Sinhalese Captain, gave orders to beat them to death. The poor people all kept together like sheep, and bore the blows without running away or stirring, without a sigh or a groan. A Portuguese Captain noticed that there were among them some innocent children in the arms of their mothers, and since he could do nothing to save their temporal lives, he wished to give them spiritual life, and hence he baptised them all. They were afterwards beheaded to give them a more lenient death." *Ceylon Antiquary II, 22.* Correa was as ardent an admirer of the Jesuits as his instructor de Azavedo, and presented to them a coconut garden.

CHAPTER X

In December 1612 de Azavedo sailed away to assume duties as Viceroy at Goa. Although from a military standpoint his eighteen years in Ceylon had been a record of failure, during that period there had been carried out certain administrative changes which it is desirable to notice at this stage.

In 1608 the King had despatched to Ceylon Antao Vaz Ferreira, a Fidalgo of the Household, with the title of Vedor, and a Commission to re-organise the Fiscal affairs of the island. Five native officials of high rank were attached to him, one at least of whom had served at the Court of Raja Sinha. The best known of them was Alagiyawanna, who had now become a convert to Christianity, under the name of Dom Jeronimo, no doubt in compliment to the General himself. A delightful story has been preserved by Tavernier as current in India in his time with reference to this conversion. At Alagiyawanna's request the Jesuits had given him a copy of the New Testament. In six months' time he came back to them and expressed his desire to be converted, adding however that there was one matter which troubled him : he could not find, he said, by his reading, that Jesus Christ ever took money of anyone, while the missionaries took all that they could get, and never buried or baptised unless they were well paid. The question was a not unnatural one from a Buddhist, whose priests could receive no payment for any services they might render ; but the Jesuits do not appear to have had much difficulty in overcoming his scruples. It is interesting to note that his new duties did not prevent Alagiyawanna from following the Muse he loved; his greatest poem, the *Kusa Jataka,* which is based on one of the Birth Stories of the Buddha, was issued in 1610 and deservedly holds a prominent place in Sinhalese literature.

The most urgent duty which fell to the Vedor was the preparation of a *Tombo,* or Register, of all the districts which acknowledged European rule. The carefully organised and elaborate system of land tenure—under which each parcel of cultivated ground was rendered liable, in accordance with the caste of its possessor, to contribute its quota of service towards the maintenance of the common wealth—had for centuries reduced to a minimum the actual pecuniary expenditure on administration and defence of the central government. The system depended for its success on the accuracy of the Tombo being beyond dispute, and the elaborate inquiries which it necessitated engaged Ferreira for several years. Each Korale was visited in turn by the Vedor, who summoned a few of the notables of the District to assist him in scrutinising the lists which the *Mohottalas* or Secretaries of the Disawas produced. The descriptions of the various holdings, together with the titles of those who held them, the income yielded by each, and the dues to which they were liable, were entered in the new register, each page of which was signed by the Vedor and numbered.

The initial difficulty to be encountered was that the Mohottalas' Rolls for several of the districts were missing. In such cases the officers responsible were called upon to take an oath to the effect that the Rolls were not in their possession. These lists, which had been inscribed on palm leaves, had in fact perished in the course of the recent desolating wars, and de Azavedo was in a position to assure the Vedor that it was useless to make further search for them. Their loss, however, was the less serious, in that there was amongst the natives little disposition to evade the summons to produce title deeds, although it called forth considerable obstruction on the part of the various Portuguese corporations, not least on that of the Camara or Municipal Chamber of Colombo—"the *Cidade* of Sao Lourenco" as it was called. It was intended that when complete the Tombo should be laid before a Junta or Board which would be ordered to assemble at Colombo for the purpose of revising it and of deciding on the quit-rent for each village, as a preliminary to its allotment. From the villages which the piety of Sinhalese Kings had set apart for the service of the Temples, a sufficient number was to be allotted for the maintenance of the various religious establishments throughout the Island, the grants being made during the King's pleasure with a view to such changes as the developments of the future might necessitate. Any of these villages which should remain after such allotment were to be dealt with in the ordinary course. The preliminary investigation revealed that several of them had recently been granted away without authority, and the cancellation of all such grants was ordered. This resolution was the source of much trouble with all the Orders concerned. The Jesuits who held the sixty-two villages of the Munnesseram Temple were, like the Dominicans and Augustinians, granted money allowances in compensation, but it was found to be more difficult to meet the claims of the Franciscans.

A Franciscan had accompanied de Almeida to Ceylon in 1505, and the Franciscans were the first missionaries to be sent out at the request of Bhuwaneka Bahu; but if they were missionaries of the Church of Christ, they never forgot that they were also subjects of the King of Portugal. Wherever there was danger to body or soul, there the Franciscan was to be found, not only nursing the wounded and providing the consolations of religion to the dying, but leading with crucifix and sword in many a bloody battle. It was claimed by the Franciscans that as early as 1554 an *Alvara* had been signed by the Portuguese King confining the work in Ceylon to their Order. However that may be, it is certain that a proclamation to this effect was issued on the 10th of March, 1593, and four years later an attempt was made to obtain the consent of the Pope to the arrangement. The trouble arose over the grant which Dharmapala had made to them in the first fervour of his conversion. This grant had been subsequently confirmed three times; but in 1598, shortly after Dharmapala's death, King Philip, on the advice of the Bishop of Cochin, had declined to ratify it, holding out to the Order the dubious consolation that this would be entirely in accordance with their Statutes. The Franciscans, however, were not prepared to submit to so great a deprivation without a struggle, and succeeded in obtaining from the *Mesa de Consciencia*[1] a ruling to the effect that the King of Portugal as the heir of Dharmapala was bound to uphold his grant. An attempt on the part of Ferreira, acting under the directions of the Viceroy, to take forcible possession of the villages under dispute led to an appeal to law on that of the Franciscans, who brought a suit against the King's Proctor. The question was therefore re-opened with a result which will be shown later.

The villages which had formerly belonged to the Temples being thus dealt with, the ancient *Gabadagan* or Royal Villages were next separated for the benefit of the King's Treasury. These had been wont to supply the Court with most of the provisions which were required for the maintenance of the various great establishments which went to compose it, but it was obvious that it was no longer to the interest of the Crown to utilise them on the ancient lines. A large revenue was expected from them, and they were disposed of like the rest of the villages, some being allotted to private parties, when they were known as *Nindagan*, some rented out, and a few reserved to provide for the military needs of the country. These last were selected in such a way that the troops on the march could thus be conveniently supplied with provisions from them, while the Captains in charge of the various stations occupied by the Portuguese were allowed certain villages to assist them in feeding their men.

Of the remainder of the villages which were now available for distribution, the best were reserved for such of the Portuguese as had specially distinguished themselves in the work of conquest in India and Ceylon, and for native Christians who had served with loyalty in high office, the smaller ones being allotted to the Mudaliyars, Arachchis and Lascarins, either as gifts or by way of remuneration for services rendered. Those Portuguese to whom lands were granted were obliged as an essential condition of the grant, to take up their residence within the Island; grantees who were of Sinhalese nationality were expected to live with their families in the various fortresses along with the Portuguese who had their villages in the neighbourhood. Great hopes were entertained that the social intercourse which was expected to follow from the proximity of the two races would lead to greater security, while educating the natives and rendering them more acquiescent in the rule of the foreigner.

In the case of the Portuguese the grants were for two or three lives, with succession open to the female line also and a restriction against alienation; the natives of the country, however, at first held their grants only during pleasure, as appears to have been the custom under the Sinhalese Kings; though a more liberal policy was subsequently adopted, the grants being made for life.

The intention of the Sinhalese Kings in assigning these villages had been to make such provision for the favoured individual as would maintain him in comfort in accordance with the simple standard of living which prevailed at the time. So long as he held his Nindagama he was entitled to all the benefits which the King was wont to receive therefrom. The provision extended to every detail of the grantee's domestic economy, as well as to the safeguarding of his *Walauwa* or residence, and person, and the due maintenance of his position; and all this without any expenditure of money on his part. The tenants of his village cultivated his rice fields and conveyed the produce to his store, which they themselves built and kept in repair. Every night they guarded him against the inroads of robbers or the attacks of wild beasts; and in the morning, whilst some swept the immediate precincts of his mansion, others attended him to the bath and prepared food for his use, or handed to him the betel which was his only stimulant. In like manner the damsels of his village were the attendants of his wife and the companions of his daughter. If he had to appear at Court, his tenants escorted him thither and carried the various necessaries for the journey, holding over him the while the palm-leaf umbrella which was as much an emblem of his dignity as a protection against the sun. In war they defended his person, sacrificing their lives to save his; in sickness they waited at his bedside; and at his death they conveyed his corpse to the funeral pyre.

The entire social scheme of the Sinhalese centred round the idea of caste, "which," to quote Knox, "is not according to the Riches or Places of

Honour the King promotes them to, but according to their Descent and Blood." "Riches," he adds, "cannot prevail with them in the least to marry with those by whom they must eclipse and stain the Honour of their family.... It is the Birth and Family which ennobleth them." Persons of the highest caste were known among them by the proud title of *Handuru—Swami daruwo*, the Lord's Children[2]—a term which strictly speaking pertained to Royalty alone. The wearing of a covering above the waist, the length of the cloth below the knees, the colour of the cap, and other petty distinctions separated the high-born from the less fortunate.

In the hands of the Sinhalese the system had worked satisfactorily and had produced a people who were in the main happy and contented with their lot. There was little oppression, and no man needed to lack the few things essential to existence in the favoured climate of Ceylon. The lord of the Nindagama was the father of the village, and under him all the inter-dependent castes worked in perfect harmony. When, however, the stranger took the place of the Sinhalese nobleman, he found ready to his hand a rod of tyranny which he was not slow to use. Taking no interest in the villagers themselves, his one anxiety was to make the utmost profit he could out of his unhappy dependents during the brief period of his authority over them. His natural callousness to suffering led him to acts of appalling cruelty; and his insatiable craving for gold brought into being a state of affairs which, perhaps, has found its counterpart only in the Crown Domain of the Congo and in the rubber forests of Peru. Bright and cheerful as is the Portuguese side of the picture as presented to us by Joao Ribeiro, it had a terribly dark background which will be set forth in a later chapter.

It has already been said that the Disawas of the four great Provinces were responsible for their administration. This they carried on through minor, officials styled *Korale Vidanes,* who performed certain judicial functions and had also the control of large numbers of tenants liable to render various services to the Crown without remuneration. It was, however, found in practice that these tenants did only what the Vidanes ordered them to do, and that the latter utilised their services for their own private benefit, to the great loss of the Treasury. The Vidanes exercised, moreover, an undesirable influence over the fighting men, a circumstance which had been an important factor in the various rebellions which had recently occured. Correa for instance was the Vidane over nine Korales, and the only service which he had to render was to maintain six hundred fighting men. With a view to eliminating this source of danger the King recommended that the Sinhalese Vidanes should be replaced by Portuguese, and that Correa himself, who had always been a suspect, should be deported to Goa. It was, however, pointed out to him that such a policy would create a degree of dissatisfaction among the more influential natives, which might prove a serious menace to the peace of the country; and that it would be better to introduce the practice by slow degrees, starting with the more settled districts.

One of the tasks imposed on the Vedor was to see to the proper enforcement of the claims of the Crown to the services of the various tenants. Above all they were to be prevented from selling the guns which they made to anyone save the King, who was anxious, if possible, to concentrate all the gun-smiths—whom in spite of their holdings it was found necessary to feed and clothe while on the King's service, since these holdings sufficed only for the support of the family during the absence of its head—in Colombo and Galle, to prevent their trading with the enemy. Strong objection was, however, raised to this proposal, and it was finally decided to be in every way undesirable to alter a practice which had existed from ancient times.

The skill of the artisans of Ceylon, inherited and perfected through generations of the caste system, was the subject of admiration throughout India, where their gold and silver work, their carvings of ivory and their weapons of steel were preferred to all others. "They make the fairest barrels for pieces that may be found in any place, which shine as bright as if they were silver." John Huyghen van Linschoten has recorded that an ivory crucifix presented in 1585 to the Archbishop of Goa by a native of Ceylon was considered such a masterpiece, that that prelate "caused it to be put in a case and sent unto the King of Spaine, as a thing to be wondered at, and worthy of so great a lord, to be kept among his costliest jewels."

Another of the Vedor's duties was the supervision of the collection of the royal dues, whether money dues or dues paid in kind. The proceeds of these latter were stored in the Factory at Colombo, whence nothing was issued save by his order. Such issues were made only for despatch to Portugal by way of Goa, or for the service of the navy. Whatever remained unused at the end of the year was sold under his direction and the proceeds deposited in a chest secured with three keys, with the management of which the Captains of Colombo were strictly forbidden to interfere. All receipts were entered in a book which was itself locked up in the chest, and separate acknowledgments were given in respect of each transaction. In similar manner every payment had to pass both the Vedor and the Factor, who in turn were restricted by the annual statement of authorised expenses.

So long indeed as the war of Conquest was in progress the General was permitted to make extraordinary requisitions on this chest, but such requisitions also had to bear the Vedor's *vise*, and the General was responsible for them to the Viceroy. Moreover they could in no case be made on any of the sub-accountants. Needless to say the Generals regarded the Vedor as a natural enemy, and the friction arising from the attempts of the former to interfere with the public funds was so great as seriously to embarrass the conduct of affairs, and to be a source of vexation to the King himself. Particularly did this friction arise with regard to the trade in cinnamon, which has been described as "the bride round whom they all dance in Ceylon.[3]" The jealousy with which this trade was guarded may be judged from the fact that in 1584 Dharmapala himself in his poverty had to apply for the special authority of the King of Portugal to export fifty quintals[4] of the article to Portugal, and was refused the necessary permission, being instead presented with a thousand cruzados. Indeed from a very early period of the Portuguese occupation the Sinhalese King had to content himself with exporting for his own benefit the quantity allowed him by the authorities at Goa. In 1558, in consideration of the fact of Dharmapala's having become a Christian, this quantity was increased to one hundred bahars.

The actual handling of the cinnamon was rented out to the Captains of Colombo, and was a serious trial to the honesty of these officers. The King did not approve of his Treasury paying all the expenses while the Captains took all the profits, and in 1589 he ordered an inquiry to be made into the matter. De Azavedo had secured the right for himself for a period of three years, and had to be sharply reminded that such a proceeding was improper in a General entrusted with the work of Conquest.

Later, in 1614, the trade was declared a strict royal monopoly, and private parties attempting to collect or deal in cinnamon were made subject to banishment for five years to the armada of the South, while the amount to be collected annually was fixed for the time being at a thousand bahars.

Once a year one of the King's ships set out from Colombo, to which port the trade was confined in 1594, with the annual cargo of this spice. The Captain in charge of the voyage was originally allowed a specified quantity of the cinnamon as remuneration, but this was subsequently commuted for a money payment. This shipment to Goa was made about the time of the expected arrival of the annual fleet from Portugal. A specially trustworthy person was elected to conduct the negotiations, and the General was expected to be in Colombo in person at the time in order to prevent any smuggling, while the Vedor issued a certificate setting out the number of the bales shipped, which had to be checked at Goa. On being landed the cargo was sold as early as possible, to enable the officer in charge to return to Ceylon with the proceeds by the next monsoon. This money was kept in a separate chest apart from the other revenues, and the statement of the amount realised submitted to the Vedor, was by him forwarded for his information to the General, who in turn sent it on to the Viceroy.

Over-production of cinnamon had led to a great depreciation in value, but it was hoped that by restricting the supply for some years the price could be forced up to its former figure, when it was anticipated that the profits of this trade alone would meet all the expenses of the conquest. With a view to securing its more efficient working, a Portuguese was placed in charge of the entire department as Vidane.

Of the minor sources of revenue of which the Vedor had the oversight, the Elephant department was managed by Sinhalese Vidanes under his general supervision, the villages which had originally been assigned to it by the Sinhalese Kings being re-distributed among the men who were engaged in the capture, taming and maintenance of the animals. The Pearl Fishery, which had formerly been rented out by the Captains of Manar, who had sent armed vessels to guard the place, had latterly suffered in consequence of a policy of showing favour to the divers who had begun to turn Christian, and as a result the revenue obtained therefrom had steadily diminished. The Jesuits who were in charge of the work of conversion accused the Captains of oppression, while the latter retorted that the true explanation of the unsatisfactory state of affairs lay in the laziness of the divers, who were pampered by the Jesuits. It had been the custom to assign the whole of one day's fishery to shoe the wife of the Captain, and the interfering action of the Jesuits in stopping this convenient perquisite did not tend to increase the good feeling between the parties. Moreover the Fishery sustained yet further damage from the quarrels which arose between the Jesuits and the Bishop of Cochin. The loss to the Treasury was serious. No fishery at all was held from 1604 to 1612, and it was even proposed by the King to settle a colony of the Parawa divers on the West of Ceylon, that the work might be carried on without friction. The suggestion however was not acted upon.

In view of the disturbed condition of the country little profit was to be obtained from the gems, though the experiment was tried of sending what few could be got together to the markets of Goa and Cochin. The lands which bore the gems were concealed from the Portuguese by the natives of the country, and though a Portuguese was appointed Vidane over the work of collecting them, it only proved to be one more field for peculation.

An attempt was made to stimulate the cultivation of pepper by compelling the payment of a portion of the village quit-rents in this spice, but without adequate results. The arecanut, on the other hand, which had always been a source of revenue to the Sinhalese Kings, was at this period in great demand in India, as has already been stated. De Azavedo was not slow to take advantage of this. He secured for himself the seignory of every village where the nut was produced in any quantity, paying for it at a moderate fixed rate. The increase in the profits arising from the trade was so great that it led to what in the financial jargon of today is called a "boom," the terrible consequences of which to the unfortunate villager will be set forth later. At the same time the competition of the subject led not unnaturally to a great diminution in the profits of the King.

Under the native Kings where a man had died without male issue all his property had escheated to the Crown, and in other cases his estate had been liable to a third of its extent. This oppressive exaction, which was known by the name of *Marala*, which in meaning corresponds almost exactly to the term Death Duty, obtained also under the Great Mogul, and was calculated to prevent all accumulation of wealth in the hands of private individuals, as well as to stifle all desire to improve property. This too was probably one of the reasons why it was customary for villagers to bury such money as came into their possession; for the villager knew no Bank so secure as the ground under his fireplace. The levy was continued by the Portuguese, though in order to encourage conversion, its severity was relaxed in the case of Christians.

The 50,000 odd headmen also were each expected to pay a pardao a year, and the amount so contributed appears to have been at the disposal of the General. Various other sources of income helped to swell the King's revenues. Breaches of the peace were punished by the imposition of fines varying with the position of the offender and the gravity of the offence. Where again any person committed suicide through inability to avenge an affront, the offending party and often his entire village were mulcted in a sum of money. Certain kinds of permanent plantations also were liable to taxation, for instance coconut lands, which usually paid a tenth of their produce. Fishermen were taxed at a fixed rate on their nets, in addition to paying a percentage of all fish caught by them. In various districts where oil was manufactured a similar payment in kind was exacted. Tolls were levied at the fortified outposts which guarded the frontiers, on passengers entering and leaving Portuguese territory, and a tax was put upon the privilege of cremation. In addition to all this the villagers were responsible for the upkeep of the village paths, bridges and resting-places, while every adult male among the Moors had to work for three months in the year on the roads and fortifications.

Under the Sinhalese rule of the Island the power of life and death had been jealously reserved to the King alone, and no man could even be sentenced to lashes except by his order. Legal process and citations were unknown, for the mere summons of the one party to the other to appear before the tribunal, if made in the King's name, had such binding force that none dared disobey. In case of conviction a common form of punishment was for the accused to be placed in *Welekma*, by tracing a circle round him on the ground and forbidding him in the King's name to step outside it; nor would he dare to do so. To supervise the collection of the Maralas mentioned above, there were appointed a number of officials termed Maraleiros, who also acted as circuit judges. In addition to their itinerant Courts, a tribunal consisting of eight Mudaliyars, established by de Azavedo, sat at Malwana and dealt with matters affecting the Sinhalese, though all important cases were reserved to be heard by the General himself, from whose decision there was no appeal. Matters concerning the village alone came before a Council of the village elders or headmen. All these tribunals recognised decisory oaths, which together with the ordeal were a popular means of settling disputes. Often the form of oath consisted in placing a number of pebbles on the head of a son of the party swearing, who then imprecated his death within the number of days represented by the pebbles if he himself was speaking aught but the truth. The form of ordeal most in favour consisted of touching boiling oil or a red-hot iron with the tip of the finger, and this method was largely employed where the chastity of women was in question.[5]

Sinhalese customary law had always recognised the practice of borrowing money on the security of the borrower's person. Such slaves were treated with great kindness and were allowed lands for their maintenance, so that they frequently acquired much wealth. With the Portuguese, however, the systematic kidnapping of children to be sold into slavery was developed into a lucrative profession, and there was a large importation of Africans whose descendants even today, in spite of three hundred years of intermarriage with the Asiatic races, as well as the admixture of European blood, revert in not a few instances to the original African type. In Goa the torture and murder of slaves grew to be so gross a scandal as to call for a special Alvara from the King. The Portuguese also maintained a large number of female slaves, from whose industry and from the commerce of whose bodies their masters derived a considerable revenue.

From the Sinhalese point of view, to appear before a great person with empty hands betokened a lack of respect. Accordingly on the three occasions during the year upon which all the Chiefs presented themselves at Court, they brought with them various offerings regulated strictly in accordance with the office and holdings of each individual and consisting of jewels, weapons, and what not, together with any rarity which was considered likely to be acceptable to the King. This custom the Generals as representing the King consistently maintained. Similarly in their progresses through the country they were received with royal honours, the roads being decorated with fruits and flowers and white cloth, and the people prostrating themselves in that reverent obeisance which Oriental etiquette demands.

NOTES TO CHAPTER X

1. A Tribunal created by Dom Joao III to decide matters of conscience. A similar Mesa was established at Goa in 1570, but did not exist long.
2. Cf. Rajput, *Raja putra*, Sons of the King.
3. Ryclof van Goens, 1675-1679.
4. A quintal=1.97 cwt.
5. Queen Emma, mother of Edward the Confessor, when accused of guilty intercourse with Alwyn, Bishop of Winchester, cleared herself and the Bishop by walking unharmed over nine red-hot ploughshares.

CHAPTER XI

De Azavedo was succeeded in Ceylon by Dom Francisco de Meneses Roxo. The main preoccupation of the new General was the acquirement of wealth, rather than of glory, and the military situation was allowed to go from bad to worse, while depots were established on the frontiers, by means of which de Meneses and his partners, the Disawas, maintained a brisk and extremely profitable trade with the enemy in cloth and opium, which they exchanged for areca-nut and pepper. The Moorish commerce had long ago been driven out of the sea-ports of Ceylon, and this very year orders were received from Goa to forbid the further settlement of Moors in the Island, orders which however did not prevent the General from employing a low-born Moor as his accomplice in his nefarious practices in the Disawani of Matara. Harsh fines, which went to swell the General's income, were inflicted on the people on the slightest pretext; the gems and elephants which belonged to the Crown were dealt with by him as if they were his private property; the revenue was misappropriated, and the scandalised natives were on the verge of rebellion; for while the General was busy with his trade, his soldiers were engaged in raiding villages for food, robbing the inhabitants and ravishing the women, till whole districts were abandoned and the people had to arm themselves in self-defence.

That discipline had ceased to exist in the army is scarcely a matter for surprise. The depopulation of Portugal had gone so far that it was no longer possible to fill the yearly navy with volunteers, and the very scum of Portugal was being shipped to the East. Boys of nine years of age and upwards were being kidnapped from all parts of the country in the hope that some of them would survive to be soldiers; and of the recruits obtained for the army no small proportion were malefactors, since a pardon was offered to any criminals who should enlist. So perilous was the war in Ceylon admitted to be, that banishment to the army there was a punishment frequently promulgated in the Royal Alvaras. The voyage to India itself was a terrible undertaking. The unwieldy caravels, crowded with their living freight and kept in a condition of appalling filth, were by the time they reached their destination pestiferous sinks. The crew and passengers were often reduced, by the devastating effects of scurvy and dysentery, to one half their original number in the course of the voyage; and the arrival of the yearly fleet at Goa crowded the spacious hospital there with helpless invalids.

Fortunately for the Portuguese, internal dissensions prevented Senerat from taking full advantage of the prevailing anarchy. He had indeed made an effort, which just failed of success, to surprise Balane, while a small fleet of Sinhalese vessels had appeared off the Western coast and captured some merchantmen: but the death of the Queen on the 20th of July 1613 following that of Astana Bandara, the heir to the Crown, served to distract the attention of the Sinhalese till the arrival in November 1614 of the new General, Manuel Mascarenhas Homem, who brought with him detailed instructions, such as the great experience of the Viceroy had enabled him to give. Rigorous discipline was to be maintained in the army, and the war carried out without intermission. Believing that the only effective policy was to wear out the enemy by captivity and death, de Azavedo recommended that the system which he had employed of making two incursions in their territory every year should be continued. No male above fourteen years was to be left alive, and the native troops were to be reorganised under reliable leaders. Effective supervision was to be exercised over those who had services to render in the way of the preparation of arms, and every effort made to cut off the foreign trade which the Sinhalese still maintained by means of their eastern ports.

The new General was instructed that the revenue from the cinnamon monopoly should be ear-marked for the expenses of the war, and advised to make Malwana his headquarters. As, however, there were no hotels to be found there, and the *ambalan* or caravanserais which the Sinhalese Kings had maintained on the chief roads for the convenience of travellers had been destroyed or had fallen into decay, he would have to keep open house for all who came to see him. He must, moreover, attend carefully to the administration of justice, and continue the Tribunal which de Azavedo had established at Malwana. Above all the work of converting the heathen[1] was not to be neglected.

In the same year King Philip issued an order which sheds a pitiful light on the financial condition of Portugal at this time. A Captain on receiving the King's Commission had been expected to spend all the money he could get together, if funds were not forthcoming, in the King's service. On the termination of his commission the Chief Commander issued to each Captain a certificate setting forth the service he had rendered and the expenditure he had incurred on the King's account. After seven years, when a certain number of these certificates had been collected, the Captain was at liberty to leave for Portugal and present them at the Office of Remembrances. There, especially if he had influence or was prepared to bribe the proper authorities sufficiently, he would be rewarded by receiving an appointment as Captain in charge of a port, Judge, or Factor as the case might be, for a certain number of years. On arriving at the station assigned to him, his sole object would be to make all the profit possible within the limited time at his disposal; and this was both the explanation of and the excuse for the amazing dishonesty which disgraced the Portuguese administrative officials.[2] Not infrequently these grants were made to females as a reward for the services of their male relatives, and in such cases the appointments were given to their husbands. Succession to such posts had been disposed of for several years to come by patents which were to take effect after the expiry of previous grants. Now, however, instructions were issued to put up to auction the Captaincies of the fortresses, the profits of the trade voyages, and the various offices of the State of India, for a period of three years, as a means of replenishing the Indian coffers, the purchasers being given precedence over all other grantees. No more significant indication could be found of the condition of helplessness into which the Home Government had fallen.

De Azavedo's instructions with regard to the conduct of the war were carried out to the letter. Twice in every year a ferocious band of freebooters penetrated to within the mountain zone, carrying with them death and destruction. No able-bodied man whom they found was left alive; and such of the women and children as could not conveniently be removed as prisoners shared as a rule the same fate. The cattle were all driven down from the mountains to feed the hungry Portuguese in Colombo; no house was passed by unburnt, and no fruit tree was left undestroyed.

The Sinhalese could regard the loss of their flimsy houses with something approaching indifference; but the felling of their trees was to them a terrible blow. A jak tree would last for several centuries and would keep the family of a villager supplied with food for several months in each year. The coconut palm again was almost a friend. It would not, so the villager believed, flourish except within sound of the human voice. From its branches he got the *cadjans* with which he thatched the roof which sheltered him from the rain; its trunk supplied the rafters and the pillars which held up that roof; its fruit was essential to every meal, and the oil which it yielded was the offering that he took with him to the temple. The treacle which he obtained from it was an ingredient of the only dainties his children knew, and the ivory-coloured tender leaves decked his house when his daughter was given in marriage, while a few of the trees themselves were the best dower that she could take her husband. It flowered twelve times in the year and yielded fruit for a hundred years. It is not therefore astonishing that the wanton felling of the tree was a criminal offence punishable at law.[3]

The Sinhalese, however, were rapidly learning their lesson. At the news of the approach of the Portuguese every soul would vanish into the thick forests, and as the Portuguese straggled in single file along the roads which as the consequence of neglect had degenerated into mere forest tracks, a silent arrow or the ball from a matchlock fired by an unseen hand would lay one and another lifeless. Defensive armour had long ago been discarded, for it had been found to be more of an encumbrance than a help in the case of foot-soldiers fighting in the tropics; and their collars of buffalo-hide and round bucklers afforded little protection against the bolts of the Sinhalese. Moreover the clothes which they wore were little better than rags, and very few of them were provided with shoes.

To make matters worse, a wrong system had come into vogue with regard to the appointment of officers. Not only were Portuguese officials taking the place of Sinhalese even in the high office of Disawa, but inexperienced men who had no knowledge of the country or of the ways of the enemy and their methods of warfare were being placed in command of armies in preference to experienced veterans such as were still to be found in Ceylon. Such a system not unnaturally bred dissatisfaction among the men, whilst it frequently involved the raiding expeditions in disaster.

The army would toil through the forest and over the mountains till disease, the result of continued exposure, broke out among the men who were already exhausted by the long marches and by lack of food. All this while a close watch would be kept upon them by the Sinhalese from the mountain tops. Each narrow passage through which they had been allowed to penetrate unmolested would be jealously guarded, and on all sides light-armed troops would lie hidden among the dense vegetation. The majestic trees which towered overhead, as if defying time and the strength of man, would all be skilfully cut round, being sustained in their position merely by the giant creepers which hung like cables from their tops; and cunningly devised stone shutes would lie snugly concealed on every crag. When at length the critical moment came and the weary Portuguese turned homeward, with a few strokes of the hatchet the great trees would crash down and block the road, the fearful shutes would come thundering from above, while unseen in the tangled jungle the Sinhalese would pour into the midst of the retreating army their arrows and leaden bullets, carefully picking out the officers among the Portuguese. As a rule the invading army came back with greatly reduced numbers, and this death-roll was extended to pitiable dimensions by the ravages of diseases contracted in the course of the campaign.

In the midst of these alarms of war there occurred portents of Nature which gave rise in the minds of the Portuguese to gloomy forebodings. A fiery comet with three tails, first seen on the 7th of March 1615, filled the whole country with terror and dismay; and this was followed by an outbreak of disease which affected both man and beast. Fish, it is related, died in such numbers as to pollute the atmosphere and add to the prevailing infection. To crown all, at seven o'clock on the evening of the 14th of April a severe earthquake shook the land, heralded by what are described as peals of thunder. The terrified inhabitants rushed into the streets to escape from the swaying houses which were tumbling down on all sides. Great fissures emitting sulphurous fumes opened on the surface of the ground. A portion of the city wall with one of the bastions collapsed, and a stone bridge was entirely destroyed, while, to add to the horrors of that terrible night, fire broke out. Two hundred houses fell to the ground, and the dead alone were estimated at over two thousand.

In May of the same year Senerat despatched Boschouwer to obtain for him the long-promised assistance against the Portuguese. The following March Dom Nuno Alvares Pereira succeeded to the office of General, his succession thereto being marked by no departure from de Azavedo's plan of campaign. Shortly afterwards Antao Vaz Ferreira—probably one of the very few honest Portuguese in the East —whose health had given way under his arduous labours, left the Island. He had completed his Tombo, which is still preserved in Portugal, but he had not succeeded in dealing with all the opposition which his administrative acts had called into being. The Camara or Municipal Chamber of Colombo was still insisting on its claim, based on a *Sannas* of Dharmapala, to a quantity of cinnamon every year. It obstinately refused to produce its title deeds to the lands and coconut plantations which it claimed as its property; and it maintained a tenacious fight for its rights over the great ferries by which Colombo was approached from the North, and also to an unrestricted trade in areca-nuts. On the other hand, it had the independence to resent all attempts on the part of the General and the Captain of Colombo to interfere with its legitimate functions, and still more with its money chest. Needless to say these latter officials did not like the Camara, nor appreciate the persistency with which it urged the importance of keeping the fortifications of Colombo in repair.

At this point another strange figure appears in the bloodstained arena. Nikapitiya Bandara had died at Coimbra in 1608, but in spite of this a mysterious rumour travelling along the pilgrim routes, which were still kept open by the footsteps of white-clad devotees, had spread from mouth to mouth among the Sinhalese to the effect that he was still in the Island, and would soon bring salvation to his people. To heighten the effect of this dramatic interlude, its *mise-en-scene* was the ancient city of Anuradha Pura, which to the Portuguese was but a shadowy name.[4] They had indeed heard that buried within the depths of the interminable forest there lay the remains of a City of Kings, but very few of them had ventured near the mysterious spot. Herds of wild elephants alone trod the broad processional paths of the Abhayagiri and Ruwan-weli-seya, which for so many centuries had been thronged with all the peaceful pomp of Sinhalese civilisation. The graceful monoliths which guarded the Tuparama in eternal silence could hardly be distinguished amidst the trunks of the forest trees which crowded in upon them. The roofless colonnades of the Lowā Mahā Paya still pointed to where Gamani's ivory throne had been placed, but the scent of flowers seldom rose from the great stone altars to the great stone Buddhas who looked so wistfully over them into eternity. Yet, though the dams of the mighty tanks had given way, the handful of fever-stricken villagers who still maintained the struggle for existence below them did not cease regularly to sweep the circuit of the aged *Bo* tree, which incessantly quivered and sighed as if in sorrow for the misery which had overtaken that country, into the heart of which it had struck its roots. Still, too, year by year at the great festivals, worshippers gathered round the Tree from the remotest parts of the Island, there to hold communion with the past and to draw fresh inspiration for the future.

In this romantic setting a wild figure clad in skins and with the matted hair of the ascetic appeared and claimed the allegiance of the Sinhalese as their rightful King, Nikapitiya Bandara. The moment was well chosen. Horror-struck by the inhuman barbarities of the Portuguese, the country was passionately demanding a leader; the atmosphere was tense with excitement; and as it happened Colombo itself was denuded of its usual garrison. On the 5th of December 1616 the self-styled Nikapitiya Bandara entered Metiyagane, the ancient royal city of Dambadeniya, as King. In eight days the whole of the district was in arms, and two thousand Sinhalese troops had arrived from the Uda Rata to assist the pretender. A Portuguese force hurried up to crush the revolt ere it should gain head, and on the 18th the armies met at Gandolaha, close to the Maha Oya.

The Sinhalese, exasperated by the long tale of cruelty, bore themselves with reckless courage, and for a long time the issue hung in the balance. At last the Lascarins began to waver and even to desert to the Sinhalese. The day seemed lost when Dom Constantino Navaratna, who was now married to a Portuguese lady in Colombo, and who had risen into great prominence during the war, hastened to the rescue. Throwing himself in front of the waverers he shouted to them that if they desired their own King he was there, for he was royal by seven branches, as they all knew. The day was saved for the Portuguese. The Lascarins hesitated a moment; then, raising Dom Constantino in their arms, they saluted him as their King.

The fight still raged furiously, but at last the Sinhalese retired to behind the Maha Oya, leaving the Portuguese too exhausted to move. Meanwhile Philip de Oliveira, an officer who was destined to achieve in Jaffna what the Viceroy de Braganza had failed to effect, hurried up with a small army on receipt of the news of the battle, which was only too horribly confirmed by the sight of over a thousand corpses lying unburied on the field of the recent struggle. To add to their sense of insecurity the Portuguese discovered a palm-leaf scroll which was made fast to a tree, and contained a Sinhalese proclamation to the effect that all the Portuguese in Ceylon had been put to death and that Colombo itself had fallen. They accordingly drew back to Attanagalla for safety. In the meantime Nikapitiya with a great following was making a royal progress through the country; extravagant grants of land served to cement the bonds which hatred of the cruel foreigner had already fashioned, and at Nakalagama, almost within sight of the Portuguese capital, the pretender caused himself to be proclaimed Emperor.

For the Portuguese the moment was critical, and they awaited with bated breath the issue of events. Elated with his success, however, Nikapitiya took the impolitic step of sending an impertinent message to the King, demanding one of the latter's two Queens for his own wife. He received the contemptuous reply that the request could be attended to as soon as he had finished with the Portuguese, while at the same time the two thousand Sinhalese who had been sent to his support were recalled, to the great delight of the Portuguese, whose army was again advancing to meet him. They found the country prepared as for a triumphal procession. The roads were swept and decorated with greenery and flowers in the manner which is still common on every occasion of rejoicing, and tender coconuts, flashing like red gold in the blazing sun, hung from the branches of the trees on the road-side to refresh the weary traveller; for all were expecting their deliverer to pass that way. The armies met at Kal Eliya, and after a short hand-to-hand fight Nikapitiya disappeared into the forest, and crossing the Maha Oya was soon once more in safety at Dambadeniya.

In the meantime Baretto, who had risen to be Disawa of Uwa, made a dash into the Rayigam Korale, and drove the Disawa of Matara into Galle for shelter. Nevertheless Senerat, who was still incensed with Nikapitiya, determined now to make peace; but the garrison at Balane, not content with treacherously putting his messenger to death, retorted to his dignified protest against this amazing breach of honour, with a defiant gibe. The punishment however was swift and severe. A large army appeared before the fort, and the Sinhalese, sheltering themselves behind wooden mantles, advanced steadily up to the walls. The blocks of stone which formed the ramparts, and which were not secured with mortar, were rapidly dislodged by means of deer horns fastened to long poles, and the garrison, despairing of resistance, surrendered on condition of their lives being spared—a condition which, in spite of their previous shameful action, was scrupulously observed.

So desperate had the condition of affairs in Ceylon become, that the Council at Goa decided that the Viceroy should proceed thither in person to restore order. India, however, had neither men nor money to spare, and other matters of equal weight made calls upon the Viceroy's attention, so that the resolution of the Council was never put into execution. But the desolating struggle continued till the occurrence of the festival of the New Year, for which the Lascarins were allowed to return to their homes, afforded a short breathing-space.

The 365 days occupied by the Sun's apparent circuit in the heavens were divided by the Sinhalese into twelve months, named after the signs of the Zodiac. The year began with the entry of the Sun into Aries, which takes place usually about the 13th of April, and the occasion was observed as the great social festival of the race. For several months beforehand preparations would be made in every household; the poorest would lay aside any small coin he could spare, to purchase new clothes for the members of his family; the idlest would go out and work, to secure the means with which to entertain his relatives and friends. For the celebration of this occasion the whole family would be assembled at the *Mul gedera*, the family homestead. The criminal hiding from justice would creep in stealthily by night, and the soldier on service would be present on leave for during this festival there was no *Rajakariya*.

The exact moment when the New Year began was calculated by the King's astronomers, whose apparatus for measuring time consisted of a light copper bowl with an almost imperceptible perforation at the bottom. This bowl was set floating in a tub of water, till it filled and settled down at the bottom. The time occupied from the moment it was placed in the water till it reached the bottom amounted to a *peya*, sixty of which made a day and a night.

At the auspicious moment the King would mount his throne in the presence of the assembled courtiers, while a salute of artillery announced the event to the public. This done, there followed the ceremony of the Anointing. The King's Physicians would have prepared the necessary unguent from the juices of various medicinal herbs, and at the hour appointed for the purpose he would take his seat facing south-east. Above his head would be suspended leaves plucked from trees which varied according to the position of the planets, and here he would be solemnly anointed, while a company of maidens holding lighted tapers in their hands invoked blessings on his head. At the same time in every household a similar rite was performed, the head of the family anointing and blessing every member thereof.

A third hour was fixed for the first eating of the food cooked in the New Year, and yet another for beginning the Year's work, when every labouring man would handle the tool by which he earned his living. This last ceremony was the occasion for the greatest rejoicing. All through the country there would be entertaining of friends and exchanging of presents, followed by ceremonial bathing. The festival which lasted several days, was brought to an end by the great Chiefs appearing before the King, carrying on their heads covered with white cloth the presents which were to be offered to him, while the King in his turn made offerings to the *Danta Datu.*

Immediately on its conclusion Nikapitiya marched into the Disawani of Sabaragamuwa, but finding the Portuguese there in strength he hastily retired northwards, and after a severe fight in the neighbourhood of Anuradha Pura, escaped into the wilds. Baretto in the meantime had revolted against Senerat and obtained control of the entire eastern part of the Island, while his armies over-ran Matara and Sabaragamuwa. The rapidity of his movements bewildered the Portuguese, who did not know which of their outposts would next be selected for attack. Their army moreover was completely demoralised, being in fact little more than a company of brigands, whose lawless excesses made them as much an object of terror and hatred to their own countrymen as to the Sinhalese. The coffers were empty, for, in consequence of the misconduct of the Generals, the revenue which the cinnamon monopoly was expected to provide for the maintenance of the war was not forthcoming. As King Philip bitterly complained, the Generals had issued so many licenses for the benefit of themselves and their satellites, that about three times as much was collected on their account as was collected for the King. The royal rights under the monopoly were in fact enforced only as against the poor; by the more powerful they were flouted with impunity.

It is therefore no matter for surprise that the Portuguese were well satisfied to conclude on the 24th of August 1617 a treaty with Senerat. Under the terms of this treaty the Portuguese acknowledged the sovereignty of Senerat, who for his part agreed to pay an annual tribute of two elephants, to suppress any rising within his dominions, to restore the Portuguese captured at Balane and all other Christian prisoners, and to send persons of position as hostages. Baretto, however, continued in occupation of the Disawanis of Sabaragamuwa and Matara. The former was entirely abandoned by the Portuguese, and the garrisons which were there withdrawn, while in the latter they met with a severe reverse at the hands of the energetic rebel. At about this same time Nikapitiya again made his appearance in the Seven Korales, accompanied by the Prince Mayadunna, a member of the Sitawaka royal family; but finding that the inhabitants were weary of war and would not support him, he once more disappeared into the wilds.

On the 17th of November 1617 the Conde de Redondo landed at Goa as Viceroy in succession to de Azavedo, whom a dungeon below the castle of Lisbon, where he dragged out the remaining eight years of his miserable life, awaited.

In the following September Constantino de Sa y Noronha arrived at Colombo as General. Of his coming the courtier-like Alagiyawanna sang :

> "As when the fat fields are parched with drought and the loud-roaring rain-cloud bursts,
> Or as when to the dying man some gifted healer comes with rare drugs from the gods themselves,
> Thus he arrived among the people who were scattered through fear of the foe, bringing joy to the hearts of men".

Indeed he had not come a day too soon, for the condition of disorder which prevailed was appalling. The peace had relieved the Portuguese of all fear from the side of Senerat, and the soldiers had taken the opportunity to abandon the field for the city, and had brought with them the unrestrained licence of the camp. The honour of no woman was safe, and the Casados were compelled to take up arms against their own countrymen in defence of their families. Predatory bands met in the streets in open fight, while the more timid exchanged their swords for the yard-measure and harassed the inhabitants with their threatening importunities. The severe discipline of de Sa rapidly reduced to order the six hundred unprincipled vagabonds who formed the army, and bands of reliable veterans were enrolled for the purpose of giving the less experienced that confidence and example of which they were so badly in need. De Oliveira was placed in chief command, while instructions were issued to the Disawas to organise the native levies on a war footing.

The energy of the new General electrified the foul and lethargic atmosphere. All the outlying posts were visited in turn and strengthened as best they might be under the circumstances; and an army of spies was distributed throughout the country to discover and report the plans of the Sinhalese. A special mission with rich presents secured the neutrality of Senerat, whilst an expedition commanded by the General himself defeated Baretto, who had retired with Mayadunna to the mountains of the Adam's Peak range, with such heavy loss that his power was broken, and de Sa was enabled to return to Malwana to attend to other pressing administrative problems. De Oliveira was sent with an army to reduce Jaffna, where the Prince Chankili had seized the Government; the latter fled from the country in a panic, while the struggle for independence was continued by a certain Migapulle Arachchi, who was supported by troops from Tanjor, but his efforts were of little avail.

Learning of the resistance which was being offered, de Sa sent Luiz Teixeira to assist de Oliveira. Diabolical atrocities marked his route. By his orders men were hacked in two with axes, the breasts of women were torn off, and the wombs of mothers were slit open and the infants they carried in their arms forced within. A short but sharp struggle restored to the North a semblance of tranquillity, while at about the same time a further attempt on the part of Mayadunna in the South resulted in his being defeated and forced to retreat eastward.

In the meantime the mission of the impetuous Boschouwer to Holland had proved a failure, and he had turned for help to Denmark. Five vessels commanded by Ove Giedde were placed by King Christian at his disposal, and in May 1620 these appeared off the Eastern coast. The envoy himself had died on the voyage leaving a young widow. Mayadunna's agents at once approached Giedde with an offer to purchase his assistance, and to this proposal Senerat after some hesitation gave his consent. It was however too late. The Portuguese were now close at hand, and on the 2nd of July Mayadunna was forced to take refuge on board the fleet, whilst Baretto was overtaken and slain after a gallant struggle. The Danes thereupon sailed away, abandoning Boschouwer's destitute widow, whilst Mayadunna succeded in making his way across to India.

The success of de Sa moved the Camara of Colombo to such enthusiasm that the figure of an angel which adorned its Assembly Hall was ordered to be removed to make room for one of the General. Upon imformation of this resolution reaching King Philip, however, he expressed his disapproval of the course adopted, and by his command the discarded Angel was once again restored to its niche.

NOTES TO CHAPTER XI

1. In this matter de Azavedo acted up to the instructions contained in the King of Portugal's letter. For instance, when five Patangatins, or headmen from Chilaw, were baptised at Malwana on the Feast of Our Lady of Victories, 1606, de Azavedo "was pleased to grant them many favours and privileges, in order to cause the envy of the other gentiles, who might thus be led to follow their example.'- *Ceylon Antiquaty,* II, 21.

2. Cf. in this respect the Roman provincial Governor under the later Republic, e. g. Verres.

3. There was a similar feeling in Attica about the felling of olive trees, which were left untouched during the fiercest tribal wars.

4. It is a pleasure to note that the Jesuits had, as early as 1606, commissioned, one of their number to make a study of the history and antiquities of the Island. *Ceylon Antiquary,* II.

CHAPTER XII

In 1620 the Viceroy removed de Sa from office to make room for his own son Jorge de Alboquerque. The new General's administration was chiefly notable for a mutiny in the army, the soldiers deposing their officers and setting up a Board of Twelve to manage their affairs till the General should appoint a new Captain-Major. De Alboquerque himself was, however, so unpopular that a plot was set on foot to put him to death, though, owing to the interference of the Jesuits no evil results ensued. About the same time also a conspiracy was detected among the supporters of Mayadunna who was now in India, and for their complicity in this some of the most prominent Sinhalese had to pay the penalty with their lives. Everyone therefore was pleased when in 1623 de Sa once again resumed office. He brought with him instructions to reduce the Sinhalese Kingdom once for all, and to erect a fort at Trincomalee to control the fine anchorage which Senerat had promised to the Hollanders. The resources at his disposal were indeed of the scantiest, but in spite of the dissuasions of his Councillors he set out the following year to carry the second project into effect.

The site selected was the spot where de Azavedo had, in the course of his last expedition in 1612, made an unsuccessful attempt to erect a fort. This was the lofty headland of Konesar Malai, which, rising with its three great stone temples to a height of four hundred feet above the sea, was one of the most holy places of Hindu worship. The temples were ruthlessly destroyed to make way for a triangular fort of stone and mortar, which was equipped with guns obtained from a Danish vessel that had gone aground in the neighbourhood. The fort being completed a small garrison was left in charge, and de Sa returned to Colombo.

The act was an audacious infringement of the peace which Senerat had so long and so honourably maintained, and he prepared to offer resistance, but was soothed by the specious explanation that the fort was intended only as a protection against the European enemies who were beginning to appear in the Indian waters. De Sa now set about preparing for his further task. All manner of blandishments were employed to win the natives over to his side, and they were freely promoted to positions of trust and responsibility. At the same time the finances were organised on a sounder footing, the fortifications of Colombo and Galle were strengthened, and at the first-named place a powder-mill was erected to supply the local demand. De Sa saw to it that the soldiers were regularly paid, suppressed with vigour the illicit trade maintained by the officers, and, in spite of the opposition of the Vedor, Ambrosio de Freitas, succeeded in establishing a small local mint. He also warmly encouraged intermarriage between the races, but the system had already proved a failure; for Christianity would tolerate no other religion by its side, and the Sinhalese who married a Portuguese wife found himself cut adrift from his own people, while the position of the wife was far from being a happy one.

In the midst of these preoccupations de Sa found time to turn his attention to the question of the Moors, who, in spite of all the orders of King Philip to the contrary, still continued to make their way into the country in increasing numbers. Not only were they to be found along the Coast, but there were whole villages of them settled in the inland districts, where, as the only channel of trade, they performed a very important function. The

Semitic blood which ran through their veins was no doubt very limited in quantity, but it retained in a high degree its distinctive characteristics. The instinct for trade which had made the Arab a great sailor was also the dominating passion with the Moor of Ceylon. Tenacity of purpose marked all his actions in life; and though the Sinhalese were glad to see him appear, the cringing obsequious hawker with a pack on his back, in their remoter villages, they soon learnt to resent his attempts to settle in their midst. Once established in the village the hawker soon grew to be the money-lender, and he in time became the land-owner who, adding field to field, gradually absorbed the holdings of the villagers. The lust of gold which overwhelmed the Portuguese officers gave the Moorman his opportunity, for they found in him just the instrument that they needed. The Moor was an excellent man of business and was never at a loss to discover where his interests lay; when a Moorman collected six hundred *amunam*[1] of areca in one season for the benefit of the General, how was it to be expected that the latter should bring himself to enforce the orders for the expulsion of so useful a class? No doubt the Holy Office at Goa was scandalised by their employment under the State, but even that powerful Tribunal was unable to overcome the passive resistance of the Ceylon Government.

The honesty of de Sa was bitterly attacked by the Vedor, with whom he was never able to work in harmony; his connection with a monopoly of salt appears to demand explanation; and it is beyond dispute that he sent an ivory bed worth 4000 pardaos home to Lisbon. The documents bearing on the period of his administration are however not yet available to the student, and it is therefore right to suspend judgment. Meanwhile one fact stands to his credit, that he was able to shake himself free of the attractive trammels of the Moors. By his orders they were in

1625 driven away in large numbers. The bulk of them found an asylum within Sinhalese territory, and a large colony of them was settled in the district about Batticaloa.

De Sa now set about strengthening Menikkadawara, for it was his intention to use this place as a *point d'appui* for the operations which he had in view against the Sinhalese; and followed this up by making a dash to the Eastern coast, where he erected a small fort on the Island of Puliyan Tivu not far from Batticaloa. The site indeed was badly chosen and the Portuguese never received from it any benefit which adequately compensated for the expense and anxiety of maintaining it; but they were in a state of great trepidation, for the Sinhalese were whispering to each other a saying in their ancient writings that a nation with eyes like those of a cat in colour would soon make its way to the Island. Senerat himself was naturally indignant at this new breach of faith on the part of the Portuguese, but hesitated to draw the sword and attempted instead to buy them off. His attempts were however in vain. In 1627 war was declared and a small Portuguese army penetrated into Uwa and burnt the town of Badulla; but though the King and his three sons looked on, they refused to be drawn into an engagement.

At this point there first appears on the stage of events the great Commander who was destined for the last time to fan the smouldering energy of the Sinhalese into a blaze. The Court was in hiding at Mahiyangana when the Maha Biso Bandara, as the Queen was called, gave birth to Maha Asthana, the future Raja Sinha; but auspicious omens had attended his birth. And indeed to the Sinhalese mind no place of better augury could have been selected for this important event than that historic spot so closely interwoven with the remotest legends of their religion and race—a spot rendered sacred by the visit of the Buddha himself, and which had witnessed the gathering together of the avenging armies of Wijaya Bahu. On that very night, it was said, the Portuguese Commander had dreamed that he saw a tiny spark, no bigger than a firefly, floating from the west and growing in size as it travelled through the sky, till it waxed exceeding great over the port of Colombo and set everything there on fire; and the appearance of the infant Prince had been signalised by the success of the King's arms at Balane. It is customary for the horoscope of every Sinhalese child to be cast; Diyakelinawala, the great astrologer, was entrusted with the preparation of the Prince's, and sedulous care was lavished on his education to fit him for the high destiny which, it was prophesied, awaited him in life.

In 1628, when the Prince was sixteen years of age, Senerat summoned his three sons, and divided his kingdom among them by lot. He had seen clearly that of the three the youngest was also the strongest, and to his great delight it was to the youngest that the Uda Rata proper fell; Maha Asthana thus became *Aga Raja* or Chief King with the title of Raja Sinha; his brothers Kumara Sinha and Wijaya Pala received respectively the districts of Uwa and Matale.

In March 1629 de Sa again took the field. The result was unsatisfactory, for heavy rains had drenched the country, and the cold on the mountain ranges was severely felt by the ill-clad Portuguese, several of whom died of exposure. The leeches also proved a terrible plague to men marching through the sodden forests and across the swollen streamlets. Ambushes lay in wait for de Sa and his army in the most unexpected places, and it was necessary to advance with the utmost circumspection. Each village that they passed through was ravaged and every living thing therein slaughtered, but still the Sinhalese army refused to shew itself. Senkadagala, which was found deserted, was burnt, and then the weary Portuguese turned homewards; but the Sinhalese now began to press on them and continued to harass them all along their line of march, defeating them in a severe engagement at Ambatenna, whence the Portuguese, who had sustained heavy loss, were glad to make a precipitate retreat.

The exposure of the men to the inclemency of the weather was followed by its natural results. The General himself was soon prostrate with fever, and so critical was his condition considered that the Viaticum was administered to him. To the great relief, however, of the Portuguese his sickness took a turn for the better and he gradually regained his health.

In the meantime four of the chief Mudaliyars' in Colombo, men who had been treated with the greatest favour by de Sa who had promoted them to high office and to positions of emolument and trust, had entered into a conspiracy with Senerat. Before long a raiding expedition commanded by Kumara Sinha had crossed the frontiers of Uwa, and for a whole month the Portuguese looked helplessly on while their territory was ravaged; for with the limited resources at their command they dared not take the field. The position was disheartening and shameful, and to make matters worse there came two despatches from the new Viceroy, the Conde de Linhares, severely censuring de Sa for his supposed inaction. The Viceroy expressed strong disapproval of the policy of temporising which de Sa had been compelled to adopt, and the latter, the second Portuguese officer in the East, was sharply reminded that he had been sent to Ceylon to supervise the war and not to superintend the trade. De Sa took the matter deeply to heart, and in spite of the remonstrances of his most experienced officers, determined to invade forthwith the Sinhalese Kingdom.

Seven hundred Portuguese and 13,000 Lascarins were soon in the field. Toiling up the steep mountain ranges they moved slowly but unopposed till they reached Badulla, where two days were spent in sacking and burning the town. On the third morning the Sinhalese banners were seen flashing among the neighbouring hills. Skirmishing began at once, but the Sinhalese would not come to close quarters, and the Portuguese, seeing that they were gradually being encircled, prepared for the conflict which could no longer be avoided. Having set fire to their surplus stores and made confession, they began early in the morning to retire. The Lascarins of the disaffected Mudaliyars led the van, the remainder of the native troops forming a ring around the Portuguese. The army had not advanced far on the road before it found itself confronted by the Atapattu Guard, the pick of the King's forces. The Portuguese were already straggling, and Dom Cosme, a member of the conspiracy, seized the opportunity to run his sword through one of them, whereupon placing the head on a pike covered with white cloth, he immediately deserted accompained by his banner to the Sinhalese, and was followed by the bulk of the Lascarins.

And now the real struggle began. The Atapattu Guard charged from the front, while the rest of the Sinhalese, protected by the forest, poured into the ranks of the Portuguese their clouds of arrows and hail of musket-balls. For three days, losing heavily and without rest, the latter broke their way through the roughly constructed works of the Sinhalese. By the third day the pressure on the rear had become so severe that it was no more than a disorganised rabble, terror-stricken and cut off from the main body. Luiz Teixeira, the Disawa of the Seven Korales, and the Sergeant Major, with all of their officers and men who had not been shot down, were captured as they attempted to conceal themselves in the forest, for the King's orders were that the Portuguese were to be taken alive. At length on reaching the level tract of Randeni Wela the Portuguese found themselves completely surrounded. Some, however, of the Lascarins succeeded in breaking away and fleeing to Colombo, and de Sa was able to despatch a messenger to inform the city of his desperate plight.

There on the plain of Wellawaya the Portuguese spent that awful night. The Lascarins rapidly melted away, till not more than five hundred were left to share the fate of their white companions in arms, and it was impossible to erect any protection against the arrows and bullets that came whizzing past throughout the hours of darkness. The General himself exchanged his usual dress for a doublet and trousers, arming himself with a sword and a small shield, as there was heavy work to be done the next day. For none was there any sleep that night. The very elements indeed seem to have conspired to punish the Portuguese for the horrors to which they had subjected that unhappy country. A terrific downpour of rain lasting several hours drenched the army and rendered the firearms of the Portuguese useless. Their swords too were of little avail against opponents so agile as the Sinhalese; though the attempt to capture them alive resulted in a terrible waste of life. Gradually however the circle narrowed round the doomed men. By two o'clock in the afternoon two hundred of the Portuguese were stretched in death. The fight was thickest round the General, whom two servants kept supplied with loaded arquebusses. It was said indeed that he killed sixty men of those that hemmed him in with his own hand. At last orders were received to shoot him down. His servants were soon dead by his side, and as he drew his sword and rushed on the Sinhalese two arrows pierced him and he sank on his knees to the ground. Another arrow ended his life, and though round his corpse the struggle redoubled itself in fury, it was not for long, and with wild shouts of triumph the head of the brave de Sa was at last severed from his body.

A pyramid of Portuguese heads was raised on the field of battle, that of the General being laid at the feet of the aged and triumphant but compassionate King, who apostrophised it with these bitter words: "How often have I prayed you not to make war on me and destroy my realm, but to let me live in peace, while you kept the best part of Lanka: but if your successors follow in your footsteps, you will not be the last."[1]

It is hardly possible to exaggerate the gravity of the disaster which had overtaken the Portuguese, and once again if the Sinhalese had but had the means of blockading Colombo by sea, the complete destruction of their power in Ceylon would have been assured. Twenty-six days after its great victory the Sinhalese army, which had captured *en route* the fort of Saparagamuwa with the whole of its garrison, appeared before Colombo and laid it under close siege. Two fierce assaults were delivered and were repulsed with desperate courage; but such was the scarcity of provisions within the town, that cannibalism was freely practised, and hundreds of starving wretches had to be driven outside the walls. These refugees were kindly treated by Maha Asthana, though a number of them with base ingratitude attempted to set fire to his camp.

The chance arrival of some soldiers from Malacca, however, strengthened the garrison and enabled it to hold out till, after the end of three months, sickness compelled Maha Asthana to retire with a portion of his forces. On his way back to Senkadagala he captured Menikkadawara, and took with him thence two hundred Portuguese prisoners. Shortly afterwards the remainder of the Sinhalese army withdrew to Kaduwela. Assistance now came to the Portuguese from various parts of India, and they were enabled to show themselves outside the walls, but could do little else. A conspiracy was also discovered at Colombo itself, and the ringleader, a distinguished Sinhalese soldier, was punished by being blown from the mouth of a cannon. The situation was so helpless that the authorities at Goa found it difficult to persuade any prominent official to accept the vacant post of General, and it was not till the 21st of October 1631 that the aged Dom Jorge de Almeida landed as the successor of de Sa.

On his arrival negotiations were opened with Senerat to secure the release of the Portuguese prisoners, but the King was not prepared to sell cheaply the advantages which he had gained. He assured the Portuguése envoy that times had changed since he entered into the peace of 1617. "Then," said he, "my chief anxiety was to bring up my sons. Today they are men who can lean upon their spears and sleep." Large reinforcements were however soon received from Goa, and the General attempted to replace diplomacy by military force. In January 1000 Portuguese, 1000 Lascarins, and 1200 Kaffirs and Canarese took the field and advanced upon Malwana. The inhabitants of the district came together to render their submission, and, with the object of striking terror into them, the horrible expedient was adopted of delivering one of their number over to the Kaffirs, who cut him up and ate him in the sight of his wife and children, while others were given as slaves to the Portuguese Captains. Kaduwela was next occupied and step by step the Sinhalese were forced to withdraw before the advancing army.

Envoys were however sent to Goa from both sides to discuss the terms of peace, though hostilities did not relax, and on the 15th of April 1633 a treaty was signed between the Viceroy and the Sinhalese ambas. sadors under the terms of which the Portuguese agreed to recognise the three sons of the Queen as heirs to the whole of the Sinhalese Kingdom, while in return the King was to pay a nominal tribute of an elephant a year and to allow a Franciscan to reside at his Capital, besides setting at liberty all his Portuguese prisoners and handing over the fort of Batticaloa. The King at first refused to ratify the agreement, for he was unwilling to acquiesce in any such token of vassalage as the tribute of an elephant would imply; in the following year, however, Diogo de Melo de Castro having in the interval arrived as General in succession to de Almeida, the terms were after much wrangling agreed to.

King Philip IV. of Spain who had succeeded to the throne of Portugal in 1621, had been instant in urging on his Viceroy the importance of not slackening hostilities, but his country was unable to supply the men required to meet the unceasing drain. "It is of the utmost importance," wrote the Conde de Linhares on the 29th of November 1634, "that armadas should be despatched to the parts Your Majesty has indicated. Senhor, with what am I to create armadas if Your Majesty does not send me the men?"

The period of King Philip's reign was indeed one of great misfortune to Portugal. Her association with Spain had forced her into hostilities with the Hollanders and the English, and she now found herself treated, not as an independent kingdom, but as a Province. Spaniards were appointed to the highest offices of State, and Portuguese territory was freely given away to foreigners. Her revenue even was not spent for her own benefit, and her Cortes had ceased to exist.

Her naval power at home was broken, and her foreign commerce was being rapidly destroyed. The China trade was well-nigh closed to her; that of the Spice Islands was controlled by the Hollanders, who had established themselves at Batavia; Shah Jehan captured the headquarters of the Portuguese in Bengal; Ormuz, of which they were as proud as of Goa, was taken by the Persians; the English blocked their intercourse with West India; the Danes had acquired a centre at Tranquebar; and even the French were beginning to appear in the Indian waters. At the same time the wealth of the great Portuguese settlements in America was being conveyed by the shipload to enrich the shareholders of the trade companies in Holland; Goa itself was blockaded from time to time, and all Portuguese vessels which were met with on the high seas were plundered.

National bankruptcy was the natural result of this interference with the commerce of the country. No money could be found to pay for such soldiers as were secured, though at this very time the monks and friars' who were supported by the State were in a condition of affluence. The numbers of these latter had now assumed astonishing proportions, and in 1623 the Viceroy had reported that in Goa there were twice as many friars as all the other Portuguese put together. The bulk of the men who were sent to serve in the Indian army hastened to enter a religious Order, and the amazing dishonesty practised over the recruiting of the Portuguese forces, whereby shiploads of infants were despatched under the name of soldiers, contributed in no less degree to fill the Convents. The arrogance of some of the Orders was beyond belief. The Jesuits had made themselves masters of Travancore and of the pearl fisheries off that coast; they maintained armed men at their own expense, and even fought on the high seas with the King's officers. They had also succeeded in securing a general supervision over the works of the fortresses in the North, of which they refused to render any accounts. The private possessions of the Orders were so large as to be a scandal, and legislation had to be passed to prevent further acquisition.

This condition of decadence was reflected in events in Ceylon. The army had again got out of hand, and in 1635 rose once more in mutiny. It elected twelve Senators to administer its affairs and occupied the approaches to Colombo till it was allowed to elect its own officers. In 1636 King Senerat died and Maha Asthana, who had been administering the Government for some years, was proclaimed King under the title of Raja Sinha. He was prepared to maintain the peace his father had entered into, but the action of the officer in charge at Batticaloa in assisting some rebels against him compelled him to reconsider his position. Not unnaturally he turned to the Hollanders, who were now firmly established at Pulicat, and on the 9th of September 1637 he sent a letter offering them one of his ports if they would assist him against the Portuguese. As a result of this message two envoys appeared at Senkadagala on the 19th November of the same year with a promise of the required assistance, on condition of the Hollanders being granted a monopoly of the cinnamon trade.

Diogo de Melo was greatly alarmed at this development, for Raja Sinha's relations with him were so strained that the King had refused further communications. De Melo had been attempting to sow discord between Wijaya Pala and Raja Sinha, and had hinted that he was willing to support the former if he pressed his claims to the Throne. He now again wrote to Wijaya Pala, complaining of his brother's dealings with the Hollanders. He described the latter as "subjects and rebels of the King of Portugal, well-known to the whole of India as pirates, hated by all Indian Kings and potentates," and concluded with a threat to appeal to the sword.

Meanwhile the Hollanders had come to an agreement with Raja Sinha, and had returned to Pulicat accompained by three Sinhalese Commissioners who had been ordered to report on the Hollanders' navy. These Commissioners arrived back in the Island on the 2nd of April 1638 accompained by three vessels under the command of Wilhelm Jacobsz Coster, to find that a great change had taken place in the circumstances of the Portuguese.

Avarice had hastened that appeal to the sword which de Melo had threatened. The covetous General robbed a Portuguese trader of an elephant which Raja Sinha had presented to him, and in revenge the King seized on two handsome horses which the General had sent for sale within his Kingdom. A contemptuous message from Raja Sinha that the horses would be restored as soon as the elephant was surrendered inflamed the General's rage, and the arrival of a large contingent from Malacca added weight to the vehement protestations with which he wrung an unwilling consent from his Council. Nine hundred Portuguese, 5000 Lascarins, and a number of Topasses, Canarese, and Kaffirs, formed the army of invasion.

Realising the danger which threatened him the King sent the friar who was at Court, armed with a crucifix, to adjure the General in the name of that God Who, he believed, had come into the world to die for men, to desist from his unjust enterprise. De Melo replied with a brutal scoff, echoing the words of his Captain Major, Damiao Botado: "The little black is frightened. We will drag him out by the ears."

Once again the Portuguese were allowed to enter the Capital unopposed, and having set on fire the city, the palace and the temples, they retired on Balane, for in their haste they had left their communications unprotected. Night however overtook them at Gannoruwa before they could cross the river and they were compelled to halt, as the soldiers were exhausted and hungry. Raja Sinha's opportunity had come. A host of the finest woodsmen in the world were soon making their axes ring against the roots of the great forest trees, and the Portuguese realised with horror that they were trapped. The troops from Matale blocked the road back to Senkadagala ; from the surrounding forests a harassing and intermittent fire picked off every straggler ; while in front a strong force rendered it impossible to obtain water from the river except at the most serious risk.

The battle which now impended, that of Gannoruwa, was the last great battle of the Sinhalese race, and it produced a poet who is none the less notable that his very name is unknown. The *Parangi Hatane*, the Story of the Feringhees, is almost an Epic. It is the most spirited piece of literary composition in the language. It is no mere medley of tinkling bells and scented flowers, of lovely women and precious gems. It rings with the passion of Pindar ; it is Miltonic in its resounding roll of names ; it laughs with the glee of Chevy Chase. Amidst the roar of the cannon, and the glint of the sword blades, and the shouting of honoured names—the contempt for the eater of beef and the scorn for the drunken Kaffir—one central idea runs through it all : "twas all but the Merit of the King."

The morning of Palm Sunday, the 28th of March 1638, was dawning as the Portuguese once more resumed their retreat in the effort to reach the ford across the river ; but no sooner had they started than the Sinhalese fell on the Lascarins who were in charge of the baggage and succeeded in separating them from the main body, whereupon the coolies threw down their loads of rice and bread and biscuit, their jars of arrack and baskets of fowls, together with the munitions, and escaped as best they could, while the Lascarins by a desperate rush succeeded in rejoining the main army. The slopes of Kiriwat Talawa lay at no great distance, and the object of the Portuguese was to entrench themselves there; but they had hardly reached the high ground when they found themselves surrounded on all sides. The jingals and other larger guns of the Sinhalese were hurried forward and opened fire, and de Melo was soon constrained to beg for an armistice. Raja Sinha vouchsafed no reply, but on his orders his drummers made proclamation that if those Sinhalese who were with the Portuguese did not immediately leave them, they would all be put to the sword the next day.

The General watched with dismay as the ranks of the Lascarins grew rapidly thinner, and then the attack began. With a terrific shout the Sinhalese rushed up the hill in an irresistible wave. Throwing their bows over the heads of the Portuguese they dragged them down to the ground, and slashed at their necks with their swords. The burly Kaffirs were mercilessly beaten as they sprawled over the slippery surface of the hill-side. To attempt resistance to the overwhelming numbers of the Sinhalese was certain death, and many threw themselves on their knees and implored for mercy. The Sinhalese in their triumph were like a crowd of riotous and cruel schoolboys. The Portuguese were stripped and flogged remorselessly before they were put to death, many a one of them cursing the General with his last breath as the cause of this disaster. The Canarese were dragged away like bulls with their hands tied behind their backs, but they and the Kaffirs and thirty-three of the Portuguese were spared alive. A great pile of heads was laid at the feet of the triumphant King, who had conducted the fight from beneath the shade of a tree; the body of the General could not be found though careful search was made, but his sword was discovered and presented to the victor.

The destruction of the invading army was complete; and at Dodanwala Dewale the grateful King offered his headdress of gold and his sword of steel as a humble thank-offering to the Power that ruled the fate of the battle.

NOTES TO CHAPTER XII.

1. An Amunam varies from 24,000 to 26,000 nuts.
2. Their defection gave the death-blow to the policy of intermarriage, for they were closely connected by marriage with the chief Portuguese families in Colombo.
3. The exploits of de Sa made a great impression on the Sinhalese, by whom he was deified, along with the bloodthirsty Simao Correa, who seems to have come to a violent end some time previously. De Sa's body was ceremoniously cremated on the King's orders.
4. If reliance is to be placed on the stories heard by Niccolao Manucci, who was in India from 1656 to 1717, the morality of the Friars in Ceylon was not different from that of the rest of their countrymen in the East. (See Storia do Mogor, Irvine's Trans, iv. 152-153.)

CHAPTER XIII

To crown Raja Sinha's joy, on the 10th of May following Admiral Adam Van Westerwold joined Coster at Batticaloa with the rest of the promised fleet. Raja Sinha himself arrived four days later accompanied by 15,000 men, leaving Wijaya Pala with the rest of the army to menace Colombo. On the 18th the combined forces attacked the Portuguese position, and after a bombardment lasting four hours, Westerwold's guns compelled the garrison to surrender.

Five days later a treaty was entered into between Raja Sinha, "Emperor and King of Ceylon and Candia," and Westerwold, acting on behalf of "Their Illustrious High Mightinesses the States General of the United Netherlands and His Princely Excellency Frederick Hendrick, Prince of Orange," by which the King accepted the Hollanders as his "friends, allies and protectors" against the "great and intolerable deceit and impertinence of, and annoyance created by, the Portuguese." It was agreed that the booty found in all forts captured by the allied powers should be equally divided between the two High Contracting Parties, and that, should the King so desire, the positions should be occupied by garrisons with sufficient artillery for their protection against the Portuguese. The King for his part undertook to strengthen the fortifications where required, to pay the salaries of the garrisons employed in holding them, and to allot the Hollanders suitable places for the storage of their merchandise. He agreed not to begin hostilities without previously consulting them, to render them assistance by counsel and deed, and to repay in kind all expenses incurred by them on his behalf. The Hollanders were to be allowed unrestricted freedom of trade, with a monopoly of the commerce in cinnamon, pepper, wax and ivory. The trade in elephants was, however, reserved to the King, though a most-favoured-nation clause was inserted by which he undertook to supply the Hollanders each year with as many of these animals as he sold to others.

The Treaty further guaranteed the extra-territoriality of the Hollanders, and while it secured for their merchants untrammelled access to the country, made it incumbent on the Sinhalese to provide the necessary transport for all goods purchased by them. Provision was made for the extradition of criminals; communication for the purposes of trade or otherwise between the Portuguese and the Sinhalese was forbidden, and the Portuguese declared the eternal enemies of both parties. Catholic priests in particular, "who alone are the cause of commotion, dissension and disturbance, and are the destruction of kingdoms and countries wherever they happen to be," were not to be allowed to enter the country. Finally all prize ships captured on the high seas were to be the property of the Hollanders.

Such were the terms of this important Treaty. On its conclusion de Melo's sword was presented to Westerwold, who sailed away to Batavia on the 4th of June 1638, accompanied by two Sinhalese ambassadors, and taking with him a supply of cinnamon, wax, and pepper, which had been sent to him by the King, while Coster remained in charge at Batticaloa. On the 29th October the ambassadors returned with a despatch from the Governor-General Antonio van Diemen and the Council of India, directed—with the fulsome obsequiousness which the practice of the Spanish Court had rendered familiar among the diplomatists of Europe—to "The Great and Mighty Radio Singha, Emperor of the Island of Ceylon; King of Kandy, Cote, Seytabaca, Dambadoney,

Anarrajapore, Jaffnapatam; Prince of Uva, Mature, Dinavaco, Quatre Corles; Grand Duke of the Seven Corles; Count of Cotenwe, Trinquemale, Batacalo, Vilacam, Vintana, Dumbra, Pandjapato, Hewerta, Putalon, Balane, Gaele, Beligaon, Calature, Columbo, Negumbo, Chilao, Madampe, Calpety, Aripature, Manaer; Lord of the Pearl Fishery, Gems, and the Golden Sun."

This letter contained a confirmation of the Treaty which the Council, adopting the Sinhalese metaphor, hoped would last "as long as the Sun and the Moon shall lighten the earth with their rays." The King, who was unaccustomed to the craft and diplomacy of the Hollanders, was completely deceived by their show of deference, and regarded with delight the powerful assistance which he had succeeded in purchasing ; but the views of the Hollanders were different. They had already made up their minds that the expulsion of the Portuguese did not necessarily imply the cessation of European interference in the country, and Raja Sinha was in their eyes nothing more than a convenient tool and source of supply for the funds necessary for the war with the Portuguese. They stood to lose nothing in case of the failure of the attempt, while it was incumbent on the King, if he was to achieve the object on which he had set his heart, to assist the Hollanders in rendering their fortifications impregnable. Once the Portuguese were gone and the Hollanders were safe within those fortifications, who was there to drive *them* out of the country ?

In pursuance of this policy they did not shrink from tactics of a dubious nature. The third section of the treaty, for instance, dealt with the occupation of the captured forts; but whereas in the Portuguese copy which the King could read there was a proviso to the effect that they were to be garrisoned *only if the King so desired,* this clause was deliberately omitted in the Dutch version. Bearing this in mind, it becomes possible to get a clear understanding of the subsequent dealings of the Hollanders with the Sinhalese Court.

Dom Antonio Mascarenhas was hurried across from India as General, and all available Portuguese forces were diverted to the defence of Ceylon. The war dragged on, and the reinforcements they had received enabled the Portuguese to push back the Sinhalese and re-occupy Menikkadawara; but in the meantime there was trouble at the Sinhalese Court. Kumara Sinha had early followed Senerat to the grave, and Raja Sinha had taken possession of his principality without sharing it with Wijaya Pala, as the latter demanded. This embittered the Prince, and he appears on account of it to have lent a readier ear to the suggestions of the Portuguese. Gallant warrior though he had shown himself to be, a curious vein of sentiment ran through his somewhat feeble character. The influence of his early Portuguese training manifested itself in strong pro-European tendencies, and his attempt to smuggle out of the country the prisoners who had been captured at Gannoruwa finally led to an open rupture with the King. In September 1638 the sword was drawn between the two brothers, but Wijaya Pala and his 8000 men were defeated, and the Prince himself was taken prisoner. Raja Sinha however was not prepared to deal harshly with the brother who had helped him so well in his hour of need, and merely kept him in surveillance at Senkadagala.

Early in the following year Antonio Caen reached the Island with another fleet of the Hollanders, to the great consternation of the Portuguese. Instead, however, of attacking Colombo as the King desired, he proceeded to capture the petty fort of Trincomalee, which surrendered in May after resisting a few days. In December of the same year a second fleet appeared bringing 1500 soldiers under the command of the Director General Philip Lucaszoon. The men were landed in the neighbourhood of Negombo, and the Portuguese army which was engaged in watching the movements of the Sinhalese hurried thither, and in spite of a disparity of numbers attacked the Hollanders with the utmost boldness. A fierce struggle followed but though the Hollanders were driven from their first line of defence, the weight of numbers told in the event in their favour, and the Portuguese were thrown back till they finally broke in confusion and fled. Raja Sinha's army had hurried down after the Portuguese, and on the 6th of February 1640 the allied forces laid siege to Negombo which was carried by assault three days later. The battered walls were taken charge of by the Hollanders, who proceeded at once to repair and strengthen them. Raja Sinha, greatly annoyed at the overbearing attitude of Lucaszoon, insisted that they should be razed to the ground in accordance with the option reserved to him under the third clause of the Treaty; but Lucaszoon was obdurate, and on the 13th of February Raja Sinha quietly withdrew to a distance, and refused to see the Director General again, though when, even after this, Lucaszoon fell seriously ill, the King in spite of their quarrel hastened to do what he could to assist him in his distress.

Alexander the Great had Hindus attached to his army to attend to such wounds as his own physicians could not heal, and the medical works of Charaka and Susruta, who lived at least 2500 years ago, are still valued. The Sinhalese have always paid considerable attention to the subject of medicine, and as early as the second century B. C. Gamani had not only established hospitals throughout the country, but had appointed a doctor for every group of sixteen villages. Six centuries later King Buddadassa who appears to have been familiar with the operation for appendicitis, set apart a fixed proportion of the revenue from the royal lands for the upkeep of a medical department. "I cannot but admire," wrote Antonio Teixeira, who was in the Island in 1588, "at those who call all physicians Barbarians, that are not Greeks or Latins . . . There have been, and still are, in Persia, Arabia and India many Physicians so excellent in their art that they are fit to be Professors in any country."

The Sinhalese have long known the value of the open air treatment, and so great is the efficacy of their antiseptic oils that they still treat successfully serious cases of fracture without having resort to amputation. Not only is their skill great in dealing with diseases such as dysentery which are incidental to a hot climate, but they also claim to be able to treat cases of hydrophobia and snake bite. They understand thoroughly the art of dieting a patient, and their system has been adopted by some of the most experienced of the physicians who have come to the country after a training on Western lines. As low dieting approaching to starvation is the foundation on which their treatment for all disorders of the digestive organs is based, the system—as Garcia de Orta pointed out in 1563—was not appreciated by Europeans. "The cure was for the Gentiles," he wrote, "who eat nothing with blood." Hypnotism has been always employed, though it is branded to-day by well-meaning persons under the name of "devil-ceremonies." The effects of the exhalations of different trees, of the contact of different metals with the human body, of the rays of the sun at varying hours, have like-wise all been made the subject of careful study; and the experience and observation of ages have left to the Sinhalese a great store of knowledge, of which the Portuguese, be it said to their credit, took advantage to no small extent.[1]

Such were the physicians whom the King now sent to attend on Lucaszoon, but the latter was so ill that he was obliged to sail away, leaving Coster in charge. With much tact Coster succeeded in pacifying the King, and it was arranged to make a dash on Galle, the Hollanders proceeding by sea, the Sinhalese by land.

The Portuguese fort of Santa Cruz de Galle occupied the rising ground which forms a promontory on the western side of the extensive Bay, the natural beauties of the surroundings of which do not, however, compensate for the dangers of its hidden rocks. A sandy depression connects the promontory with the mainland, which rises sufficiently to command the fort. On the side facing the sea the position was well defended by the natural ruggedness of the coast, while a line of ramparts with three bastions served to protect the landward side.

As the fleet sailed southward along the coast a body of Lascarins from Colombo kept pace with it, but was unable to prevent the Hollanders from landing on the eastern side of the Bay, and entrenching themselves close to the town outside the fort. The next day an attempt was made to drive them away from their position. The fight was desperately maintained, and the Portuguese claimed to have killed eight hundred of the enemy, but were none the less compelled to withdraw to within the fort with the loss of their Commander as well as that of seventy men—a not inconsiderable proportion of the entire force at their disposal. A heavy bombardment of the walls was now begun and this was maintained till they were sufficiently broken down to allow of an assault, which was carried out on the 13th of March. In spite of the unequal numbers the Portuguese resisted with the utmost gallantry, and over a hundred of them lay dead before the

Hollanders forced their way in. Everyone who was found with arms within the walls was put to the sword, while the rest were hurriedly taken on board the Hollanders' vessels and despatched to Batavia.

A half share of the plunder was allotted to the King, who was delighted at the success, though he was suspicious of the conduct of the Hollanders in beginning the assault before the time that had been agreed upon with his Mudaliyars, and though he was persuaded that he had been defrauded in the division of the spoil. The Kaffirs and Canarese who had served with the Portuguese were taken charge of by the Hollanders, 1500 Sinhalese prisoners were delivered over to the King, and "to prevent all future unpleasantness" permission was granted to the soldiers to marry the numerous Mestico widows and the few unmarried women who were in the town. Captain Walraven de St. Amant with 196 men occupied the fort on the King's account, and Coster also took up his residence there as President of the Company's people at Galle.

The loss of this port, the great value of which had been frequently insisted on by the King, created such perturbation among the Portuguese that there were those who urged the desirability of abandoning Colombo itself. This desperate counsel was however rejected, and all the available troops were mustered to defend the town, while reinforcements were hurried across from India. Meanwhile internal troubles which were sternly repressed kept Raja Sinha occupied at home. He called upon the Hollanders to present their bill, for he was anxious to pay them what was due before asking them for more soldiers; but this prompt settling of accounts did not suit the Hollanders, whose policy it was to involve the King in pecuniary obligations to them. The relations between the parties consequently grew so strained that Coster decided to wait upon the

King in person, and he presented himself at Court at Senkadagala on the 17th of July 1640. Unfortunately there was friction from the beginning. Coster's interpreter was arrested while having a secret interview with Wijaya Pala; the portrait of the Prince of Orange which had been presented to the King was returned without a word of explanation; and the Sinhalese courtiers bore themselves towards Coster and his suite with cold reserve.

Coster, however, submitted a Memorandum setting out the points to which he invited the King's attention. He begged that a supply of cinnamon, wax, and pepper might be prepared against the next sailing season in part payment of the Company's claim; that the freedom of trade which had been promised might be made a reality; and that parties desirous of trading with the Hollanders should not be interfered with. He further asked for some villages in the neighbourhood of Galle for the maintenance of the soldiers, at the same time requesting that directions should be given to the King's Disawa to see that provisions were regularly delivered to the garrison. He complained, moreover, of the condition of the local currency, and requested that steps should be towards the establishment of a Mint as provided for in the treaty of Batticaloa. In conclusion he urged the King to supply vessels for the purpose of guarding the rivers, and to erect a fireproof store at Kottiyar for the Company's use.

The King sent his reply in writing, expressing regret at the delay in meeting the claims of the Hollanders, and attributing the delay to the impoverished condition of the country. He undertook to supply a large quantity of cinnamon as soon as Batticaloa should be handed over to him, but asked for a detailed statement of the entire claim against him before further reinforcements were sent. He moreover declared that everyone was at liberty to trade with the Company, so long as it did not infringe the royal monopoly. The irregularity in the supply of provisions he stated to be due to the devastation of the countryside in the neighbourhood of Galle, but he promised to allow the Hollanders some villages as requested, and agreed to build the vessels and construct the store as soon as the country should be more settled. With regard to the question of the currency, he pointed out that the matter was seriously complicated by the depreciated Portuguese coin which was held in stock in the Portuguese districts.

In the meantime Coster had learnt that some Indians had come to the Court with an offer of assistance to the King, and that these men were traducing the Hollanders; and he was still further incensed at a message from the Chiefs occasioned by his having gone armed into the King's presence. He expressed himself very warmly on this latter subject to the King, who at the same interview directed that the reinforcements which were said to be on the way should be sent to attack Colombo, though he declared that he himself would be unable to render much assistance for at least three years, owing to the condition of the country. Coster was then given permission to depart.

Scarcely had he started on his way when he was overtaken by a Sinhalese courtier, named Colombo Nainde, who had been ordered to search a slave who had joined himself to Coster's train. The owner of the slave, a Portuguese priest, had missed some valuables; but though the slave was stripped and searched, nothing was found on him. Coster in a passion took from his own neck the gold collar with which the King had presented him and threw it at Colombo Nainde's feet, declaring that after the insult to which he had been exposed, that chain might be used to make good the priest's loss. Colombo Nainde, however, endeavoured to pacify him and replaced the chain with much ceremony round his neck.

The wild village of Nilgala was at length reached, and there the arrogance and hasty temper of Coster brought about his death. He called for some milk, and as there was delay in procuring it, struck the Mudaliyar who commanded his escort on the chest with his cane. The Sinhalese who witnessed this outrage raised a great tumult and attacked the Hollanders with their pikes. Coster tried to escape into a house, but, as he stooped to enter through the low door, he was run through by the spears of the Sinhalese and decapitated.

On the 8th of September Thyssen, who was in charge of the Hollanders at Batticaloa, received a letter from the King expressing his regret at what had occurred, and conveying a hope that this would not interfere with the friendly relations subsisting between him and the Hollanders. Thyssen hurried at once to Galle, only to find that the amorous St. Amant, who had fallen in love with a young Portuguese woman, had deserted to the enemy with a few of his companions, and had made his way to Colombo. St. Amant's report of the condition of things at Galle, where the garrison was suffering great want, did much to raise the spirits of the Portuguese, for Negumbo was known to be in even worse plight. At the same time the fortunate capture of an enemy vessel conveying specie to Masulipatam enabled Mascarenhas to give the soldiers a double allowance of pay.

Nevertheless the condition of affairs in the East was, from the Portuguese point of view, extremely gloomy. The Hollanders had obtained an almost complete control over the trade of the Far East, and were adopting an increasingly aggressive attitude on the coasts of India. Their fleets were continually and in every quarter harassing the ships of the Portuguese, and hovered round even in the immediate vicinity of Goa. Naval engagements were frequent, but had no decisive results. Such was the lack of funds that once again public offices had to be put up for sale. Malacca was in danger, and King Philip, while urging the importance of straining every nerve to preserve that important settlement, was obliged to confess that in view of the trouble created by the Hollanders in Brazil, it was not possible to send any assistance. The Viceroy replied that under the circumstances it appeared that the time had come to wind up affairs in the East and return home. A terrible blow was dealt to the Portuguese when in 1639 the Hollanders sailed to Murmagoa, one of the two ports of Goa, and set fire to the three great galleons which lay at anchor there. In August of the following year they began the siege of Malacca, which they succeeded in capturing a few months later.

In September 1640 the Conde de Aveiras arrived in India as Viceroy. He realised that the position of affairs was nearly desperate, and that unless help was sent to Ceylon as quickly as possible, everything there would be lost. Don Philip Mascarenhas was selected for the difficult task. Not only was he recognised as possessing great talents, but he had also much wealth which, it was thought, he would not hesitate to expend on behalf of his King; while at the same time his appointment was likely to be less irritating to his brother Dom Antonio who was then General, than that of a stranger. With Mascarenhas went Joao Ribeiro, then a boy of fourteen, who has left us in his *Fatalidade Historica*, the fruits of his eighteen years in Ceylon, a lively and valuable account of the last years of the Portuguese in that country.

The arrival in Ceylon of Dom Philip was soon followed by the re-capture of Negombo, which surrendered on the 9th of November 1640, and the defeat of a Sinhalese army which was in the neighbourhood. Raja Sinha, who had come down to the low country, retired on Senkadagala, and the entire coast from Colombo to the neighbourhood of Galle declared for the Portuguese. The Hollanders viewed the turn of affairs with anxiety. They feared, not without reason, that the loss of the Matara Disawani would result in that of the whole cinnamon trade; Galle itself was being threatened, and they were not sure as to the temper of the King. He had demurred to paying certain items in the bill which had been presented to him. Trincomalee and Negombo, he had pointed out, had been garrisoned by the Hollanders not only without any request from him to that effect, but in opposition to his expressed wish. Under the circumstances he denied that he was in any way responsible for the expenditure incurred in their maintenance. He was however very angry with Mascarenhas about a threat which the latter had held out to him to place Wijaya Pala on the throne, and he accordingly sent an embassy to Batavia to discuss matters. Before long Galle was blockaded by the Portuguese, and their armies also penetrated into the Four and Seven Korales, but could effect little beyond laying the country waste.

In the meantime Wijaya Pala himself had raised the standard of revolt in Uwa; his rebellion however ended in failure, and he was obliged to escape down the Idelgashinna Pass into Saparagamuwa, where he was received by the Captain Major with effusive protestations of the gratitude of the Portuguese for the attitude which he had maintained towards them at such terrible risk to himself. Wijaya Pala was much pleased and asked for the services of three companies of Portuguese, promising on his part to assist them to drive the Hollanders out of the Island. The Captain Major was, however, unable to comply with this request without the authority of the General, and the Prince showed in his face how grievously he felt the disappointment. To make matters worse an aged noble, who had brought up the Prince as a child and had accompained him in his flight, bluntly expressed his dissatisfaction at the manner in which the Portuguese proved their gratitude, whereupon the Captain Major in a burst of uncontrollable rage, ordered him to be arrested and executed on the spot.

The unhappy Prince realised too late the mistake he had made in placing himself in the hands of the Portuguese. For two days he refused to see the Captain Major, but at length was prevailed on to go to Malwana to meet the General. He was received by Mascarenhas with a similar ceremonious courtesy and like protestations of gratitude. Two chairs covered with crimson velvet and gold were placed on a dais, and there Wijaya Pala and the General sat down side by side. The Prince, who was now about thirty-four years of age, impressed everyone by his dignity and regal bearing. He was slim of body and carried himself very erect; his long hair was curled at the ends and his beard was worn full in the Portuguese fashion. For a whole hour the two sat there exchanging compliments, Wijaya Pala toying with the great catseye, as large as a musket ball, which was bound to his arm. Then with a passionate exclamation he poured out his grief at the manner in which his trusted adviser had been done to death. Mascarenhas did his best to console the agitated Prince, and it was finally decided that he should go on to Colombo, where again he was received with full military honours.

A Council was summoned to deliberate as to what action should be taken to assist him in regaining his principality; but after much discussion a pedantic adherence to their standing instructions regarding the conversion of heathen Princes who fell into their power, prevented the Portuguese from complying with his request, and the disappointed Prince left for Goa, where he subsequently embraced Christianity and died in 1654. His departure relieved Raja Sinha of an embarrassing kinsman, and enabled him to seize on the Matale district for himself.

In October 1641 the King's Ambassadors returned from Batavia. The communications which passed between Raja Sinha and the Council there have been preserved and form interesting reading. The Council, pursuing its policy of deferential obsequiousness, had reported to the King with what state and ceremony his previous letter had been received. "It is a proper disposition," replied the King, "in the person who occupies such a place as you do." His indignation at the attitude assumed by Lucaszoon finds expression in the following passage: "He put on one side the Articles of the Treaty which was made at Batticaloa, desiring to alter it in some matters so as to act contrary thereto. And as the Dutch nation is considered and acknowledged in all regions to be trustworthy in its professions, and as it is not befitting in Kings of my standing to abandon what has been once ordered and agreed upon, I, seeing that the aforesaid Philippe Lucas enlarged the scope of the Treaty in many matters contrary to its articles, once agreed upon and sworn to, desired not to abide by what he at that time determined upon." Nevertheless, Lucaszoon's conduct has not shaken his confidence in the Hollanders: "So long as I live I shall love the Dutch nation, regarding it as the light of mine eyes, and my successors shall do the same, yea, so long as the Sun and Moon shall shine." In proof of his unswerving good faith he had sentenced the man who had caused the death of Coster to be hanged, though he was satisfied himself that it was

Coster himself who was to be blamed for that tragic affair.

Yet in spite of all he was not prepared to pay the expense of the garrison which had been maintained at Trincomalee against his wishes. If, as he said, the Hollanders' garrisons had suffered from want, it was because they had been kept in the forts despite his opposition. If he had chosen to call the Hollanders faithless, he would have had good reason for doing so, for they had throughout acted in defiance of the terms of the Treaty. He was, however, prepared to overlook all their offences in this respect. "When Colombo is captured the booty found therein shall be equally distributed and the city itself destroyed, leaving not one stone upon another. I have for many a year had a longing to destroy the city of Colombo, and to raze it to the ground, for it is the origin and the mother of all the evil that has come upon this Island and the lawful Kings thereof."

The Hollanders had suggested that when the Portuguese were driven out, it would be well for the safety of the country to maintain four forts manned by Hollanders; but the King retorted that there was no such stipulation in the Treaty, and that he was quite as competent to protect his country, once the Portuguese were gone, as his great namesake of Sitawaka had been. Yet through all he had implicit confidence in his Allies, and he frankly told them: "If you went away I should not enjoy the honour which I have long striven after, that of driving the Portuguese away from this Island." In answer to their protestations of loyalty he replied: "I shall remind you that Kings of my position do not break their Royal word, and thus promise you, on my honour as a King, that I shall keep the word which I have given, to observe the Treaty and to give no occasion to break it."

Attempts on the part of the Portuguese to seduce the garrison of Galle were attended with very slight success; but though the blockade had now been maintained for a long period, they still feared to venture on a siege. An assault was out of the question, for though the garrison was weak the walls were strong. A siege was equally impracticable, since vessels were lacking to bring the necessary guns from Colombo. Some laid all the blame on Mascarenhas, asserting that he was too busy trading to attend to the war, and the Viceroy found it necessary to address some severe despatches to him; but the truth was that the Portuguese were afraid to face the risk of a possible defeat. As Mascarenhas pointed out to the Viceroy: "All the Sinhalese already (considered) themselves as relieved from any Christian yoke."

If the attitude of the Portuguese was characterised by a certain lack of self-confidence, that of the Hollanders can only be described as pusillanimous. During January and February 1642 their fleet kept cruising about in the neighbourhood of Colombo, but after much solemn deliberation it was decided that the position was too strong to be attempted and that it was better to recapture Negombo. On their sailing thither, however, the hearts of the Hollanders again failed them, and they hastened once more back to Galle. In the meantime great changes had taken place in Europe. France had been moulded into a mighty kingdom by the hand of Richelieu, and in December 1640 an insurrection in Portugal had ended the Sixty Years' Captivity, and placed the eighth Duke of Braganza on the throne as King Dom Joao IV. This revolution was welcomed with joy by the United Provinces, who hastened to conclude a treaty with the once more sovereign State. Under this Treaty, which was dated the 12th of June 1641 and which was to come into force in the East Indies a year after its conclusion, there was to be peace between the two nations for a period of ten years, each nation remaining in possession of what it actually held at the date of its promulgation. All Allies of the two High Contracting Parties were equally included in its terms.

The declaration of the peace in Ceylon was however delayed by negotiations regarding the territorial limits of the fort of Galle, which were claimed by the Hollanders, and hostilities continued till the matter was settled. On the 11th of May 1643 a body of two hundred Portuguese was attacked by a strong force of Hollanders at Akuressa, but so gallant was the defence that after a fight lasting five hours the Hollanders fled in confusion, leaving behind them over a hundred dead and fifty prisoners. In consequence of this defeat Van der Laen and Doncq, the two officers in command, were ordered to proceed to Batavia to be placed on their trial.

The failure of the peace negotiations, which had been referred by the General to the Council at Goa, put the Batavian authorities on their mettle, and Francois Carron, Councillor of India, shortly arrived before Galle and landed with a force of 1400 Europeans. Elaborate plans were laid for attacking the five hundred Portuguese who were encamped in the neighbourhood, but after a week's toil the attempt was abandoned as too dangerous, and Carron sailed away to Negombo, which he reached on the 7th of January 1644. Learning of this Dom Antonio Mascarenhas hurried up with 550 Portuguese, and, with the reckless courage which had throughout marked his career, attacked the Hollanders; but in spite of their gallantry the Portuguese were gradually hemmed in by the superior numbers of the enemy, Dom Antonio himself fell with no fewer than nine gunshot wounds, and very few of his men left the field alive.

The feeble garrison that was within the walls closed the gates and attempted a last desperate resistance. A shower of blazing powder barrels greeted the Hollanders as they forced their way within ; the Captain in charge, fighting sword in hand, was hacked to pieces, while the rest of his companions were either killed or taken prisoner. The Hollanders, accompanied by 2000 of Raja Sinha's men, now started by land for Colombo, but finding the Southern bank of the Kelani Ganga occupied by the Portuguese, their hearts failed them and they returned to Negombo, whence Carron sailed away on the 18th of March 1644, leaving a garrison of 500 men in occupation.

Reinforcements from India now raised the available Portuguese army to 1300 Europeans. In June 1644 they once more appeared before the town and after a month's siege attempted to carry it by assault. So mismanaged, however, was the affair that 600 Portuguese were left dead before the walls, while a remanant of 400 dispirited men dragged themselves back to Colombo. Fortunately on the 10th of January 1645 the long-discussed peace, which left each side in the possession of such terrritory as was *de facto* in its power, was agreed to, and the Portuguese once more obtained a breathing space.

NOTES TO CHAPTER XIII

1. An organised effort is at last being made among the natives themselves to foster as much of their medical science as has survived a century of neglect and ignorant opposition.

CHAPTER XIV

The conclusion of peace was followed by a disagreement between the Hollanders and Raja Sinha, who had found strong ground for complaint in the manner in which the negotiations had been conducted so far as they affected his interests. All the arts of cajolery were brought to bear in the effort to pacify him, while at the same time the Hollanders proceeded steadily with the work of establishing themselves in the Seven Korales. The King insisted on the removal of the garrison which had been left at Pannara from his territory, but under pretext of doing so the Hollanders smuggled in ammunition in casks of rice. Thereupon he sent an indignant letter pointing out that while the Council of Batavia was inviting him to take possession of the district, the local authorities were strengthening their forces in order to rob him of it, and adding that he was coming in person to find out what they were about.

On the 13th of May 1645 Adrian van der Stel, late Commander of Mauritius, left Negombo for the camp at Pannara with one hundred and fifty men and two guns. Nothing further was heard till three days later, when a naked Hollander appeared at Negombo with a pitiful tale. Gorgeously clad in scarlet and carried in a palanquin, van der Stel was proceeding on his way when he was met by a Sinhalese officer who politely inquired from him what he was doing there with so many armed men, as the

King himself had given a promise to see that the garrison at Pannara was escorted safely to Negombo. Van der Stel, with that arrogance which had previously brought disaster upon Coster, replied sharply that this was no concern of the King's. The officer earnestly begged him to consider his position; the Sinhalese were there in strong force, and if he insisted on pursuing his course not a limb of the Hollanders would leave the place.

The Hollander, however, was obdurate, and the Sinhalese opened fire. Van der Stel ran out his two field guns and fired on them with grape, but the Sinhalese skilfully withdrew to cover, whence they poured such a deadly hail of bullets into the ranks of the Hollanders that before long few of the latter were left alive. The Sinhalese then rushed on the demoralised remnants sword in hand. Van der Stel, begging for quarter, had his head cut off by the stroke of a sabre, and when one hundred and three lay dead on the ground, the remainder broke, and fled into the jungle. The King hearing the firing hurried up and issued a proclamation by beat of drum, promising to spare the lives of those Hollanders who had escaped. The head of van der Stel, placed on a silver dish and covered with a white cloth, was courteously sent to the commander of the garrison at Pannara, to be buried according to the rites of his people.

The Sinhalese army now appeared before the camp. A long line of ghastly heads fixed on pikes was carried round the stockade in procession, that the soldiers might see for themselves what had taken place; and then Raja Sinha called upon the garrison to surrender. In the course of the night he ran up earthworks of sufficient height to make it possible to fire down into the camp, and the next morning the entire force, numbering five hundred men, surrendered with all its baggage and ammunition.

The immediate result of this *coup* was that the Hollanders set about preparing for war, but upon calmer reflection they were fain to admit that they had put themselves in the wrong, and accordingly attempted to enter into negotiations. For six months the King met their overtures with a contemptuous silence, till in their perplexity they were obliged to beg for permission to send an ambassador to the Court, at the same time entreating that His Majesty might be pleased to hear him. It was not, however, till July 1647 that the indignant monarch vouchsafed a reply. The Portuguese too were making overtures to him, and the King for many months amused himself by keeping the ambassadors of the two nations dancing attendance at his Court, and by confronting them each with the other.

The year 1648 dragged on into 1649 and no progress had been made; but in July of the latter year, to the great relief of the Hollanders, ambassadors appeared from the King with a conciliatory message and fresh proposals of his own. The ambassadors were received with a salute of eleven guns and three salvoes of artillery, and the signing of the new agreement was celebrated by the ringing of joy-bells and the discharge of rockets. Nevertheless at this very moment Maatsuycker, who had succeeded Thyssen at Galle, was writing to his Principals in Batavia that the only means of dealing with the King was to employ force. The policy of double dealing adopted by the Hollanders, indeed, made a final settlement impossible, and the King bluntly accused them of "tergiversations, subterfuges, and courtesies." He was enraged at the chicanery of the *casta Hollandeza*, as he contemptuously called them, and he coldly asked for a detailed statement of the expenses they had incurred in his service, pointing out that this had never been submitted to him in spite of his repeated demands. At length, however, after much angry correspondence, the quarrel was patched up.

The ensuing period of peace was a great relief to the Sinhalese, who were utterly weary of devastation and slaughter. The people settled down once more to cultivate their fields and to rebuild the villages which had been destroyed, while the King spent most of his time in Badulla and Bintenna, away from the harassing cares of Government. He did not realise that the Hollanders had already decided that none of the territory which yielded cinnamon, and which was now in their power, was to be restored to him, and with a light heart he turned to those diversions which had always attracted him. His fondness for animals was well-known, and strange beasts were among the most welcome presents which could be sent for his acceptance. A rhinoceros or an ibex was received with as much pleasure as an Arab steed. He had the reputation of being a good rider, and his skill in the hunting field is still celebrated in song. He was very particular about his kennel, and once wrote to inform the Hollanders that the mastiffs which they had sent him were fit neither to guard the palace gates nor to frighten people away, while their bearing and appearance were not pleasing. He liked hawking, and wrote with regret to inform the Hollanders of a hawk which he "had brought up with great love and tenderness, and taking him with me one day to the chase, I gave him wing, and he disappeared for ever." He appreciated the Bird of Paradise plumes which were sent to him, and showed his appreciation by wearing them. Like his father, he preferred European to the native Sinhalese music, and a fifer who had been captured at Pannara was received into high favour because he played "softly and with sweetness." When this man died the Hollanders sent him another, but he found "his manner of playing the instrument a little harsh."

He had a strong objection to the custom of intermarriage, and learning that a Sinhalese woman at Galle had married a Hollander, he wrote to express his great annoyance. He admitted that such marriages had once prevailed while the Sinhalese had no native King to look after them, when the Portuguese baptised, fed and clothed them, and that "some women, casting honour and shame on one side, intermarried with them," but he was determined not to tolerate the evil usage now that they had a King of their own.

On one occasion the Hollanders wrote to expostulate with him because he allowed himself to be addressed as "God," a custom which has obtained among peoples so diverse as the Romans and the Japanese. In reply he argued that the very God who created Kingdoms and Kings had shown his approval of the custom by punishing his two brothers, who had acted under the influence of jealousy because similar honours were not paid to them.

The years of peace gave the Portuguese an opportunity to place the administration of the country in some state of order, but good administration was the last thought that entered their minds. They had found in Ceylon a contented race and a fairly prosperous country, with a system of government regulated by clearly defined and universally accepted customs. It is melancholy to reflect that the intervention of the most enterprising race in Europe had succeeded in producing nothing but chaos. Out of the long list of high-born Fidalgos whom Portugal sent to Ceylon, it is difficult to point to one name as that of an enlightened statesman or high-principled administrator. Except for the seeds of Christianity which were sown among the population of the Coast, and their language—which has, curiously enough, survived among the descendants of those who took their place—the Era of the Portuguese has passed away like a nightmare. No stately fabric remains as compensating gain for that religious fanaticism, to which ample witness is borne by the desecrated ruins of those lovely structures which the piety of generations had strewn broadcast over the face of the country. No great monument exists to perpetuate their name, which is chiefly familiar to the peasant as that of the foulest disease which desolates the fever-haunted villages of the dry regions.[1] No principle of legislation which is in operation to-day derives its origin from the epoch of their rule. A failure so complete and so pitiful, where the possibilities of success had been so great and the original prospects so bright, can hardly be matched in the History of the Nations.

Except in the case of the priests, no Portuguese who came to Ceylon, whether as official or soldier or in the pursuit of trade, gave any consideration to the fact that he had a duty to perform towards the country. Whether he intended to settle down in the Island or not, he regarded it only as a means for the rapid acquisition of wealth. The power of the Generals was well nigh absolute and was subjected to the gravest abuse. Capital punishment was inflicted on the slightest pretext, often with little or no justification, and was usually accompained with circumstances of revolting cruelty. In spite of the positive injunction of the King to the contrary, Christians were frequently sold into slavery by way of punishment. The hundreds of villages which under the Sinhalese Kings had been utilised for the remuneration of public servants and as the reward of good service were, under the Portuguese regime, distributed not with an eye to the benefit of the State, but to satisfy those who had by any means established a claim on the General. Even preferment which had received the Royal sanction was ignored where it did not suit the King's representative in the Island.

The Public Service was a mass of corruption. The trickery which was practised in the sale of elephants was notorious; and cinnamon and precious stones proved no less fatal to the integrity of the Generals, whose trade speculations extended from arecanut to butter. The services of the Royal tenants and the supplies from the Royal villages which would have been invaluable for arming the forts, where the gun-carriages lay rotting, were diverted for the purpose of building the General's trading vessels; and not infrequently fictitious lists of soldiers were prepared with a view to the embezzlement of the pay drawn upon them.

Needless to say the lesser officials followed the example set by the General. With the Portuguese Disawas who had displaced the great Sinhalese of the type of Samarakon and Navaratna, war was only a pretext for filling their own pockets at the expense of the King, and they carried on a brisk trade with the enemy even during the continuance of hostilities, levying contributions of areca-nuts from all and sundry. The Vedors, indeed, were sometimes honest men, but that was not often. The great villages which they controlled kept their households in luxury, even while the patients in the Hospital, for which they were responsible, were starving. The Factors again entered all manner of fantastic items of expenditure in the Accounts, and helped themselves to what they wished at the King's Stores at their own price. The Ouvidors or Judges were rarely men of competent education, and justice was freely bought and sold. The circuits of the Maralleiros[2] were triumphant progresses during which their many hangers-on lived on the villager and extorted what money they could, while the Maralleiros themselves, by means of inquiries of an oppressively inquisitorial nature, took every opportunity that offered of penalising a poverty-stricken people, whose property consisted of little more than their instruments of tillage. Even in the General's Court, the work of which was controlled by his Secretaries, nothing could be transacted without the assistance of a bribe.

In the military sphere things were no better. The Captains, who were expected to supply the soldiers with food, robbed them of their rice, as well as of a proportion of their pay which they received at long and irregular intervals. The soldiers naturally developed into brigands, and plundered the country-side till entire villages were abandoned by their inhabitants. More than once, as has been seen, the army in desperation was forced into mutiny. The forts had no proper garrisons nor adequate supplies of munitions, their stores were depleted, and their ramparts were in ruins; and all the while the ports were being carefully watched to prevent complaints from reaching Goa.

The villages held by the religious Orders were a source of much heartburning. Those which had been granted by Dharmapala's *Sannas* to the Franciscans were resumed by the Crown, till it was found that the cost of supporting the Order from the Treasury was excessive, and the villages were restored to it, to be taken back and again restored, according to the exigencies of the Revenue. In the same manner the Jesuits were deprived of the Kalpitiya Peninsula, which they had successfully exploited. The Government could not even spare a village for the maintenance of perpetual Masses for the repose of the soul of Dharmapala, and for the up-keep of the Chapel in which he was buried. There is unhappily no reason to doubt that the Orders had suffered from the same degeneration as had manifested itself at Goa. They were charged with oppressing the villagers, with imprisoning, fining and flogging them, and with refusing to bury their dead without previous payment. Their defence was that what they did was, as a rule, done in the interests of religious discipline, and that such charges as they levied had been duly authorised. At any rate, they argued triumphantly, none could accuse them of the dishonesty, robbery and oppression which characterised the actions of the officials as a class. That the quarrels between the Civil and Religious authorities had a very bad effect on the work of conversion the Portuguese in Ceylon, who had grown indifferent to Church matters, did not greatly care.

"Treat the natives with justice and kindness" the King had written to his Viceroy on the 12th of January 1607, "for the work of conquest will progress more by such means than by force of arms." The spirit in which his Officers in the East carried out their master's orders has been seen.

"At the death of the King, the Lord Dom Joao Dharmona Pala Asthana, Emperor of Cota, when the Lord Dom Jeronimo de Azavedo succeeded to the Government of the Empire in the name of His Majesty, at the Cortes which was held at Malwana to settle on the laws under which we natives were to live, promise was made to us to maintain our own laws, under which we had elected to live, because they were humane and kindly. It was with the aid of these laws that our Kings had ruled us and fostered our well-being for the 2200 years and more during which our native Princes bore rule over this our Island." Such are the opening words of the first paragraph of a petition presented in 1636 to Diogo de Melo by the Sinhalese. The promise therein referred to was the condition upon which the Sinhalese had accepted the King of Spain and Portugal as the King of Ceylon, but the terms of that promise had not been better observed in Ceylon by the Portuguese officials, than those on which Portugal recognised the King of Spain as being her King by Philip III and Philip IV.

The laws of the Sinhalese were customary laws based upon certain broad principles of Equity.

They were the growth of many centuries and obtained their sanction from the acquiescence of the people. A Code of law, as the term has been understood at Byzantium, was unknown amongst them, and everything was handed down by word of mouth among those whose duty it was to administer Justice. The decisions of these last were subject to a final appeal to the King, though the Law was always recognised as being above the King, and cases had been known where the King himself had been fined by his own Courts. It was probably owing to their utter indifference to everything connected with the welfare of the people, that the Portuguese, when they became responsible for the administration of this law, failed to take any steps to have it committed to writing. So long indeed as the Mohottiars who had belonged to the Courts at Jayawardhana Pura and Sitawaka were alive to assist them with their knowledge, and so long as great Sinhalese noblemen presided over the Tribunals, the rights of the people were not endangered; but when a foreigner possessing few qualifications apart from an entire ignorance and an unlimited avarice stepped into the place of the native Judge, and was allowed to exercise as much authority as he chose to arrogate to himself, the consequences which followed can well be imagined.

The key-stone of the fabric of Sinhalese social life was caste, a word which has acquired for the European mind a somewhat evil connotation. It is probably not to exaggerate to assert that at this period, the middle of the seventeenth century, there could not have been found one Sinhalese who did not consider the system of caste an essential factor in a well-organised State. It must be firmly realised that the Sinhalese were not a commercial race, that they were without a foreign policy, and that they were utterly indifferent to everything outside their own country. It must also be borne in mind that the Monarchy which prevailed in Ceylon was the only form of government of which the Sinhalese could conceive, and that sufficient land was available to support everyone, according to the prevailing standard of living, in comfort. The object on which each set his heart was contentment, and that the system as it obtained in Ceylon succeeded to a great extent in bringing about.

The disabilities created by caste were mainly social; and social distinctions under various names have existed among all peoples and at all times, and are of minor importance in the life of a nation. The real question is whether the system prevented the utilisation of the best intellects of the country to the fullest advantage; and though caste did not interfere with the recognition of the merits of the soldier, and the skilled doctor and the artist would be sure of their reward, that question can only be answered in one way. Thanks to the spread of European education this is being realised more and more every day, and in another two hundred years will probably be admitted by all Sinhalese.

The Portuguese ignored the distinctions which were cherished among the people of the country, not because they were opposed to caste as such, but because these distinctions stood in the way of the satisfaction of their own greed. The allotment of villages among them had placed them in a position of control over large numbers of dependants, whose services were strictly regulated by custom according to their social position; and they proceeded to enforce their authority with a reckless disregard of all existing prejudices, and in a manner which was characterised by gross oppression and tyranny.

The high-born man could take his share in any agricultural work, but he might not carry a burden. That task was confined to the lowest castes, and therefore, though the use of the palanquin had always been a privilege which had been guarded with the utmost jealousy,[3] the labour of bearing it has at the same time been regarded as one of the most degrading occupations to which a human being could be subjected. Now, however, every Portuguese claimed the right to keep his palanquin, and followed this up by compelling men of all ranks to act as bearers. The humiliation which this inflicted on the high-born man was intense; and the humiliation was aggravated when the low-born agents of the Portuguese began to claim the same privilege. Cases were not unknown where unfortunate persons submitted to death rather than incur such disgrace.

In like manner all castes without distinction were forced to labour at erecting the houses which formed a prominent feature of Portuguese social ambition—houses which, not unnaturally, were frequently marked out for destruction in the course of rebellions. This work again was the duty of special castes, who were at the same time entitled to their food, though the Portuguese never thought of fulfilling this their share of the contract. As landlords they were entitled to cooked provisions from their tenants when they visited their villages, and they took advantage of this to reside in them for long periods at a time, together with their families and their numerous dependants. At their departure the tenants would find their stores depleted and themselves reduced to the brink of starvation. The position was even worse when some low-born Vidane or Superintendent was permanently stationed in the village to look after the lord's interests.

When the rice crops on the lord's fields were reaped and were ready for partition between him, the tenant who had cultivated them, and the various parties who according to custom were entitled to a share, the landlord's agent would come and quarter himself on the cultivator for several days, during which time the unfortunate man was obliged to keep him sumptuously supplied with food. The landlord's share was then separated, a specially large measure being used for the purpose, though where rice was sold on the landlord's account a measure of smaller capacity was employed. The tenant's fruit trees, which supplied him with so large a portion of his sustenance, were recklessly cut down whenever his Portuguese land-lord required timber; and the produce of his garden and of his fold was taken by the landlord at the latter's own valuation for the purposes of his trade.

During the arecanut boom in particular every tenant was compelled to obtain the nut for the landlord's benefit, and where sufficient was not available from his own holding he had to secure it as best he could, being often compelled to travel several days' journey for the purpose. Even when he had collected a sufficient quantity, he was still obliged to convey it himself wherever it was required to be conveyed, to receive in the end for all his trouble about one-fourth of the market value. It was indeed a common occurrence for men to pawn their own persons or sell their children to enable them to obtain the necessary amount, and a case has been recorded where a Portuguese had one of his tenants crucified on the ground for failing to supply the quantity which had been demanded of him. In addition to the landlord's exactions, the agent also frequently insisted on a further twenty per cent as his own private perquisite.

The Chaliya caste, that of the cinnamon peelers, was exposed to special oppression, so much so that entire villages fled to within the Sinhalese territory. So strictly were they kept to their work that they found little time to attend to the cultivation of their own lands, and were in consequence soon reduced to a condition bordering upon beggary.

The hold of the Portuguese over their possessions, such as it was, could never have been maintained except by the aid of the native troops, for it was on the exertions of the latter that their armies when in the field depended for their supplies. The lightness of foot and suppleness of limb of the Lascarins rendered them invaluable in guerilla warfare, and the King repeatedly urged that everything possible should be done to keep them contented with Portuguese rule. Nevertheless they were treated in the same reckless fashion as the other natives: their villages were taken from them on the slightest pretext; little provision was made for the maintenance of the families of those who died in war or from disease; they were kept engaged in all manner of work to which they were not legitimately liable; and while they were absent in the field, their women were exposed to the brutal lust of the soldiery.

Under the Sinhalese customary law corporal punishment by flogging could not be inflicted except by the special order of the King; but every Portuguese had fancied himself a King within his own village. The high-handed treatment of the natives of the country was the more mischievous in effect in that the Sinhalese was intensely sensitive of his dignity. The manners of a gentleman were natural to him, and the lowliest spoke with no less correctness of diction than those of gentle birth. Those peculiarities which differentiate in other lands the spoken language of the uneducated from that of the educated have never prevailed in Ceylon. "The ordinary Plowmen and Husbandmen do speak elegantly. In their speech the people are bold without sheepish shamefacedness, and yet no more confident than is becoming," wrote the experienced Robert Knox. Their language itself teemed with niceties which marked the various social distinctions, and the manner in which the

Portuguese behaved towards a people accustomed to sedateness of bearing and formal decorum gave rise to a feeling of humiliation which could ill be borne.

In a word, all that the Portuguese had achieved was completely to estrange from themselves all classes of the populace.

Mascarenhas had shortly after the declaration of peace been appointed Viceroy, and had accordingly returned to India, leaving behind him in Ceylon a great reputation not only for wealth, but also for skill in poisoning. He was succeeded as General by Manuel Mascarenhas Homem, who proved singularly incompetent to grapple with the critical situation which confronted him. He ignored the certainty of the speedy recrudescence of hostilities, and omitted to take advantage of the opportunity afforded by the peace of making adequate preparations therefor. Thus everything was in a condition of neglect when in October 1652 two Hollanders arrived to announce that war had again been declared.

On all sides it was realised how utterly unprepared the Portuguese were. There were suspicions as to the loyalty of the General himself, and ugly stories were in circulation to the effect that he had sold to the enemy provisions which were meant for the army. The popular discontent came to a head when an attempt was made to assassinate a leading fidalgo who dared to voice it openly, and the soldiers rose in mutiny. The General was deposed, three Commissioners were placed in charge of the administration, and Gaspar de Figueira—the one brilliant apology for the system of intermarriage, for he was the son of a Sinhalese mother by a Portuguese husband—was entrusted with the command of the army. His feats alone relieve the sombre story of the downfall of the Portuguese power in Ceylon. Under Figueira's leadership the Hollanders who were guarding the road to Negombo were forced back and their garrison of five hundred men at Anguruwatota, which controlled the passage down the Kalu Ganga, was captured. The Sinhalese who had advanced to the support of the Hollanders were repulsed, and their main army was driven out of its fortified camp at Udapola Kanda.

Stress of weather had scattered the Hollanders' vessels which were continually cruising about the neighbourhood of Colombo, when on the 10th of May 1653 there arrived in the Island the aged Francisco de Melo de Castro, once Governor of India, who had been persuaded to undertake the thankless task of restoring order in Ceylon. In the course of the following month Adrian van der Meyden took over the control of the interests in the Island of the Company. In the meantime the Hollanders' Lascarins from Galle were ravaging the Coast right up to the neighbourhood of Colombo, destroying the palm groves, driving away the fishing population, and preventing the collection of cinnamon. A sharp fight at Tebuwana on the banks of the Kalu Ganga, however, enabled the Portuguese to reoccupy Kalutara, and to place an army on the Northern bank of the Bentota river. A strong force of the Hollanders appeared on the opposite bank, and thus the two armies continued to confront each other for five months, till the 16th of December 1654, when the Hollanders by a skilful manoeuvre succeeded in getting across. The Portuguese promptly withdrew, and forcing their way through two other bodies which had been sent to cut off their retreat, fell back on Kalutara. Simultaneously Raja Sinha's army invaded the Four and Seven Korales, and drove in the Portuguese outposts, but retired on the appearance of Figueira, who was living in retirement and was hastily summoned to save the situation.

The following March the Hollanders once more appeared before Kalutara. At the same time the

King came down the Galagedera Pass with a strong force, but was repulsed by Figueira after a hotly contested fight at Kotikapola, whereupon the Hollanders in turn retired. It was clear that the critical moment in the long-drawn-out struggle for the possession of Ceylon was near at hand, but not even the gravity of the military situation availed to prevent Raja Sinha from returning to his Capital to take part in the celebration of the *Esala Perahera,* the most important of the religious festivals observed by the Sinhalese. As the name implies, the main feature of the festival consisted of the *Perahera* or processions which were held during the Sinhalese month of Esala.[4]

The legend in which the story of the origin of the festival is enshrined takes us back to the very dawn of civilisation in the East, to the days when the gods walked among the children of men. An evil spirit--no doubt some ferocious pirate—is said to have haunted the waters of the sea and to have levied toll of human lives, seizing men and women and taking them on board a vessel where it put them to death. Thereupon the gods met in conclave to discuss what should be done to relieve the sufferings of the world, and with their approval the God of War took upon himself the task. Rendering himsely incarnate in human flesh, he descended to the abodes of men and engaged the evil spirit in single combat on board its own vessel; after which he cut off the head of his conquered foe, and filling his golden pitcher with water rose again to heaven and laid the head before the assembled gods. Then there was gladness within the celestial walls, and the gods danced for joy, and Sekraya the great god made order that mortals should thenceforth for ever commemorate yearly this great deliverance. Thus it came about that year by year, in every Dewale in the Island, the New Moon of Esala witnessed the beginning of the festival, which lasted for a fortnight.

Naturally enough it was at the Capital that the celebration was carried out with the greatest splendour, the four chief Dewales which were situated there combining in the event. Day after day for four days the mysterious Emblems of the gods were borne in solemn procession round their temples. On the fifth day the procession emerged from the temple precincts and paraded through the four principal streets of the city. On the tenth day it was joined by the Emblems of the female divinities which were carried in palanquins.

The King himself now supervised the arrangement of the procession, and all the resources of display at his command were drawn upon to render due hononr to the gods, "who were regarded by all the people as the fountain of prosperity."[5]. His finest State elephants with their gleaming coverings of cloth of gold, his artillery and his men-at-arms, the great Officers of State with their banners and trains of attendants, all took their part in the ceremonial, together with the hundreds of the Dewale retainers, whose duty it was to render honour to the gods at this high festival. The King himself, surrounded by a brilliant throng, joined in the procession, while the palanquins of the goddesses were followed by princesses and by the noblest ladies of the land. On the fifteenth day, when the Moon was full, the Festival culminated in an outburst of splendour. At midnight offerings of food were made to the gods at their temples, and then the procession, with its myriad flambeaux and amid the ceaseless din of the tom-toms, made its way to the Maha Weli Ganga at Gannoruwa. There the four priests with their attendants were rowed out into the stream to await the rising of the Sun; and as the first rays of light flashed from the East, the priests raised aloft their golden swords and cleft the water, at the same time plunging in the golden pitchers which they held in their left hands. The water thus taken was then solemnly carried to the temples, whither the procession, having at length fulfilled the great god's command, finally returned.

Despite these distractions, guerilla warfare continued briskly all along the King's Western frontier till on the 15th of August 1655 the new General, Antonio de Sousa Coutinho, reached Colombo, bringing with him funds to pay the soldiers [6] whose wages were eighteen months overdue. On the 15th of September the reinforcements long awaited by the Hollanders, consisting of 3000 Europeans under the command of Geraard Hulft of Amsterdam, once Secretary of the City and now Director General of India, were sighted off the Western Coast.

The Fates appeared to have conspired against the Portuguese. An outbreak of murrain had so reduced the number of cattle as seriously to impede the cultivation of the rice crops, and the price of food-stuffs had risen to an unprecedented figure. Military stores of every kind were lacking. The gun carriages were old and in dis-repair, and there was no timber available for the construction of new ones. There were, moreover, no trained artillery men to handle the 150 heavy pieces on the ramparts. Eight hundred men formed the total European force in the Island, and of these less than a third were at Colombo, while the Lascarins who still remained were few in number and of doubtful loyalty.

The Hollanders in the meantime landed in force to the North of Colombo, but the drenching showers of the north-east monsoon so disheartened the men, whose limbs were stiff after their two months' voyage on crowded vessels, that they were taken back on board and the fleet sailed southwards. Their main body disembarked at Beruwala and appeared before Kalutara on the 29th of September. Another force landed at Panadura so as to cut the line of communications with Colombo; while yet a third watched the Kalu Ganga. On the 8th of October Figueira, who had been summoned in haste from his camp on the Sinhalese frontier, reached Colombo, and the arrival of four vessels from Goa enabled him to take the field with 600 Portuguese and his Lascarins. He started for Kalutara on the sixteenth morning, but was met on the road by the news that the fort had fallen two days previously. Nevertheless he pushed on and the next day met the Hollanders on the sandy plain which stretches from Moratuwa to Panadura. The Portuguese charged with an impetuosity which nothing could resist. The Hollanders, opening their ranks, let them pass through, then raked them with a terrific fire from their field-pieces. Before long five hundred and twenty of the Portuguese lay dead on the field, and the remainder were in headlong fight.

NOTES TO CHAPTER XIV

1. *Parangi*, a syphilitic disease, probably imported from the Western Hemisphere.
2. Ch.
3. For instance the use of palanquins in Goa had been the subject of special Alvaras from the King in 1602 and 1605.
4. July-August.
5. Mahawansa.
6. So pressed were the authorities at Goa for money, that in 1653 they seized a portion of the Trust funds held by the Misericordia there, nominally as a loan, in order to pay for the expedition which was being prepared for the relief of Ceylon.

CHAPTER XV

Figueira reached the terrified city the same evening with 160 men. The consternation there was indescribable, and the streets were filled with lamentation and weeping. There was, however, no time for vain regrets. The gates were immediately closed, and Figueira with desperate energy set about strengthening the fortifications, women, children and friars all joining in the common task. Everyone contributed from his private resources, and Figueira's great stores were freely devoted to the need of the hour. The bastion of Sao Joao, commanding as it did the road from -Mutwal by which the Hollanders would approach the fort and forming the protection to the draw-bridge across the moat, demanded the first attention. A stockade connected it with the seashore, and a rampart with the great central bastion of Sao Estevao where the moat began. From Sao Estevao the rampart continued in a south westerly direction past the small bastion of Sao Sebastiao to that of Madre de Deos which overlooked the lake. These two latter guarded the Porta Rainha or Queen's Gate, the principal entrance to the city, the only approach to which from Sao Sebastiao Hill was by a bridge which was broken down. The Rua Direita or Straight Road ran from this gateway by way of the Assembly Room of the Camara right up to the Hospital on the bay, where another road, the Rua de Misericordia,[1] led past that institution to the General's residence.

The chief defence to the south of fort was the crocodile-infested expanse of the lake. The

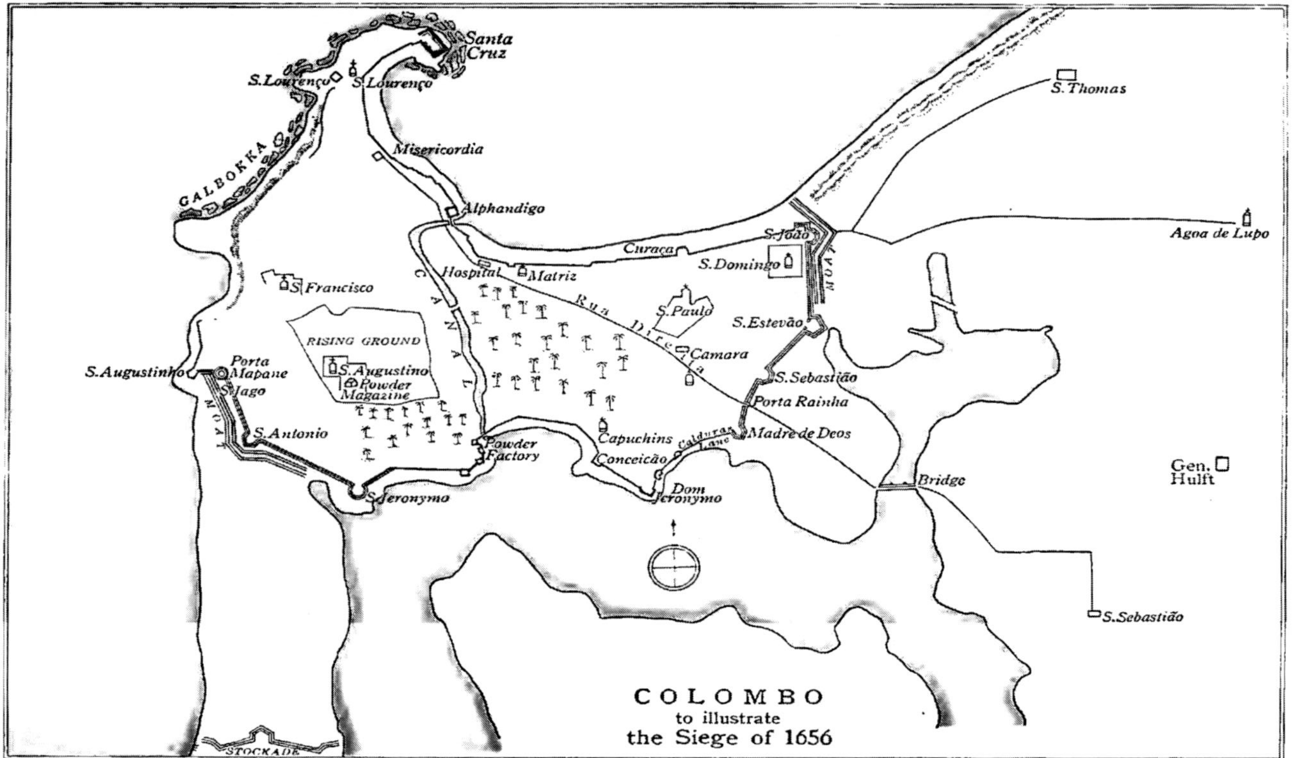

WAXTYPE
GEORGE PHILIP & SON, LTD.

powerful bastions of S. Jeronymo, S. Antonio and S. Jago with their rampart and moat protected it on the South-west. The last of these three guarded the Mapane Gate, which was arched above and mounted with guns. A stone breastwork connected S. Jago with the lofty rock of S. Augustinho over which the flag of Portugal fluttered in the breeze. From this point the rough coast ot the Galbokka, running northward and skirting the establishment of the Franciscans, was sufficiently defended from the sea by a line of palisades and a few guns. The hill on which the Augustinian Convent stood formed the strongest part of the city, and within the convent enclosure was the chief powder magazine. The Galbokka ended in the historic rock of S. Lourenco, which was occupied by a bastion facing westwards out to the sea, and by a church dedicated to the saint after whom the rock was named; while on the extreme point of the reef stood the strong bastion of Santa Cruz, the sixteen guns of which commanded the entire Bay. From the bastion of Santa Cruz the low shore ran south and east till it reached the Alphandigo or Customs, where there was a bastion of the same name; east of this again was situated the Curaca or breastwork of S. Paolo, opposite the important establishment of the Jesuits, which in its turn was connected with the bastion of S. Joao. Eighteen companies of about twenty five men each, with the Casados[2], Lascarins and Kaffirs, made up the force available for the defence.

The Hollanders began their attack by constructing batteries on St. Thomas' hill so as to threaten S. Joao, the engineers engaged in the work being subjected to constant harassment by the Portuguese from sand pits on the shore. A number of these 'snipers', as they would now be called, were captured, and as the Hollanders found their maintenance expensive they were after three or four days taken into the jungle and shot in cold blood. Other batteries also were begun in the neighbourhood of the monastery of Agoa de Lupo, the site of which is now known as Wolvendahl, and of that of S. Sebastiao, while Hulft himself took up his residence in one of the comfortable houses in the hamlet, still called after him Hulftsdorp, where the Portuguese had been wont to spend the hot weather among their shady coconut palms in enjoyment of the cool breeze from the sea.

As ill luck would have it Raja Sinha was for the moment detained in his Capital by one of those periodical attacks of fever which were the sequel to the arduous life of exposure which he had led. He sent, however, 1200 of his men to join the Hollanders, and a letter in his own hand and dated the 25th of October served as further confirmation of his anxiety that the task which lay so near his heart should at length be carried through to a conclusion. At the same time, in spite of his satisfaction at the success of the Hollanders, he was not prepared to abate one jot of his Royal dignity. Sinhalese etiquette demanded that everything meant for the King's use should be wrapped in white linen, and Raja Sinha took occasion to point out that the last letter which he had received had not been so covered, and that some of his Royal titles had been omitted—formalities which, he said, should not be overlooked even in the hurry of war.

Before October was out the effect of the Hollanders' bombardment began to be apparent, for the walls were crumbling under the incessant cannonade, though all night long the Portuguese toiled to make good the damage caused during the day. They more than suspected that the first assault would be directed against the low wall connecting the bastion of S. Sebastiao and that of Madre de

Deos, and they prepared for this by opening two portholes low down in the wall, and mounting in them two *pedreiros*, which were kept ready loaded with grape. The lake was of great service to the besieged, for across it was brought the timber required for the works, as well as the tough bark of the *hibiscus tiliaceus* which, growing in abundance by the water's edge, was invaluable in place of rope and match-cord.

On the 4th of November one of Raja Sinha's courtiers, Tennekon Appuhami, appeared in the Hollanders' camp. He was a member of a great Low-country family which claimed descent from one of the Royal houses of the Choromandel Coast, and which had sought refuge among the mountains. Tennekon himself rose to be the foremost of Raja Sinha's Generals, though in his old age he returned once more to the sea coast and settled down in Matara. He now brought with him a letter of congratulation from the King, who was still very ill, but who sent to Hulft a gold pendant studded with precious stones as a token of his esteem.

Hulft now resolved to attempt an assault. Before doing so he sent a summons to Coutinho "in the name of His Imperial Majesty Raja Sinha and that of the Most Noble Dutch East India Company" to surrender. The General replied that he was accountable to his King for the fort which had been entrusted to him, and that he could not surrender the place till he had been shown the most cogent reasons for so doing.

Early in the morning of the 12th of December four of the Hollanders' vessels sailed across to Santa Cruz, while simultaneously three detachments of infantry advanced on the Curaca, S. Joao and the Porta Rainha, while Raja Sinha's men made a feint of attacking the Mapane Gate. Of the four vessels the *Maid of Enckuysen* alone drew close to the bastion, against which she maintained a terrific bombardment. Her fire was, however, replied to with an equal vigour and in a short time all her masts were laid low, and so many holes had been made in her side that she was abandoned by her crew and sank; whereupon her sister ships, which had been content to open fire from a distance, sailed away out of range.

In the meantime two hundred men had crossed the lake in boats and landed on the eastern side, to be greeted with pans of powder from the windows of the neighbouring houses and musket shots from every point which afforded cover. They pushed on. however, till they reached a Lane, where they found themselves hemmed in by two bodies of Portuguese which appeared at either end. Again and again they tried to break through, but were cowed by the fire of the *bacamartes* or blunderbusses, which picked them off mercilessly. Two more companies of Portuguese now came on the scene, and opened fire from the neighbouring gardens. Further resistance was hopeless, and the seventy-four who still survived, and who were nearly all wounded, laid down their arms.

While this was going on van der Laen, who had returned to Ceylon after being honourably acquitted at Batavia, had crossed the moat with one of the detachments of infantry, and had pushed on to the Curaca,' which was in a state of disrepair. Ladders were hurried up and grenades thrown within the walls ; but as the Hollanders dashed up to the fortifications, the Portuguese who had been sweeping the shore with their three guns poured into their ranks a destructive fire from their matchlocks, so that soon both defenders and assailants were completely hidden in the smoke, and nothing could be heard save the clash of steel on steel and the rattle of the musketry. The men at the adjoining station hastened to the assistance of their countrymen, and among the newcomers was to be seen the inspiring presence of Figueira, who had been busily employed at Sao Joao. The little garrison took fresh heart, the Kaffirs with their *assegais* fighting manfully. The slaughter was great and numbers of wounded lay on every side. At length, burnt and bleeding, the Hollanders drew back, leaving the shore strewn with corpses.

The attack on the Porta Rainha was commanded by Hulft in person. In spite of the fire directed against them from three bastions his men were advancing on the gate, when, to their great consternation, the two concealed *pedreiros* opened fire on them with grape, mowing down scores. At the same time the garrison poured down volley after volley from the ramparts on to the confused throng below. The Hollanders were so taken aback that the sailors refused to move up with the scaling ladders. Hulft was filled with rage and despair. Hurrying to the front he seized a ladder and called on the rest to help him ; but none would stir, and Hulft fell shot through the leg. He was hastily dragged out of the zone of fire, and without more ado his men turned and fled in confusion, while the Lascarins and Kaffirs threw themselves from the walls in pursuit and drove the Hollanders into their camp.

Fortunately for the Hollanders the Portuguese were too exhausted to follow up their success, or the siege would have had to be raised. Even as it was the blow was a terrible one to Hulft, for he had lost eight hundred in dead alone, and there were five hundred wounded. To aggravate his sense of failure he received the same evening from the King a letter full of the latter's confident hope that the Hollander would soon place Colombo in his hands. Hulft could only return an apologetic letter informing the King of what had happened. Raja Sinha, indignant that the Hollanders should have attempted a task of such magnitude without first consulting the party who would have to pay the cost of it, replied by warning them sharply not to make another similar attempt till he was near to assist. For several days therefore, they remained in their own lines, while the Portuguese were busily engaged in repairing the damage caused by the bombardment. However, some despatches from Goa which fell into the hands of the Hollanders revealed the fact that there was no fear of reinforcements reaching the garrison from that quarter, and once more the work of the siege was energetically taken in hand.

A great crowd of non-combatants had, on the approach of the enemy, sought refuge within the walls, but so scarce were provisions that on the 12th of December a large number of them had to be turned out of the fort. The Hollanders, however, would not allow them to pass their lines, and the miserable wretches were compelled to return. Meanwhile the Hollanders' batteries had been brought up closer and were pounding away at the wall to the south of the bastion. On the 10th of January 1656 the besiegers attempted to fill in the moat near S. Joao and to run a gallery across; but after a fight lasting from ten at night until dawn, they were compelled to abandon their materials and withdraw. They now brought to bear a novel species of projectile made of tow and other combustibles and fitted with a score or more of small tubes, each carrying two bullets. The explosion of these projectiles a short distance above the ground led to many deaths, and greatly harassed the Portuguese.

In spite of the desperate resistance of the garrison, the Hollanders doggedly continued with their plans against S. Joao. The condition of the moat favoured the attackers to no small extent; the preceding year had been marked by a prolonged drought which had dried up the water and enabled the Hllanders at last to fill it up in the neighbourhood of the bastion. Having accomplished this they began to mine underneath it and break through the foundations of the rampart. To meet the new peril the Portuguese began a countermine. With the increasing need of timber, however, the difficulty of obtaining a supply had also increased, and at last the precious coconut trees—the great resource in the prevailing lack of food—had to be sacrificed. The beams also of the houses destroyed by the Hollander's guns were carefully extracted from the ruins and used to protect the magazine.

Death, wounds and sickness had now greatly reduced the number of men available, and those who had so far survived were worn out with the incessant toil and the lack of food. The bastions too were in some cases so badly damaged that a horse could easily make its way on to the battlements. Meanwhile the peril in which the city stood caused every Church to be crowded with supplicants. The Host was kept exposed at the Convent of the Capuchins, and before it women and girls knelt all day long, imploring the God in whose name their husbands and brothers had for so many years deluged the country with innocent blood to have pity on them. A stone image of S. Thomas which had been discovered by the Hollanders was shot by them in derision from a cannon and fell into the moat, whence the armless trunk was recovered by the garrison and removed with great reverence to the Jesuit Church. The image was however successfully claimed by the Franciscans, who conveyed it in solemn procession to their own Church, while crowds followed and besought the saint to take the city under his protection.

The ravages of disease steadily increased, and soon the task of burying the dead grew beyond the powers of the numerous volunteers, so that on every side decomposing bodies polluted the atmosphere. Some of the starving inhabitants were successfully smuggled out of the city and across the lake, but in the first fortnight of February 620 of them were turned back. The garrison, however, would not allow them to re-enter the fort, and they were left to die between the walls and the Hollanders' camp, their unburied corpses providing a ghastly spectacle by the water-side. This, however, did not stop the exodus, and Hulft decided to adopt more effective measures. He accordingly sent a letter to the General warning the latter that all refugees would in future be severely dealt with. The event showed that he had made no idle boast. Men, women and children were flogged by the hundred and sent staggering back, to perish of starvation under the eyes of their countrymen before the walls of Colombo.

When these measures in their turn proved unavailing, the Hollanders took to shooting at sight, like the stray dogs which prowl round the out skirts of a village, all who were seen between their trenches and the town. Even this did not suffice, and we must leave it to one of the soldiers who took part in these atrocities to describe the culminating horror of which the fertile imagination of his countrymen was capable: "As we had no means of driving them away from our camp, we had to strike still greater terror into them. Therefore when a woman came and brought small children, we forced her to put her child into a wooden mortar and to pound it to death with the pounder, and then to go away again with the dead child."[1]

The Portuguese, however, still hoped for the succours from Goa which never came, and no thought of surrender had entered their minds. Match-cord was exhausted, but the soldiers tore up the shirts on their backs to take its place, and supplemented them with the shrouds of the *Maid of Enchuysen* soaked in vinegar and wine and daubed with gunpowder. No boat could approach with provisions from India, for the Hollanders' vessels blocked the entrance to the harbour every night, and the King's Disawas had constructed a palisade from the sea to the lake to prevent the Portuguese from breaking through on the side of the Mapane Gate. S. Estevao was so battered that it had been almost abandoned, and Madre de Deos was a heap of rubbish. Near S. Joao a fresh battery had been constructed at a distance of only ten paces from the moat, while the greater part of the Portuguese guns had been put out of action. The prevalent desire among the Portuguese was to stake everything on one last desperate fling, but the General still had hopes of relief from Goa, and could not be induced to consent.

On the 21st of March the mine at which the Hollanders had been working so doggedly came into contact with the tunnel the Portuguese had driven to meet it. As the latter passage was much the narrower of the two, the Portuguese were able without exposing themselves to any extent to inflict great losses with their pistols and *bacamartes* on the Hollanders, who came crowding to the defence of their own work. By way of reply the Hollanders barricaded the passage with stout beams in which they bored observation holes, while the Portuguese hurriedly buried a large cask of powder in such a position that it could easily be exploded by a pistol-shot in case of need, and broke down their tunnel, leaving only sufficient space for one man to crawl through. Volunteers for the task of guarding the spot were now called for from among the retired Captains, and two by two they took each his turn at keeping the dreary watch, in darkness so dense that they lost all sense of direction. Throughout the siege the weary vigil continued, for the Portuguese were determined to blow up the passage if the enemy should attempt an entrance. So great was the strain that in the end, out of the forty original volunteers, only three were found to have remained faithful to the duty.

On the 10th of March the General had addressed a pitiful letter to Raja Sinha. "The City of Colombo," he said, "is an ancient inheritance of the Portuguese, bestowed upon them by the Kings and Emperors of Ceylon, your predecessors, who always were ready to honour them with their protection .... it being always the ambition of great Monarchs to take the less powerful under their protection." The General concluded by hoping that the King "will be pleased not to leave us in this extremity." Raja Sinha in reply advised Coutinho to surrender, promising that the inhabitants should be allowed the possession of the lands required for their sustenance. On the same day the King sent to Hulft, "the most trusty servant that ever he had in his life," his *Sannas* whereby he appointed him Director General over all his dominions; for, he said, his services could not be requited by the usual presents of raiments and jewels.

The fever and dysentery which had prevailed were followed by an epidemic of plague which raged with terrible fury during March and April. These months form the hot season of the year, and the sufferings of the inhabitants were aggravated by the drought, for no rain fell during the whole period of the siege. At first the corpses were buried piled up in shallow graves, the earth over which soon swelled out and gaped in the blazing sun; but in a short time their number was so great that it was no longer possible to bury them, and the bodies lay rotting in the public streets. A pound of dog's flesh was a rare luxury; fourteen out of the fifteen elephants were killed and eaten up to their very skins; while cannibalism was of common occurrence.

One unhappy mother who had killed the infant at her breast for food was blown from the mouth of a cannon; but even this severity proved of no avail in stopping the practice, and in April two of the miserable wretches who still continued alive between the lines were reported to have devoured their newly born babes.

On the 5th of April Hulft set out for an interview with the King, who received him in audience at Rakgaha Watta. On entering the hall in which the interview was to take place Hulft went down on his knees, but a nod from the King gave him permission to advance. Moving halfway up the passage he again sank on his knees, whereupon the King rose up on the dais and commanded him to approach yet nearer. Still remaining on his knees Hulft delivered a carefully prepared oration to the following effect.

"Most Potent Monarch, Your most humble servant approaches Your Imperial Throne with a most warm affection and with confidence in your generous inclinations and wonted clemency, the which have encouraged me to address myself to Your Majesty (whose name is renowned throughout the world,) with a most sincere wish that God Almighty will be pleased to bless Your Most Illustrious Imperial Majesty and the Prince." The King thereupon ordered Hulft to rise; but the latter, pretending not to understand him, referred to the presents which he had brought with him; which, he said, though of little value in themselves, were such as were usually received with approval by Kings, being the banners of his conquered foes. Then, pointing to the pendant he had received from the King and which hung about his neck, he approached the throne, and kneeling on a cushion kissed Raja Sinha's hand, declaring that to be allowed to do so was the greatest honour he was capable of receiving. The King took a collar of gold and placed it round Hulft's neck; and drawing off his own ring, the bezel of which covered the greater portion of three of his fingers, he commanded Hulft to put out his hand, requesting him to wear the jewel in remembrance of the King who had placed it there. Hulft was overwhelmed at this act of condescension, but with ready and courtier-like wit put out the broken middle finger of his left hand, assuring the King that the finger which had been so ill treated by His Majesty's enemies was now well recompensed by the honour done to it.

These compliments over, Hulft proceeded to business. He recounted all that he had so far accomplished on the King's behalf, and after a further private interview was given permission to depart. He reached Colombo the next day and went the same evening to inspect some works which had been erected in his absence. While he was thus engaged the Portuguese made a determined attempt to set fire to the gallery of the Hollanders. Hulft hurried to the spot and was busily employed in helping to extinguish the fire, when he was seen suddenly to throw up his arms and to fall to the ground, exclaiming "Good God, help me." He was hastily carried away covered with blood and laid on a bed, where he expired without further word, for he had been shot through the heart with a musket ball.

Immediate information of this terrible disaster was sent to Raja Sinha. His grief was no less intense than that of the Hollanders, and he sent his chief Minister and his Disawas to view the body before it was removed to Galle for interment. On being led to the spot where Hulft had fallen they made a profound obeisance, and solemnly taking up a handful of earth gave instructions that thereafter no man should be permitted to set foot on that hallowed soil. The whole Court went into mourning; the silver drapery in the Royal quarters was replaced by black cloth; and so great was the King's distress – for he appears to have conceived a real affection for Hulft, as the only Hollander in whom he could repose confidence—that for three days he would see no one.

Hulft was succeeded in his command by Van der Meyden, and the siege continued. In spite of the misery prevailing in the city the Portuguese, with a gallantry and a courage which must ever be a subject for marvel, met every attempt of the Hollanders by some desperate counter-move. The wall between S. Sebastiao and Madre de Deos had been so battered down, that the cannon balls of the Hollanders swept the streets freely and the Rua Direita had to barricaded with palm trees. All the sappers were dead, and to replace them recourse had to be had to the male and female slaves who were allotted, to enable them to keep body and soul together a few weeks longer, the pittance of a quarter of a *medida*[4] of rice each day. Coutinho however, sturdily refused in any way to alter his previous resolution, "which" he said, "is to take care of and to defend the city to the utmost of my power in the service of the King my Master."

Every day it was becoming increasingly clear that an assault could no longer be delayed, and with this Raja Sinha's eagerness to visit the camp increased proportionately, to the discomfort of the Hollanders. Van der Meyden's hints brought on him a sharp retort from the King: "You are of opinion that it would be more convenient for me not to come to the camp till after the taking of the city: but what business should I have in the camp then unless it were to see that the conditions were performed?" However he finally gave a reluctant consent to an assault being delivered if necessary in his absence, for he was still suffering from attacks of fever. On the 6th of May a deserter informed the Hollanders that the guns had been largely removed to the streets, which had been barricaded, and that the next morning there would be only a handful of men on the walls. It was accordingly decided to make an assault without further delay.

A chilling shower heralded the dawn of the 7th of May. The weary company of soldiers and citizens who had watched through the night had gone to Church to attend Mass before returning home for a little rest. Three Portuguese, two of them boys under fourteen whom the struggle for life had armed with muskets, with a number of Lascarins, were on the crumbling bastion of S. Joao. The boys and about eight of the Lascarins lay buried in slumber, as three companies of Hollanders carrying scaling ladders crept quietly up to the wall. One volley killed all those on the bastion, and then the alarm-bells rang out. The Hollanders swarmed up the battered walls with ease, and despite a handful of Portuguese who opened fire with two guns, pushed steadily on, while the Sinhalese who had come up to their support poured in a cloud of arrows. The fight was too unequal and the Portuguese fell back step by step, disputing each yard of ground, into the barricaded street, where they were joined by a small band of soldiers. Throwing away their arquebusses after the first volley, the Portuguese charged sword in hand with reckless courage and forced the Hollanders back three times to the bastion. The Hollanders, however, were there in overwhelming numbers and the Portuguese had to desist from the attempt to reoccupy it, though their opponents who had lost five of their banners dared not venture out again in the open.

The latter indeed soon found that the bastion was no safe position for them, for they were exposed to an annihilating fire from Santa Cruz and from the Curaca. Meanwhile the Portuguese outside had been joined by the General Coutinho, and so greatly did his presence encourage them that once again they dashed at the bastion. The handful of soldiers who were watching this exploit from the Curaca were so carried away by the audacity of the attempt, that headed by the aged Francisco de Melo de Castro, the late General, who was now past eighty years of age, they poured out into the street shouting "Victory" and urging everyone to join in the attack. De Castro had to be dragged back forcibly, while once more the Portuguese, despite their gallant endeavours, were obliged to retire.

Another body now attacked the woodwork of the stockade behind S. Joao, which was held by several hundred Hollanders, and succeeded in firing a mine, the explosion hurling Hollanders and Sinhalese alike to destruction. Then, sword in hand, they drove the Hollanders within the bastion, and pressed on behind them to the gate. This they battered down without difficulty and a dozen of them entered. Inside the bastion the scene was an amazing one. The Hollanders, crowded together in the limited space, were obliged to be cautious in discharging their firearms, while the Portuguese were able to lay about them freely with their swords. Bottles filled with gunpowder were flung into the crowd, till an open barrel caught fire and burnt the Portuguese so severely that they could no longer continue the fight. Once again they had to give way, nearly every one of them being wounded or burnt, and some of them having as many as five bullet wounds.

It was seven o'clock at night when the fighting at length stopped. The starved and wounded handful had kept up the astonishing struggle for nearly twelve hours aud one hundred and twenty of them were either killed, wounded or seriously burnt. If the darkness, however, was welcome to them, it was no less welcome to the Hollanders, who had lost so heavily that only 1287 Europeans remained fit for service. The night was spent by the besiegers in erecting defences of timber and in turning the guns abandoned by the Portuguese on to the city. By morning they commanded with their fire the Curaca, where the remnants of the garrison were now concentrated. Two days later the Council met; they recognised that the condition of affairs was hopeless, and resolved to make a cautious attempt to obtain favourable terms from the enemy. The next day the white flag was hoisted, and three envoys were sent across to the Hollanders' camp. The proposals of the Council were returned the next day with the counter-proposals of the Hollanders, and these latter were in the end agreed to.

In accordance with them the city was to be surrendered the next morning, the soldiers of the garrison marching out of the fort with all the honours of war. Special provision was made with regard to the Clergy, the Generals and the chief officers; the Casados, together with the minor officers and merchants, were to be transported to the Choromandel Coast with as much property as their slaves could carry. Such of the Portuguese as should be willing to acknowledge the supremacy of the Hollanders were to be well treated and to be allowed to retain their property. The natives were to be dealt with at the discretion of the General, though a special condition was inserted that the Mudaliyars, Arachchis and Lascarins were to be treated with favour. The Hollanders further undertook the care of the sick and wounded, and it was agreed that any Portuguese vessel arriving up to the 30th of May should be allowed to sail away unmolested till out of sight.

The Terms of Capitulation were signed on the 12th of May, and at mid-day two Hollanders were sent into the city to receive the keys, and to take an account of the provisions and arms. At three o'clock the same afternoon the Hollanders together with Raja Sinha's troops were drawn up outside the fort to receive the Portuguese garrison. The gates were flung open, and with colours flying and drums beating there marched out the men to bring whom to the point of surrender had cost seven months of arduous toil and so much blood and treasure. First there staggered forth seventy-three living skeletons, not a few of them moving painfully with the aid of a crutch or supporting themselves with a stick grasped in the one hand which was left. Four cannon accompanied them as far as the gate, but they had not the strength to drag them further. A short distance behind came about a hundred Casados and other inhabitants of the city, all in similar plight. It was some time indeed before the Hollanders could believe that this was the garrison which had forced such favourable terms from them. The pitiable handful of men passed on to Van der Meyden's headquarters, where they surrendered their arms, after which they were conducted to a walled garden which had been selected for their occupation.

The Hollanders now entered the fort in triumph. Van der Meyden and his staff proceeded straight to the Curaca where the two Portuguese Generals, haggard and wild-eyed with the sufferings they had so unflinchingly borne, came out to receive them. Sentries were posted round the city, the Lascarins were disarmed, and the entrances to the mines placed under guard. Six musty loads of rice were all the provisions to be found in the stores, and the quantity of gunpowder remaining was but 6500 pounds, together with a little saltpetre and brimstone. In the treasury there were left onlv 1500 coins. A service of thanksgiving at the Church of S. Francisco, before the tomb of the hapless Dharmapala, celebrated the transfer of his ill-used heritage to the Hollanders, and within two days six of their vessels had set sail with the majority of the Portuguese, whose daughters however were kept behind as wives for their captors.

The latter now began to put off all pretence and to show their hand openly. When Raja Sinha's troops attempted to enter the fort they were forcibly prevented from so doing, and only a few officers of high rank were admitted. Raja Sinha himself had not even been kept fully informed of what was toward. At three o'clock on the morning of the 11th of May a letter had been despatched to him by his Disawas at Colombo to inform him of the arrival of Plenipotentiaries, but the rumour that the terms had been settled was so persistent that he sent an urgent message demanding an explanation. Van der Meyden replied by sending him a copy of the Capitulations.

For five and twenty years Raja Sinha had toiled laboriously and incessantly to drive the Portuguese out of Colombo. "When our Imperial Self summoned you to this our Empire," he wrote to the Hollanders, "the principal cause was that you might help us, and more especially to capture the city of Colombo. Ever since that the most serene and famous Raju, King of Ceitavaca, laid it several times under siege and could not take it, for this reason we took into our Imperial heart to capture it." He had been passionately set on winning for himself the honour which his deified namesake had failed to achieve, and now, at what had seemed the moment when his long-cherished hope was to be realised, he found that he had been over-reached by the cunning of a trading company. No Attic poet could have conceived a more poignant tragedy.

He fiercely demanded why he had not been consulted before the terms were agreed on, and he found a chilling answer in the tenth Clause of the Capitulations, whereby the Hollanders undertook to treat the Mudaliyars, whom by the terms of their agreement with Raja Sinha they were bound to hand over to him as traitors, with favour. "When our Imperial self heard this," he wrote in the bitterness of his soul, "We had no desire to know more respecting the other points, inasmuch as we did not bring the Hollanders to this our Empire, nor did we labour up till now, that they should act thus towards us."

A few days later the Sinhalese forces withdrew back from Colombo, and intercourse with the Hollanders totally ceased. The inhabitants of the villages in the neighbourhood of the city were removed to a distance, and trade with the foreigners was forbidden. The effect was speedily felt and the Hollanders were brought to the verge of famine. Disease too broke out, and twenty and thirty died each day. Many of the Portuguese who still remained in the island, as well as of the Lascarins who were with the Hollanders, deserted to Raja Sinha. Figueira was still in Colombo, and the King, who had a chivalrous admiration for a gallant foeman, sent him a tempting invitation to join his standard ; but the Hollanders, who had a bitter experience of the prowess of the erstwhile leader, hurried him over to India.[5].

Meanwhile the Hollanders were rapidly strengthening the defences of the city, abandoning two-thirds of it, and concentrating the fortifications round the high ground where the Augustinian Convent was situated. During the progress of the work an angry correspondence was carried on with the King, who replied with impatience to the evasive letters of the Hollanders. "Write" he said, "these rigmaroles to whomsoever it may seem well to you to write them, but not to our Imperial selt." His Disawas now began to appear to the South of Colombo.

There was unrest all along the coast, and the peeling of cinnamon was seriously hampered. Matters reached such a stage that before long the Hollanders were glad to send a submissive letter to Raja Sinha begging for a restoration of the former amicable relations and offering to restore Negombo to him. Van der Meydenf urthermore entreated him to let them know what other satisfaction he required at their hands, declaring that they would gladly render it to him. Raja Sinha's only reply was the curt message "Propound me no riddles", while his troops attacked the Company's outposts.

"If you will not understand," he wrote to Van der Meyden on the 23rd of October 1656, "God will find a remedy. You state in your letter that the Governor-General of Batavia will be displeased. If the Governor-General and the Company are persons who keep their word they will have reason to be displeased ; and if things go on after this manner, there will follow more and more sorrows." His frank avowal that the Portuguese, who were known to be making active preparations to win back what they had lost, were anxious for his friendship, was a source of great anxiety to the Hollanders. At length, however, they ventured to come outside the city and attacked the Sinhalese forces, whereupon Raja Sinha withdrew to Ruwanella. From there he watched with gloomy rage the last phase of the struggle between them and the Portuguese.

In January 1657 the Portuguese fleet sailed out of the harbour of Goa, but was encountered by the Hollanders and three severe engagements followed. Early in the following year, 1658, a powerful Dutch armada under the command of Ryckloff Van Goens appeared before Tuticorin and reduced the Portuguese settlements of the Fishery Coast. A few weeks later three thousand Europeans with a force of Bandanese and Sinhalese from Colombo landed in

Manar; after a slight resistance the bulk of the Portuguese, crossing over to the mainland, fled in panic-stricken confusion to Jaffna, and on the 22nd of February the fort of Manar surrendered. The Hollanders thereupon crossed to Mantota and began their advance on Jaffna, being allowed to reach Chundikuli, two miles from the fort of Our Lady of Miracles, unopposed.

A few stockades now blocked the road, and served to delay for a few days the further approach of the invaders, while the terrified inhabitants crowded within the walls of the fort. On the 20th of March the attack began, the Hollanders breaking up the tombstones in the cemeteries, and firing the pieces from mortars into the fort. The Portuguese however held out grimly, though famine was hovering very near; for the only food that remained was a small quantity of spoilt rice, while the supply of salt too was nearly exhausted. To intensify the horror of the siege, plague broke out and wrought havoc among the crowded refugees. Yet though the parapets and walls, which were of soft coral stone, were visibly crumbling before, the fire from the batteries, the Hollanders after their experience at Colombo dared not attempt an assault. Three months passed and the store of powder was well-nigh spent; the water in the wells, contaminated by the putrefying corpses, had become a source of infection, and not even enough arrack to dress a wound could be procured. It was realised that further resistance was impossible, and on the 22nd of June the fort surrendered. The Hollanders were not inclined to be merciful in their triumph, and though the garrison was allowed the honours of war, all the property of the Portuguese and their adherents was confiscated.

On the 22nd of June the garrison, including the brave Figueira, who had once more returned to his country to draw his sword against the hated Protestant, began to March out of the citadel. Three days were spent in the evacuation, women and men alike irrespective of age and rank being stripped and subjected to a minute and degrading scrutiny, to prevent the concealment of any valuables about their persons. The place was then methodically sacked and thoroughly cleansed so as to render it once more habitable; while with characteristic foresight the Hollanders proceeded to plant the space within the walls with three hundred coconut trees.

On the 23rd of June 1658 the army assembled within the church of Our Lady of Miracles; and where the triumphant strains of the *Te Deum* had so often celebrated the victories of de Oliveira, there rose the deep guttural voices of the Hollanders, rendering thanks to Almighty God that at length this blood-stained country was entirely rid of the Portuguese.

THE END

NOTES TO CHAPTER XV.

1. This charitable organisation was considered a branch of the Misericordia at Goa, regarding which see Senhor Martin's exhaustive work, *Historia da Misrricordia de Goa*.

2. All Portuguese leaving for the East were either Casados, married men, who could not be compelled to go to the wars save in very exceptional circumstances, or Soldados, though the latter term did not imply that they were engaged as soldiers.

3. Johan Jacob Saar.

4. A Portuguese measure equal to about a quart.

5. Huratala—The Little Pet—the great decoy elephant whose dexterity was estimated to have yielded the Portuguese 50,000 *patacas* a year, and who alone out of a herd of fifteen had escaped uneaten during the siege ,was another object, of the King's desire ; but the Hollanders would not part with him and he lived to see the Standard of England float where so many Portuguese had shed their blood.

INDEX